Dissenters, Radicals, Heretics and Blasphemers

The Flame of Revolt that Shines Through English History

John Hostettler

Dissenters, Radicals, Heretics and Blasphemers
The Flame of Revolt that Shines Through English History
John Hostettler

ISBN 978-1-904380-82-5 (Paperback)   ISBN 978-1-908162-07-6 (E-book)

Published 2012 by
Waterside Press Ltd.
Sherfield Gables
Sherfield on Loddon
Hook, Hampshire
United Kingdom RG27 0JG

Telephone +44(0)1256 882250
E-mail enquiries@watersidepress.co.uk
Online catalogue WatersidePress.co.uk

UK distributor Gardners Books, 1 Whittle Drive, Eastbourne, East Sussex, BN23 6QH. Tel: +44 (0)1323 521777; sales@gardners.com; www.gardners.com

North American distributor International Specialized Book Services (ISBS), 920 NE 58th Ave, Suite 300, Portland, Oregon, 97213-3786, USA. Tel: 1 800 944 6190 Fax 1 503 280 8832; orders@isbs.com; www.isbs.com

Copyright © 2012 This work is the copyright of John Hostettler. All intellectual property and associated rights are hereby asserted and reserved by the author in full compliance with UK, European and international law. No part of this book may be copied, reproduced, stored in any retrieval system or transmitted in any form or by any means, including in hard copy or via the internet, without the prior written permission of the publishers to whom all such rights have been assigned worldwide.

Cover design © 2012 Waterside Press. Design by www.gibgob.com

Cataloguing-In-Publication Data A catalogue record for this book can be obtained from the British Library.

e-book *Dissenters, Radicals, Heretics and Blasphemers* is available as an ebook (ISBN 978-1-908162-07-6) and also to subscribers of Myilibrary and Dawsonera.

Printed by MPG Books Group, Bodmin and King's Lynn.

Dissenters, Radicals, Heretics and Blasphemers

The Flame of Revolt that Shines Through English History

John Hostettler

ALSO BY JOHN HOSTETTLER

Sir William Garrow: His Life, Times and Fight for Justice (with Richard Braby)
   2010 | Paperback ISBN 9781904380696 | Ebook ISBN 9781906534820

Champions of the Rule of Law
   2011 | Paperback ISBN 9781904380689 | Ebook ISBN 9781908162021

A History of Criminal Justice in England and Wales
   2009 | Paperback ISBN 9781904380511 | Ebook ISBN 9781906534790

Thomas Erskine and Trial by Jury
   Reissued 2010 | Paperback ISBN 9781904380597 | Ebook ISBN 9781906534868

and many more at **WatersidePress.co.uk**

Contents

About the author   *xiii*
Dedication   *xv*

1. INTRODUCTION ... 19
    Heroes ... *19*
    Dissenters ... *19*
    Radicals ... *20*
    Heretics ... *21*
    Blasphemers ... *22*
    Rebels ... *23*

2. EARLY CONFLICT OF RELIGION AND POLITICS ... 25
    Introduction ... *25*
    Pelagius ... *25*
    English Nationalism ... *27*
    Independence ... *27*
    Charge of Heresy ... *28*
    Indestructible Views ... *29*

3. JOHN WYCLIFFE ... 31
    Early Protestant ... *31*
    John of Gaunt ... *32*
    Church Indulgences ... *33*
    Bible in English ... *33*
    Politics ... *34*
    End of Pope's Power of Inquisition ... *36*
    Death ... *37*

4. RELIGIOUS MARTYRDOM ... 39
    Sir John Oldcastle ... *39*
    Abuse of Criminal Law ... *40*
    Transubstantiation ... *41*
    Found Guilty ... *42*

    Death by Fire 43
    Poor Priests. 44

5. **WAT TYLER AND THE PEASANTS' REVOLT** 45
    Hated Poll Tax 45
    Black Death 46
    Wat Tyler and the March on London 47
    Rebel Demands 48
    Meeting the King 49
    Vengeance. 50
    Heroic Message 51

6. **CROMWELL'S COMMONWEALTH AND PROTECTORATE**. 53
    Undermining the Traditional Ethos 53
    John Lilburne and the Levellers 55
    The Putney Debates 57
    Trials of "Freeborn John" 59
    Judges are Ciphers 60
    "Perverse Verdict". 61
    Women Levellers 62
    Second Prosecution of Lilburne 63
    Prophecy 64
    The Diggers or True Levellers 65
    Gerard Wynstanley. 65
    St George's Hill and Cobham. 67
    Political Programme. 68

7. **THE ISLAND BEDLAM** 71
    The Seekers and Ranters. 71
    Scourges of the Wealthy 73
    Abominable Practices 75
    Muggletonians 76
    Fifth Monarchists. 77
    Barebone's Parliament. 77

8. THE SOCIETY OF FRIENDS ... 81
Quakers ... *81*
Blasphemy ... *82*
William Penn ... *83*
Alleged Conspiracy ... *83*
Common Law ... *84*
Incredible Scenes in Court ... *85*
Bushell's Case ... *86*
Changing Image ... *88*

9. JOHN COOKE ... 89
Barrister-at-Law ... *89*
Solicitor-General ... *90*
Prosecuting the King ... *91*
"Refusal to Plead is a Confession" ... *92*
Trial of John Cooke ... *94*
Vitriol ... *95*

10. JOHN MILTON ... 97
Revolutionary Ardour ... *97*
Divorce Pamphlets ... *98*
Secretary for Foreign Tongues ... *99*
Freedom of Speech ... *100*
The Restoration ... *101*
Paradise Lost ... *101*
Optimism ... *102*

11. JOHN BUNYAN ... 105
From Tinker to Christian ... *105*
Soldier in the New Model Army ... *106*
Imprisonment ... *108*
The Pilgrim's Progress ... *109*
Milton, Bunyan, Defoe ... *110*
Affinity with the Ranters ... *110*

12. DANIEL DEFOE 113
Political Leanings *113*
The True-born Englishman *114*
Defending Dissenters *115*
Robinson Crusoe *116*

13. JOHN WILKES 119
The Hellfire Club *119*
The *North Briton* *120*
Wilkes and Liberty! *121*
Absurd Ruling *122*
Massacre of St. George's Fields *122*
Unconstitutional Ploy *123*
Unreformed Parliament *124*

14. TOM PAINE 127
Common Sense *127*
The Rights of Man *128*
Social Reform *129*
Trial for Seditious Libel *130*
Alleged Spy in France *131*
The Age of Reason *132*
Return to America *134*

15. WILLIAM WILBERFORCE 135
The Clapham Sect *135*
Crusade Against the Slave Trade *136*
Morality *139*
The End *140*

16. THOMAS HARDY AND THE TREASON TRIALS OF 1794 141
Government Repression *141*
Rehearsal in Scotland *141*
Reign of Terror *144*
Trial of the Shoemaker *144*

William Pitt's Testimony *146*
Victory Tokens *147*
Hardy to Lafayette *148*

17. MARY WOLLSTONECRAFT 151
Early Development *151*
A Vindication of the Rights of Woman *152*
Controversy *154*
William Godwin *155*

18. THE PETERLOO MASSACRE 157
"Orator" Hunt *157*
The Yeomen Charge *158*
York Assizes *160*
Eventual Success *161*

19. REFORM OR REVOLUTION 163
Franchise Anomalies *163*
The Reform Bill *164*
Rioting *164*
Bristol in Flames *165*
Aftermath *167*
Propaganda *168*
Francis Place *169*
Victory *170*

20. CHARTISM: JOHN FROST AND ERNEST JONES 173
The Peoples' Charter *173*
Women Supporters *174*
Divisions within the Movement *175*
John Frost *176*
Bull Ring Violence *177*
The Newport Rising *178*
High Treason *180*
Chartist Leaders Gaoled *182*

Kennington Common *183*
Ernest Jones, the Chartists' Advocate *184*
"The Charter and No Surrender" *186*
Red Republican *187*

21. THOMAS WAKLEY — AN ENEMY OF INJUSTICE *189*
An Improbable Radical *189*
The Lancet *190*
The Ballot *190*
Tolpuddle Martyrs *192*
Friend of Chartism *194*
The People's Judge *194*
Coroner for West Middlesex *196*
Death by Flogging *198*

22. KEIR HARDIE *201*
Self-help *201*
The Cloth Cap *202*
The Independent Labour Party *203*
The Birth of the Labour Party *204*
The Labour Party and the *Taff Vale Case* *206*
Aftermath *207*
International Impact *208*
Folk-hero *209*

23. THE PANKHURSTS AND THE SUFFRAGETTES *211*
Votes for Women *211*
Birth of the Suffragette Movement *212*
The Mud March *214*
Schism and Successes *214*
In Court *215*
Forced Feeding of Hunger Strikers *216*
More Violence *219*
"Cat and Mouse" *220*
The Derby *220*

Appraisal *221*
　　　Sylvia Pankhurst. *223*
　　　Stream of Dissent *224*

24. MARIE STOPES *227*
　　　Campaigner for Birth Control *227*
　　　The Mothers' Clinic *228*
　　　Eugenics. *231*
　　　International Success *232*

25. BATTLE OF CABLE STREET *233*
　　　British Union of Fascists. *233*
　　　"They Shall Not Pass" *234*
　　　BUF Defeat *235*

26. CAMPAIGN FOR NUCLEAR DISARMAMENT *237*
　　　The Atomic Age *237*
　　　J. B. Priestley's Call. *238*
　　　Aldermaston Marches. *239*
　　　Committee of 100. . . . . *240*
　　　Cuban Missile Crisis. *241*
　　　Greenham Common *241*
　　　Current Policy *242*

27. MODERN REVOLT *243*
　　　Rebels. *243*
　　　The Angry Brigade *244*
　　　Battle of The Beanfield *245*
　　　Poll Tax Riots *246*
　　　Conclusion. *247*

Select Bibliography   251

Index   261

About the author

John Hostettler was a practising solicitor in London for 35 years as well as undertaking political and civil liberties cases in Nigeria, Germany and Aden. He sat as a magistrate for a number of years and has also been a chairman of tribunals. He played a leading role in the abolition of flogging in British colonial prisons and served on a Home Office Committee to revise the rules governing electoral law in Britain. He holds several university degrees and three doctorates. *Dissenters, Radicals, Heretics and Blasphemers* is his 21st book.

His biographical works include those on the radical social reformer Thomas Wakley and legal icons Sir James Fitzjames Stephen, Sir Edward Carson, Sir Edward Coke, Lord Halsbury and Sir Matthew Hale.

John Hostettler's writings also encompass a succession of acclaimed works for Waterside Press, including *The Criminal Jury Old and New: Jury Power from Early Times to the Present Day*; *Fighting for Justice: The History and Origins of Adversary Trial*; *Hanging in the Balance: A History of the Abolition of Capital Punishment in Britain* (with Brian P. Block and a Foreword by former Prime Minister Lord Callaghan); the all-embracing *A History of Criminal Justice in England and Wales*; *Champions of the Rule of Law*; and the reissue of a work previously published by Barry Rose, *Sir Thomas Erskine*.

In 2009, his book *Sir William Garrow: His Life, Times and Fight for Justice*, co-written with Richard Braby (a descendant of William Garrow), rescued from obscurity the true story of one of English law's forgotten legal giants, a tale mirrored by the prime time BBC TV series "Garrow's Law".

To my wife Joy for her considerable help and many suggestions on reading the manuscript.

This book is a glorious Molotov cocktail to be placed in the hands of every citizen and lobbed at the status quo. John Hostettler's inventory of leading Dissenters throughout our history reminds us that dissent is the intellectual tradition which keeps liberty alive and energises democracy. A brilliant and exhilarating work. A counter to the politics of passivity.

Helena Kennedy QC

CHAPTER 1

INTRODUCTION

Heroes

The British men and women who merit a place in what follows have all had a profound impact on our way of life. Some were earnest and zealous individuals. Others were more hot-headed and impetuous. Frequently they are found to overlap in more than one of the categories referred to in the title. They sometimes gave their lives for liberty and the future but often they enjoyed to the full the lives they led and the esteem in which they were held by those who supported them. What they all wanted was to improve the lot of the common people against the few who endeavoured to preserve the status quo, meaning their own wealth, power and privilege. This meant, although they did not always know it, they were moving, sometimes intuitively and sometimes resolutely, inexorably towards the modern concept of democracy. They are among the heroes of the history of our land.

Dissenters

Dissent is a universal, explosive force that helps turn the wheels of history. By dictionary definition a dissenter is someone who refuses to conform. But that also applies to rebels who are a different breed, although the distinction can be a fine one. In the last chapter of this book I consider three groups of rebels whose activities have made a disturbing impact. But they did not significantly change the future.

In the main I deal with dissenters who are men and women who lead or join with others in a common cause to make the world a better place. Often they suffer imprisonment or death for their beliefs. They are frequently so-called "troublemakers" who change the society in which they live as recent events in North Africa and the Middle East have shown, whatever the final outcome may turn out to be. Dissent is a dynamo of liberty and there is no forward march for mankind without it. Nevertheless, there is a great deal of diversity in the English tradition of dissent.

It encompasses many conflicting intellectual and religious trends and adopts many different forms in changing historical and social environments. In truth, from early times to the modern day dissenters, radicals, heretics and blasphemers have often been the strongest supporters of free speech and civil liberty. Of one kind or another, and frequently despised by enemies in their own day, many of them have played a crucial part in forging the human rights and rule of law that we now enjoy. Where they have seemed to be eccentric and remote this has sometimes been an excuse for historians to ignore or abuse them when the true reason for doing so has been their open, and sometimes violent, hostility to established authority.

In reality dissent is an intellectual tradition and, in the words of E. P. Thompson, "out of this tradition came many original ideas and original men".[1] Dissenters have altered for the better the manner in which people today live their lives, their quality of life and, sometimes, whether they live or die. Without them we should not be living in the modern world. Clearly, people like Guy Fawkes and his co-conspirators are not dissenters in this sense. They were refusing to conform to the religious laws of the time which were directed against themselves as Roman Catholics and were not seeking the common good.

Radicals

Radicals are sometimes described as advocates of radical change; but that is close to tautology. More importantly, they seek fundamental change by root and branch social and political reform. Some wish to change the established order by peaceful means, whilst others work to overthrow it by violence

---

1. E. P. Thompson. (1968) *The Making of the English Working Class*. London, Penguin Books. p. 57.

and revolution. As we shall see, the Chartist movement in particular was divided by a split between two such groups, the "moral force" brigade and the "physical force" party; a discord which had the effect of undermining it. The campaign in the late nineteenth and early twentieth centuries for votes for women was similarly divided between the suffragists who wished to campaign peacefully with meetings, petitions and the like and the suffragettes who turned to more violent methods. Notwithstanding their differences, however, they all remain radicals. Another radical was Mary Wollstonecraft in the eighteenth century.

With the famous treason trials of 1794 Britain saw the eruption of fierce repression by a government which feared the spilling over into this country of the Terror of the French Revolution. Then, after the defeat of Napoleon and with economic distress and heavy unemployment across Britain, various attempts at radical change of both types were crushed, culminating in the Massacre of Peterloo in August 1819. A decade or so later the leaders of the Whig Party, Lord Grey, Henry Brougham and Lord John Russell introduced the 1831 Reform Bill. This was partly in the interests of the growing mercantile and middle classes who thirsted for the power long denied them but also to avoid the stagnation stemming from the inflexibility of men like the Duke of Wellington who had preceded them as prime minister. Subsequently, the radical, and often violent, battles for the Bill, including the Nottingham and Bristol riots, were led by people who played a crucial part in securing the enactment of the Great Reform Act of 1832 but are largely unknown today.

Modern radicals include the socialist Keir Hardie and those who fought Sir Oswald Mosley and his British Union of Fascists at Cable Street in the heart of London's East End in 1936 in order to crush the potential onset of fascism and preserve democracy.

Heretics

A heretic is not only a person whose views are at variance with those of the majority but one who engages in activities to undermine the prevailing orthodoxy. Heresy often involves an opinion opposed to the usual or conventional persuasion, or a belief or beliefs contrary to the authorised teaching of the religious community to which a person ostensibly belongs. But so far as the latter is concerned there has frequently been a political and cultural dimension to heresy as throughout history the Church has been closely associated with the state and activities against it have been prosecuted by the authorities. A prime example of a heretic is John Wycliffe whose followers, the Lollards, persisted, from the fourteenth century until their ideas were absorbed by the Protestant Reformation, in advocating not only clerical poverty but also the taxation of Church property and the exercise of religion outside the Church. Others include John Bunyan and Daniel Defoe in the seventeenth century.

Blasphemers

These have included groups of people who engaged in impious or profane speaking or behaviour and cursed and swore liberally to advertise their freedom from generally accepted rules of conduct and morality. They also often behaved profanely and spoke impiously or contemptuously of God or sacred subjects. Blasphemers existed in significant numbers during the Commonwealth of the seventeenth century and in *Chapter 7* we shall examine various groupings of them, including the Ranters and the Muggletonians, as well as their activities and influence. And although they were often disparate and unrelated, each had a political dimension.

As George Bernard Shaw put it with some hyperbole, all great men start out as blasphemers. Liberty of conscience has been their watchword and inspiration. He also wrote that, "we are obliged (if we are wise) to tolerate sedition and blasphemy to a considerable extent because sedition and blasphemy are nothing more than the advocacy of changes in the established forms of government, morals, and religion; and without such changes there can be no social evolution. But as governments are not always wise, it is difficult enough to secure this intellectual anarchy, or as we call it, freedom of speech and conscience".[2]

---

2. George Bernard Shaw. (1965) *The Complete Prefaces of Bernard Shaw*. London, Paul Hamlyn. p. 301.

Rebels

None of these categories is self-exclusive and if society is not to stagnate such men and women must abound and sometimes succeed as on many occasions they have in the course of English history. Not all of them are saints, however, and where they have flaws I have not ignored or hidden them. It is their achievements that are being recorded here not any personal failings they might have had. In the nature of things, rebels have not been so successful as dissenters in changing history, but historian David Horspool's description of them is otherwise true of all the categories written about here:

> The English rebel may only rarely be a triumphant or even a particularly likeable character. But he and she are as much a part of the fabric of English history as the monarchs, law-makers and political leaders they defied. They serve as inspiration, as warning, and sometimes simply as example. They may not always be visible, but they, too, are all around us.[3]

Some readers may regret that their favourite dissenters and radicals etc. are not included here but because they are so plentiful it is necessary within the scope of a book to choose a few and that is what I have had to do. Those presented here are my personal choice and by no means exhausts the list of such intriguing characters who helped forward the historical growth of our country. So the choice, a difficult one with so many to choose from, is mine and I trust I have made a significant selection that will be of interest to those who read the book.

---

3. David Horspool. (2010) *The English Rebel: One Thousand Years of Troublemaking from the Normans to the Nineties*. London, Penguin Books, p. xxiii.

CHAPTER 2

EARLY CONFLICT OF RELIGION AND POLITICS

Introduction

From Anglo-Saxon times until Henry VIII's breach with Rome the Church in England enjoyed substantial wealth and power. It rivalled the monarchy but at the same time gave to the crown a divine imprimatur and legitimacy. The Church was involved with all the laws that were enacted[1] and these secured substantial incomes in taxes and fines both for itself and the king. However, although the Church and the monarchy usually worked closely in harness, the crown and the nobility both coveted the wealth of the Church. The desire to confiscate that wealth, which drove Henry VIII to the dissolution of the monasteries, was already apparent in the early Middle Ages. It revealed itself in the political opposition to the Church which was often fuelled by noblemen who encouraged religious dissenters within the Church. Nevertheless, attacks on the wealth and hierarchy of the Church had a much longer pedigree. And, religious dissent generally had a political dimension. Let us start with a Celtic monk in the so-called Dark Ages.

Pelagius

Born about 354 AD, Pelagius is the first notable English dissenter, radical and heretic, albeit against a foreign occupier. His name is a Greek translation of the Celtic Morgan meaning "sea-born". Of his life little is definitely known but, apparently tall in stature and portly in appearance, he lived at

---

1. See Alan Harding. (1973) *The Law Courts of Medieval England*. London, George Allen & Unwin Ltd. p. 20.

least until 420 AD, when he is believed to have died in Palestine. As a British theologian and monk Pelagius was well educated, fluent in both Greek and Latin and learned in theology. He was an ascetic who denied the need of divine aid in performing good works. Believing in free will and man's inherent capacity for good his teachings tormented the Roman Catholic Church of his day.

For most of Pelagius' lifetime Britain was an economic colony of Rome. Following Emperor Constantine's Edict of Milan in 313 AD the official religion of the Roman Empire was Christianity. It was centralized and authoritarian and centred around bishops under the ultimate authority of the Bishop of Rome. They preached total submission to divine authority. Man, they taught, was born in sin and salvation and grace was possible only through the Church and Christian teaching.

In about the year 380 AD, Pelagius travelled to Rome to write and teach and there he wrote three books on faith and the scriptures. It was in Rome that he became concerned about the moral laxity of society which he largely blamed on the theology of divine grace preached by St Augustine. Augustine of Hippo (in modern Algeria), a reformed libertine, held that man's will was evil through original sin, that righteousness was not possible without grace and that men without it were destined to eternal hell. The terrors of this doctrine, as he intended, secured widespread obedience to the Church. Pelagius, on the other hand, apart from denying original sin, maintained the concept, startling at the time, that grace was not a source of, but merely an aid to, righteousness and that God had not predestined men to heaven or hell. In the eyes of the bishops this was rank heresy.

Yet, early in his career Pelagius had been praised by Augustine who was not only a powerful bishop but a major influence in the intellectual development of Western Christianity. He referred to Pelagius as a "saintly man". But Pelagius was to shock the Church and its orthodoxy further when he argued that, contrary to Church theory, the sin of Adam was not transmitted to every human being. Sin was not inborn in the body and man was rational and a free person who was able to choose between good and evil. In other words, he entirely rejected the doctrines of original sin and predestination and believed in man's free will and capacity for good.

English Nationalism

Not surprisingly, such views aroused fierce controversy in the Roman world and they had a particular appeal in England which saw itself as an expendable outpost of the Roman Empire. The doctrines of Pelagius proved to be a fertile ground for the growth of a spiritual formula to suit local nationalism. Indeed, Pelagianism appears to have been adopted by the English propertied class in its desire for independence from Rome. The chief clerical opponent of the Roman Church in England was a leading Pelagian named Agricola, the son of a bishop who was clearly backed by a powerful party of local magnates.[2] Pelagianism explored the importance of the political dimension of nationalism. As a consequence, in 410 his followers in England commenced an anti-colonial revolution aimed at independence from Rome. Details are provided by the Byzantium historian Zosimus (491-518) in his *Historia Nova* ("New History") written in Greek in Constantinople where he lived. He says in book six of his *History* that,

> ...in 410 an enormous army of barbarians crossed the Rhine, without effective resistance from the imperial authorities. The British revolted from Roman rule, and established a national state. They took up arms, freed their cities from the barbarian invaders, expelled the remaining members of the imperial administration and set up their own system of government.[3]

Independence

Under invasion by heathens Rome accepted the situation and this may truly be said to be the end of the Roman occupation of Britain. For the first time in the history of the Roman Empire a colony had gained its independence lawfully and Pelagianism proved to be a major contributory cause in the decline of Roman Britain.

---

2. Peter Salway. (1981) *Roman Britain*. Oxford, The Clarendon Press. p. 426.
3. Paul Johnson. (1972) *The Offshore Islanders: From Roman Occupation to European Entry*. London, Weidenfeld & Nicolson. p. 17.

A year after Rome was sacked by Alaric, king of the Visigoths in 410 Pelagius, fled to Carthage where he met Augustine. It was here that the Church seriously ceased to regard him as perfectly orthodox and considered his view to be heretical, but only after the controversy had been complicated by Nestorianism. The heresy advanced by Nestorius, the patriarch of Constantinople, was that Jesus was two distinct persons, one human and one divine. It comes as no surprise this was rejected by the Roman Catholic Church and it is unfortunate that the opponents of Pelagius succeeded in identifying him with such a doctrine. Despite his enemies, however, the views of Pelagius spread quickly and the last years of his life were spent defending them against the Catholic theologians who held he was undermining the faith of the apostles.

Charge of Heresy

Augustine now saw Pelagius as a heretic and wrote four letters attacking Pelagianism and strongly affirming the existence of original sin and the impossibility of a life without sin unless by Christ's grace. He charged Pelagius with mysteriousness, mendacity and shrewdness. He called the Council of Carthage in 418 under the Presidency of Aurelius, bishop of Carthage, and the Council strongly denounced Pelagian doctrines and set out nine beliefs of the Church that it alleged Pelagius denied. They were:

1. That death came from Adam's original sin and not man's physical nature.

2. Grace negates past sins and helps avoid future sins.

3. No good works are possible without God's grace.

4. Infants must be baptized to be cleansed from original sin.

5. Children who die without having been baptized are excluded from both the Kingdom of heaven and eternal life.

6. We confess we are sinners because it is true, not from humility.

7. The saints ask for forgiveness for their own sins.

8. The saints also confess to being sinners because they are.

9. The grace of Christ gives strength and the will to act out God's commandments.

As a consequence, the synod denounced Pelagius as a heretic along with his friend and pupil Celestius, an Italian lawyer of noble descent. Following the example of Pelagius, Celestius had set out six theses which were declared heretical. They were:

1. Even if Adam had not sinned he would have died.

2. Adam's sin harmed only himself, not the human race.

3. When born, babies are in the same state as Adam before his fall.

4. Mosaic law is as good a guide to heaven as the Gospels.

5. Even before the advent of Christ men were without sin.

6. Christ was not resurrected.

Indestructible Views

As Peter Salway has put it, "By 429 AD Pelagianism was a real issue in Britain whether religious or political or both".[4] So serious was its threat to the dominant theology that in that year Germanus, bishop of Auxerre in Gaul, was sent by the Pope to England to combat the heresy and recall the English

---

4. Peter Salway. *Roman Britain. Op. cit.*

Church to orthodox beliefs. Germanus put a band of Saxons to flight and was successful at a huge gathering at Verulamium (today's St Albans). This was a hollow victory for Rome, however, and did not put an end to the influence of Pelagius whose doctrines were to persist into later centuries.

Not surprisingly all the power of the medieval Church was directed at such threats to its existence. Nonetheless, although Pelagius and Celestius, who was said to be incredibly loquacious but also open-hearted and free in social intercourse[5], were both declared heretics the increasing hostility to the move of the Church away from the teachings of Christ, which are described in the next chapter, was sufficient to ensure that although their views were driven underground they proved indestructible. They were destined to resurface from time to time particularly in the works of John Wycliffe and Martin Luther.

---

5. See *The Catholic Encyclopedia*.

CHAPTER 3

JOHN WYCLIFFE

It should be said straight away that one historian casts considerable doubt on what we really know about Wycliffe and that we should free him "from a great deal of ignorant repainting and several layers of rich brown protestant varnish".[1] He does, however, concede that English nonconformity owes its origins to Wycliffe.

Early Protestant

Born about the year 1328 A.D. in Ipreswell (today the village of Hipswell near Richmond in North Yorkshire) Wycliffe was to live for some 60 years before dying on 31 December 1384 at Lutterworth in Leicestershire. He was a theologian, lay preacher, translator and religious reformer, known in the Roman Catholic Church as a dissident who looked to Scripture for his faith rather than to the hierarchy of the Church. And, by proclaiming a direct relationship between God and man he threatened to undermine the theology of Rome. Like that of Pelagius his heresy was revolutionary and also had a political significance. It was not only anti-clerical and anti-feudal but democratic in spirit in its implications and content, if not in form.[2]

He influenced Martin Luther, the precursor of the Protestant Reformation, and is often referred to as "The Morning Star of the Reformation". He preached anti-clerical and biblically-centred reforms and, as a celebrated critic of the Roman Catholic Church, when Master of Balliol, Oxford he was invited to draw up a document refuting the justice of the Roman Church's demands on England for money. It proved to be a task dear to his heart. He attacked the unseemly pursuit of wealth by the Church and caused the bible

---
1. See K. B. McFarlane. (1972) *Wycliffe and English Non-Conformity*. London, Penguin Books.
2. A. L. Morton. (1945) *A People's History of England*. London, Lawrence & Wishart Ltd. p. 127.

to be translated from Latin into English. As a scholar and reformer he also founded an order of itinerant preachers who became known as Lollards[3].

John of Gaunt

Wycliffe's teachings of an early Protestantism, and the concept that he who does not work shall not eat appealed to both peasants and town and city merchants but provoked alarm in the hearts of the clergy and crown alike. But John of Gaunt (named after Ghent, the town where he was born), Duke of Lancaster, a son of the king and the greatest and wealthiest subject in the land, saw an opportunity to use them. An enemy of the wealthy and powerful bishops, he believed he could draw Wycliffe with his anti-clerical ideas into his political schemes for getting the clerics out of government and seizing the wealth of the Church to promote wars and to distribute it among the nobles, as Henry VIII was to do later. To this end he sheltered Wycliffe from the rage of the clergy. Nevertheless, when Wycliffe attacked the doctrine of transubstantiation, the belief that bread was the flesh of Christ after consecration, even Gaunt warned him to hold his tongue.

But silence was no longer sufficient since the bishops felt they could defy Gaunt at least on this issue. They summoned Wycliffe to appear before Bishop Courtenay of London on a charge of heresy. Gaunt stood by Wycliffe's side, however, and threatened to drag Courtenay out of the Cathedral, in which Wycliffe was being tried, by the hair of his head. In the event, the trial could not proceed when crowds of Londoners swarmed all over the Cathedral and carried off Wycliffe in triumph. The bishops belatedly decided not to hand him a martyr's crown and they let the matter rest. Nonetheless, Wycliffe's followers were to suffer constant persecution in the future despite Parliament complaining in 1382 that it was not intended that men should be tried for heresy or be made subservient to the prelates.

---

3. The word Lollard was a popular derogatory nickname from a Dutch word meaning mutterer.

Church Indulgences

A fundamental belief of Wycliffe's was that the Church should be poor, as in the days of the apostles. Consequently he protested vigorously against the blatant sale of indulgences by the Church. It had become possible to buy from the clergy batches of indulgences for dead relatives who were believed to be in purgatory. There were also indulgences for religious vows as well as for the dubious acquisition of worldly goods and for permission to dispense with the need for confession.[4] Rome despatched commissioners across Christendom to collect the proceeds of the sale of the vastly profitable indulgences and they caused a great deal of unrest. Indulgences brought enormous wealth to the Church and Jan Hus of Prague was burned at the stake for his opposition to them, with Wycliffe's manuscript bibles used as kindling for the fire. Eventually indulgences led, on 31 October 1517, to Luther launching the Reformation by nailing his "ninety-five theses" to the door of the Schlosskirche at Wittenberg. The Christian world is still in conflict over the issues Luther raised of individual freedom of beliefs against institutional Church authority and how to read the bible.

Bible in English

Wycliffe's progress as a dissenter and heretic is shown by the fact that even as early as the end of the fourteenth century he had already produced a complete bible written in middle English. Three hundred copies of these Wycliffe bibles are still in existence. He also outspokenly referred to the Pope as the "Antichrist". He sent out his "poor priests" to preach to the lay people whom he believed could understand the bible better than the ecclesiasts and scholars who wanted to reserve it to themselves. "Christ", he said, "did not write his teachings on tablets of stone or on parchment but in the hearts of men". He considered confession was wrong since priests, he said, had no special authority nor the power to forgive sins; and he argued that priests should not hold political office but should concentrate on their spiritual mission.

---

4. See Richard Friedenthal. (1970) *Luther*. Translated by John Nowell. London, Weidenfeld & Nicolson, p. 136.

He believed that their adopted role as intermediaries between God and man and their wealth should be diminished. Furthermore, the clergy should be accountable to the civil law and not simply to the bishops. He also strongly denounced all types of wars and violence.

Wycliffe owed a great deal to William of Occam who was also a major figure in the intellectual and political controversies of the fourteenth century. He followed Occam's interest in realism, natural science and mathematics but Wycliffe concentrated on a study of theology, ecclesiastical law and philosophy and he was also interested in Roman and English law. Most of his life was spent in Oxford, one of the earliest universities in the world, where he was Master of Balliol College in 1360-61. In the latter year the college presented him with the parish of Fylingham in Lincolnshire and this meant his leaving Balliol although he continued to live at Oxford. Whilst studying natural science, mathematics and philosophy he took a bachelor's degree in theology and around 1380 he became a Doctor of Divinity. From many of his studies, particularly of realism, Wycliffe drew political conclusions.

Politics

As a consequence of the rapid changes in society following the Black Death the period witnessed a ferment of ideas with strong criticisms of both the Church and the society of the time. Wycliffe welcomed the secularization of ecclesiastical properties in England and began to express his ideas in writing culminating in his greatest work, the *Summa Theologiae*. As we have seen he was patronised by the powerful John of Gaunt, Duke of Lancaster, when he attacked the temporal rule of the clergy. Gaunt was aggressive towards clerical wealth and privilege and ruled England at the time along with Lord Percy. He asked Wycliffe to preach for the cause of disendowment in the churches of the City of London and Wycliffe obliged, arguing that in temporal matters the king was above the Pope and the sale of indulgences was both simony and venal. Following his attacks on abuses in the Church, Wycliffe had turned to strike at its constitution saying it would be better without Pope or prelates. He also asserted the right of every man to examine the bible for himself.

It was in his great political work, *De Dominio Civili*, that he made an elaborate scholastic argument for the secularization of Church property. He claimed that temporal domination of the country by the Church should be abandoned. The state should interfere to change pernicious systems of the Church and take over ecclesiastical property if it was misused by the clergy. He strongly believed in predestination; and a church of the elect rather than the institution of Rome. After putting these ideas to his students at Oxford he decided to proclaim them more widely and this caused both widespread support and hostility. He was, in fact, the greatest preacher in England at the time and recommended both to his Oxford students and a wider audience radical new views on religion and society.

On 22 May January 1377, Pope Gregory XI sent copies of a bull against Wycliffe to the Archbishop of Canterbury, King Edward III, the bishop of London and others with 18 theses of Wycliffe's which were denounced as erroneous and dangerous to the Church and the state. However, Edward died on 21 June and was succeeded by Richard II, still a boy of eleven years, who was under the influence of John of Gaunt and the bull was kept secret for six months.

Wycliffe wanted to see his ideas put into practice with the Church as poor as he believed it was in the days of the apostles. His early successes came in London with the support of John of Gaunt, sections of the nobility and the poorer people who flocked to his sermons. But his maintenance of a right in a secular power to control the clergy was offensive to the bishops. Eventually, Simon Sudbury, the Archbishop of Canterbury, and the other bishops decided to defy Gaunt and summoned Wycliffe to appear before them at St. Paul's on 19 February 1377 to answer the allegations of heresy, scandal and pride. In doing so they were acting to defend the Church in England against a political movement intent on confiscating its property. They assembled behind the altar in the Lady Chapel but Londoners again responded with considerable rioting both inside and outside the Cathedral and Wycliffe remained free.

End of Pope's Power of Inquisition

Wycliffe laid his theses before Parliament and made them public in a pamphlet. Then, in March 1378, he appeared at the episcopal palace at Lambeth to defend himself. But, whereas at the St. Paul's trial the bishops acted within the scope of the English Church courts, after the Pope's bulls there was a distinct claim of papal jurisdiction in England encouraged by the presence of papal commissioners. As a consequence, at an early stage in the trial Londoners broke into the Archbishop's chapel at Lambeth and interrupted the proceedings with violence. A Church chronicler of the time was enraged. "In this way", he wrote, "that slippery John Wycliffe deluded his inquisitors, mocked the bishops, and escaped them by the favour and care of the Londoners, although all his propositions are clearly heretical and depraved".[5] Nonetheless, the significant result was that the Pope's inquisitorial powers in England were now ended for all time. When heresy was suppressed in the next century it was by the authority of the Church courts and Statute law, not the Church of Rome.

In the meantime Wycliffe was imprisoned at Oxford by the Vice-Chancellor. However, for incarcerating one of the king's subjects on the orders of the Pope, the Vice-Chancellor himself was arrested and imprisoned whilst Wycliffe was released. Nevertheless, many of his followers were uneasy and left Oxford to add to the number of itinerant Lollard preachers roaming the villages and towns of England. They were soon to be found scattered all over the country having been transformed from academic theologians into mass evangelists. In the end Wycliffe considered the influence of the organised Church of Rome on parish work so evil that he advocated sweeping away the papacy, the whole hierarchy of the Church and monastic establishments in order to leave the parish priest virtually unfettered by clerical superiors.[6]

---

5. George Macaulay Trevelyan. (1946 edn.) *England in the Age of Wycliffe*. London. Longmans, Green & Co. p.86.
6. *Ibid.* p. 121.

Death

Wycliffe often preached in the parish church at Lutterworth against the politics of the Church of Rome and, whilst he was hearing mass there on Holy Innocents' Day, 28 December 1384, he was struck with paralysis and died on the last day of the year. Some years later he was condemned as a stiff-necked heretic by the Council of Constance on 4 May 1415.

A Statute of 1401 had later extended persecution to Wycliffe's followers and the Constitutions of Oxford of 1408 banned his writings and made the translation of the bible into English a crime punishable as heresy. His books were burned and, since he had evaded capture during his lifetime, his remains were exhumed from Lutterworth churchyard and destroyed by fire 44 years after his death. His ashes were cast into the River Swift which flows below the village of Lutterworth. Today, however, he is honoured in the Church of England on 31 December each year, but he should still be regarded as a dissenter against both the Roman Church and, as will be seen in the next chapter, the English state. Lollardy had a political dimension that was to re-emerge from time to time until it was subsumed in the Protestant Reformation. On the other hand, Wycliffe's work for the common good had a profound effect on later reformers. His influence and that of the Lollards set on foot among the lower ranks of society a belief in the liberty of thought that helped the Reformation and has survived until the present day.

CHAPTER 4

RELIGIOUS MARTYRDOM

Sir John Oldcastle

Early in the reign of King Richard II, Parliament endeavoured to protect the Lollards, many of whom were gentlemen as well as merchants, squires and knights. Precisely the sort of people who were sent to the House of Commons where they had considerable influence. As a result, although Wycliffe's missionaries continued to criss-cross the country with their heretical message, few were made into martyrs at the time. But all that changed when, in July 1382, Richard II, ignoring Parliament, ordered the arrest of all Lollards in order, he proclaimed, to destroy heresy in the kingdom. The House of Commons disapproved, however, and in October insisted on the withdrawal of the king's ordinance to which they had not assented. The Lollards were not, they added, to be tried for heresy, "nor to bind themselves or their descendants to the prelates more than their ancestors had been in time past".[1]

Nevertheless, the Peasants Revolt of 1381, in which John Ball preached Lollardy and demanded that the wealth of the Church be distributed to parishioners, had changed the political situation. The state was frightened not only by the threat to Church authority but also to the social order and as a result dropped its claims against ecclesiastical property. Henceforth, the power of the nobility which had defended Wycliffe was turned to supporting the crown in an endeavour to crush his followers. As a consequence, the king and John of Gaunt now attacked them as a thorn in the side of crown and Church alike. But they were not to be easily defeated.

---

1. *Rotuli Parliamentoram.* (1783) vol. iii. p. 141.

Abuse of Criminal Law

When Henry V, of the House of Lancaster, ascended the throne in 1413 he determined to crush the Lollards, whom he feared as a political as well as religious movement, once and for all. He quickly had enacted the Statute of Heresy by which the bishops, acknowledged as the second arm of the state, were encouraged to seize and try all teachers of "heresy", all schoolmasters "infected" with heretical teachings and all owners or writers of heretical books. The criminal law was to be abused as a weapon of the state to crush independent thinking. Anyone found guilty was to be burnt at the stake. The first layman in England to be put to the stake following the Act was an artisan, John Badby, who refused to renounce his Lollard views and alleged heresy.

To provide an example to others and in particular those aristocrats who were inclined towards Lollardy, Henry set the bishops on Sir John Oldcastle, Lord Cobham by marriage, and a knight of repute as well as a renowned soldier. Oldcastle had fought courageously for the crown against rebellion in Wales and in the autumn of 1411 he was one of the captains sent by the Prince of Wales to help the duke of Burgundy to recover Paris.[2] He had become an intimate friend of both the king and, earlier, his father. Now he was to be thrown to the wolves.

Oldcastle, who was born about 1378, was a man of sincere religious conviction and he felt no hatred towards the priests. He did, however, offer the protection of his estates and castles in Kent to known heretics. There is no doubt that he was himself a Lollard, as were many nobles and gentry of the time since they feared the growing power and influence of the bishops. Moreover, he had been in correspondence with King Wenceslas IV and the theologian, Jan Hus, at Prague in Bohemia. Both Wycliffe and Hus were influential in the world of letters and at the Council of Constance (1414-1418) were condemned by Rome as heretics. The Council ended the three-Pope schism in the Church. It also summoned Hus to Constance under a letter of indemnity but as we have seen notwithstanding the letter the saintly Hus was to die bravely at the stake for his attachment to the works of Wycliffe

---

2. K. B. McFarlane. (1972) *Wycliffe and English Non-Conformity*. London, Penguin Books. p. 146.

by order of King Sigismund when he succeeded to the throne of his brother Wenceslas.

With the same end in mind, Oldcastle, who had been arrested and was a prisoner in the Tower of London, was summoned to appear before Archbishop Thomas Arundel and the bishops of London and Winchester. They constituted an ecclesiastical court which was held in St Paul's chapter house where Wycliffe had been accused in 1377. Oldcastle's plea that he had appealed from the Archbishop to the Pope in proper form and therefore Arundel should not be his judge was set aside.

Transubstantiation

Sir John was charged with heresy in both assisting Lollards and sending them out to preach. Further, that he believed that bread remained material bread and was not the flesh of Christ after its consecration by a priest. As early as 1401 the Lollard William Sawtry, a chaplain in Norfolk, had been committed to the flames and burned at the stake in Smithfield Market for just that belief. Others had followed in swift order.

But although Oldcastle was not the first to be tried for denying transubstantiation, he was the first peer to be so and the State Tryals claim that the court was determined that he be punished according to "the devilish decrees, which they call the laws of holy church".[3] The "Lollards Tower" in the Tower of London and the "Lollards Pit" in Thorpe Wood, Norfolk are grim reminders of such persecution. Although facing the penalty of death by burning, Oldcastle wrote a bold confession of faith to his judges in which he denounced the misuse of images and pilgrimages and the necessity of oral confession to a priest. Questioned by one of his judges he also exclaimed that the Pope was head of the Antichrist; "You bishops, priests, prelates and monks", he declared, "are the tail... never will I in conscience obey any of you". Nonetheless, he repeated the creed and now affirmed his

---

3. Quotations in this section are taken from (1719) *A Compleat Collection of State Tryals for High Treason from the reign of Henry IV to the end of the reign of Queen Anne*. London, T. Goodwin and Others. 4 vols.

belief in the sacraments of the Church including the sacrament of the altar which proclaimed that consecrated bread was Christ's body.

The Archbishop was not to be denied, however, and persisted that the accused had not answered whether after consecration the bread remained material bread or not. As a fundamentalist, Oldcastle naturally replied that he believed all that was in the bible was true. But he would not agree that the issue of the bread could be determined by the Pope. He was told by Arundel that Christ had ordained Peter the apostle to be his vicar on earth and had granted the same power to his successors, the later Popes. To this Oldcastle replied that the Church should show more esteem to the poverty and lowly behaviour of Peter and the Christian martyrs. On being informed by the court that if he meekly asked for absolution he could have it as a friend of the king, he responded by accusing Arundel of fabricating base and malicious slanders against him. At this point he was excommunicated and sent back to the Tower of London to be dealt with by the king's courts.

Examined later in a secular state trial, he accepted that wine was turned into Christ's blood and bread was turned into his body. But, he continued, bread is what we see with our eyes. The body of Christ, his flesh and blood, is there also but hidden and not seen except by faith. St Paul himself had called it bread and not Christ's body but a means whereby we receive Christ's body. With Oldcastle fighting for his life but endeavouring not to give up his beliefs, the whole trial seems to mirror the interminable medieval debates on how many angels could dance on the head of a pin.

Found Guilty

Despite his close friendship with the king, and some of his testimony, Oldcastle was found guilty of being a "most pernicious and detestable heretic". To bolster the verdict the bishops then produced a recantation which they had not hesitated to fabricate. Nevertheless, Oldcastle responded to the verdict by cheerfully telling his judges, "Though ye judge my body, which is but a wretched thing, yet I am certain and sure that ye can do no harm to my soul, no more than could Satan upon the soul of Job. He that created that, will of his infinite mercy and promise save it, I have no manner of doubt".

Turning to the spectators in the courtroom he declared that he stood by his faith, and with arms uplifted proclaimed in a loud voice, "Good Christian people, for God's love beware of these men; for they will else beguile you and lead you blindly into Hell with themselves. For Christ said plainly unto you, 'If one blind man leadeth another, they are like both to fall into the ditch'".[4] He was then returned again to the Tower to await execution. However, when the king gave him 40 days respite in which to renounce his heresy, he managed to escape from the Tower and remain hidden in London under the roof of a William Fisher, a Lollard parchment-maker of Smithfield. Fisher was later executed on a charge of assisting the escape.

Whilst Oldcastle was hidden in the city he appears to have become reckless and unwisely encouraged a wild attempt by members of the nobility on Twelfth Night to seize the king in the royal manor at Eltham as part of a conspiracy to capture the capital and political power. Despite a wide network of support, the chances of success were non-existent. Yet to enlist support for the plot he called upon all Lollards to rise in defence of conscience. To their own misfortune, many of them needed little prompting since their only places of refuge from persecution were the strong houses and castles of powerful sympathisers like Sir John. However, the attempted seizure of the king was soon exposed and foiled. The plot to occupy London was discovered and frustrated by the closure of the gates of the city to prevent Lollards entering the capital from outside. Forty-one who responded to Oldcastle's call, walked into the trap and suffered death in consequence.

Death by Fire

Oldcastle managed to evade capture for four years, most of which he spent in the mountains of Wales. At the end of that time he was found and betrayed by Lord Powis whose sons arrested him and returned him to London. There, by order of the king, he was hung in chains of iron and burnt alive in St Giles' Field near Temple Bar. Other methods of execution could just as well destroy the body but it was believed that only the flames would

---

4. John Hostettler. (1998) *At the Mercy of the State: A Study in Judicial Tyranny*. Chichester, Barry Rose Law Publishers Ltd. p. 7.

cleanse impure souls. At the stake he prayed to God to forgive his enemies and called upon the large crowd which had gathered to follow the teachings of Christ and beware of false ministers. He was the first peer to be sentenced to death for religious beliefs. According to the *State Tryals* the people who witnessed the burning prayed for him to the accompaniment of priests blaspheming and cursing them. Later, Shakespeare was to write that Sir John Oldcastle had died a martyr and he is believed to have used him as a model for Sir John Falstaff.

Poor Priests

In the year 1414 the justices of the peace were made responsible for suppressing the revival of the Lollards who thereafter were frequently indicted at quarter sessions. During the next ten years there was a concerted persecution of Wycliffe's "poor priests" most of whom, in effect, were missionaries in the mould of St Francis of Assisi. As had Wycliffe himself, they journeyed around England with their tracts, clad in russet gowns and barefoot like pilgrims. Many of them were arrested and charged with treason rather than heresy, which enabled them to be executed in the barbarous manner reserved for that offence. Notwithstanding this exhibition of power by the state, Wycliffe's legacy, as the first form of English Protestantism, was to bear fruit in the Reformation. Equally, the dispute over consecrated bread did not go away and was to resurface in the reign of "Bloody Mary".

The Lollard martyrs fought a harsh battle against both the state and the power of the medieval Roman Catholic Church which had exercised rights over men's minds for nearly a thousand years. In doing so they struck a powerful blow for the liberty of thought that was, and still is, hated by tyrants the world over.

CHAPTER 5

WAT TYLER AND THE PEASANTS' REVOLT

Hated Poll Tax

The Peasants Revolt of 1381 was the most violent and widespread insurrection in England's history. And although in the end it failed in its immediate objects it was successful in heralding the end of the feudalism in this country. Led by Wat Tyler, it came close to succeeding and played a significant part in moulding our national character and traditions. In part, it is surrounded in mystery since most of the chroniclers of the time not only gave differing versions, but generally sided with the king and his advisers and gave a distorted picture of what the peasants did or did not do. Not that all those involved in the revolt were peasants. Many were farmers, wage labourers and various types of clerks.

King Richard II was only fourteen years old at the time and the rebellion was precipitated by his Council endeavouring to enforce a countrywide poll tax which amounted to three groats (i.e. one shilling) a head for everyone over the age of fifteen irrespective of income. People naturally contrasted it with another poll tax which had been introduced four years earlier in 1377 when the rate imposed was four pence. Under the new tax a man had to pay two shillings for his wife and himself in cash which, in many cases, he did not have. The government sent out commissioners to revise the taxation returns and, as they might have anticipated, the commissioners were greeted with serious riots in many parts of the country. The government, whose only concern was to raise money to finance debilitating wars with France, was dominated by John of Gaunt, the king's uncle who was acting as regent; Simon Sudbury, Lord Chancellor and Archbishop of Canterbury; and Sir Robert Hales, the Lord Treasurer who was responsible for the poll tax. They were widely regarded as greedy and corrupt officials exploiting the weakness of the boy king.

Black Death

The background to the revolt was the terrible bubonic plague known as the Black Death which had swept the country in 1348-9. In many places half to three-quarters of the population had died creating a widespread shortage of labourers and peasants with the survivors able to command higher wages and shorter hours of work. In fact it gave them a taste of prosperity and freedom not known before. The response of the government was to secure the Statute of Labourers of 1351 which set a maximum wage equal to that paid in 1346 before the Black Death. This was two or three pence a day and the Act also restricted the movement of labour so that a peasant or labourer could not move to another district where he might earn more. It was an attempt to drive the peasants back into serfdom from which they were slowly climbing.[1] One consequence was a series of earlier peasant risings which culminated in that of 1381.

This started on 30 May when Thomas Bampton, a commissioner of the poll tax, rode out from London to Brentwood in Essex to revise the taxation returns in nearby villages. Thomas Baker, the spokesman for the villagers, was so defiant that Bamford ordered his arrest only to find himself and the official party attacked with stones and driven out of Brentwood empty handed. Sir Robert Belknap, the Chief Justice of the Court of Common Pleas, was then sent to Brentwood to punish the rioters. Before he could summon jurors to present indictments, however, he was seized by a host of local men and as the revolt spread throughout Essex and Kent an armed uprising had begun.

---

1. A. L Morton. (1945) *A People's History of England*. London, Lawrence & Wishart. p. 118.

Wat Tyler and the March on London

At this point Kent, already in tumult, was the centre of the revolt with Rochester Castle being taken by storm and fighting breaking out elsewhere in the county. Canterbury was attacked and within a month the Kentish rebels followed their leader Wat Tyler in marching on London via Maidstone to join the men of Essex. At Maidstone they executed a wealthy burgess as a traitor and set free 20,000 men from the local gaol. When they reached Blackheath they camped and the Lollard priest John Ball, who had just been rescued from the dungeons of Maidstone gaol, preached a sermon which included the couplet for which he is famous and which played its part in provoking the revolt,

> When Adam delved and Eve span,
> Who was then the Gentleman?

It was rumoured, on the strength of a confession that has not survived, that Ball had admitted to having been for two years Wycliffe's pupil.[2]

According to *The Chronicle of England* Ball also declared, "At the beginning all were created equal. It is the tyranny of perverse men which has caused servitude to arise, in spite of God's law; if God had willed that there should be serfs, He would have said at the beginning of the world who should be serf and who should be lord".[3] This was in line with the long-standing tradition among medieval peasants that expressed their anger at oppression and celebrated the heroes — real or fictional–of the struggle against subjection such as Hereward the Wake and Robin Hood. It was widely believed that injustices were remedied by such popular local heroes.

Wat Tyler had served in the army against the French and had a skilful understanding of military organisation and strategy. His hold on the rebels was complete. In their name he issued a proclamation that the people in arms continued allegiance to King Richard and the Commons but would not accept a king named John — meaning John of Gaunt the acting regent.

---

2. K. B. McFarlane. (1972) *Wycliffe and English Non-Conformity*. London, Pelican Books. p. 86.
3. Jack Lindsay. (1964) *Nine Days' Hero: Wat Tyler*. London, Dennis Dobson. p. 67.

By this time more and more men were flocking to join the rebels in both Kent and Essex and the two forces planned to meet in London. In their progress, the men from Kent broke open prisons and collected and burned all rolls and records relating to taxation. However, no one living within 12 miles of the coast was permitted to join the march for fear of a French invasion. Indeed, only three years before French raiders had captured and burned down Rye in East Sussex and invaded the Isle of Wight. By 12 June 1381 some 30,000 men of Kent were at Blackheath and more were marching from Essex to the fields of Mile End. Meanwhile huge numbers in the capital, which had a population of 40,000 to 50,000 citizens, were waiting to join what was being called the "True Commons".

As the Kent contingent approached London they broke off to sack the palace at Lambeth of Simon Sudbury, the Archbishop of Canterbury. At the same time the whole of the city was now in ferment and the revolt was spreading to East Anglia, Surrey, Sussex, the West of England and the Midlands. Meanwhile the king and his councillors were seeking safety in the Tower of London. The gates of London were opened to the rebels and by 13 June they were peacefully in complete control of the city. Prisoners were released from the Marshalsea and Fleet gaols and financial records at the Temple and Lambeth Palace were destroyed. Although the city was in the hands of the peasants the only serious violence within its precincts was the destruction of John of Gaunt's palace, the Savoy, where two looters were killed. Otherwise there was little disorder, although outside the city the slaughter was considerable against perceived tyrants and corrupt officials.

Rebel Demands

The rebels now began to prepare the demands they wished to put before the king which included a list of the men who were to be executed for their part in oppressing the people. This meant John of Gaunt, Sir Robert Hales, the Bishop of London, Archbishop Sudbury, Chief Justice Belknap and Thomas Bampton who had sent out the poll tax commissioners. The other demands included freedom from serfdom, common justice, freedom of trade and easing the conditions on which land was held. The annual rent of land was to be no more than fourpence an acre. Although not won at the time all these demands, except the last, were to be met in succeeding centuries and laid the basis for modern Britain. However, at the time no one knew if the king would even consider meeting them. William Walworth, the Lord Mayor of London, wanted to use the military to attack the rebels. On the other hand the more shrewd and realistic Earl of Salisbury saw defeat facing them if such a move were made and proposed talks and conciliatory promises until the rebels returned home. Salisbury's tactic prevailed and to this end the king and his councillors agreed to meet the rebels at Mile End, a mile or so from the Tower and outside the city walls.

Meeting the King

The meeting with a nervous king took place the following day. As he approached the rebel army the men shouted "For King Richard and the True Commons" and fell on their knees in welcome of the man they considered a semi-divine monarch. At this point the rebels believed that the king had only acted earlier on bad advice from his councillors, who were the true villains. Wat Tyler put to the king the demands already agreed upon and after some prevarication the king accepted them including the abolition of villeinage. Clerks were immediately put to work to draw up the charters that would give the amnesty and freedoms the rebels required. The latter were jubilant with their success whilst paying little heed to the possible duplicity of the king's advisers.

Impatient nonetheless, a group of rebels stormed the Tower of London and on Tower Hill summarily beheaded those most closely associated with the poll tax including the Archbishop of Canterbury and Sir Robert Hales, the Lord Treasurer. John of Gaunt had fled to Scotland to avoid certain death as the most hated man in England.

At Wat Tyler's request the king now agreed to a further meeting, this time at Smithfield, to hear new demands even more radical than those put forward at Mile End. However, instead of the king approaching the rebels William Walworth called upon Tyler to leave his army and come forward to meet the king. Foolishly, armed only with a dagger, Tyler did so and put forward a number of fresh demands.

Tyler read out the list. First, "Let no law but the Law of Winchester prevail".[4] Secondly, "Let no man be made outlaw by the decree of judges and lawyers. No man shall exercise lordship over the commons; and since we are oppressed by so vast a horde of bishops and clerks, let there be but one bishop in England". And then, "the property and goods of the holy Church shall be taken and divided according to the needs of the people in each parish, after making provision for the existing clergy and monks, and finally let there be no more villeins in England, but all to be free and of one condition".[5]

Richard promptly agreed and asked that the men return to their homes. By now it was dusk as the Council had intended and the king's retinue surrounded Tyler who was cut off from his own men who could not see clearly what was happening. As the king's men pressed closer upon him Tyler took out his dagger to protect himself. Walworth at once attacked him and when Tyler responded his dagger could not penetrate the breastplate which had been carefully hidden under the mayor's robes. The courtiers then joined in and Tyler was killed. Sensing something was wrong the rebels began to surge forward but Richard rode up to them crying, "Tyler has been knighted. Your demands have been granted". To which he then added that Tyler was waiting for them at St. John's Fields in Clerkenwell. The crowds began to move towards Clerkenwell but when they got there they discovered that their leader had been killed. Disheartened, the peasants and others agreed to disperse still believing that the charters and concessions would be honoured.

Vengeance

In fact the Council were now ready to wreak their vengeance. An organised militia of seven thousand men traversed the countryside and in the disturbed districts, where peasants and labourers were expecting the king's promises

---

4. This Statute of the reign of Edward I provided that people should be responsible for the maintenance of law and order in their own area.
5. Jack Lindsay. *Nine Days' Hero: Wat Tyler. Op. cit.* p. 173.

to be kept and serfdom destroyed. There they carried out wholesale killings and hangings without trial. When people at Waltham in Essex pleaded the promises made by the king they were brutally answered, "Serfs you are and serfs you will remain, not as before but incomparably harsher". Leaders such as John Ball and Jack Straw were captured and executed. Men still responded in an effort to achieve their rights, however, and there were renewed uprisings in parts of Norfolk. In Sussex crowds stormed Lewes Castle and burned all the rolls, rentals and charters of the Earl of Arundel. Conflicts also arose in London and East Suffolk and continued into the next century in Exeter, Bristol and Lincoln. All over England the ferment had been at work.

Nevertheless, the peasants had suffered a heavy defeat, which was inevitable since they had no means of exercising a permanent control over the policy of government. They could combine and terrorise the country's rulers but were bound sooner or later to return to their villages and leave the state in the hands of the king and such nobles as had not been executed. The terror struck into the country's rulers by the revolt also turned them decisively against the new religious movement of Wycliffe.

Heroic Message

On the other hand the revolt foreshadowed a general increase in wages, a relaxation of villeinage and commenced a radical tradition in English politics that has never been lost or destroyed. The power of the government to keep order in the country was weakened and dissenters in subsequent centuries often took courage from the lessons learned from the revolt. Indeed, its effects were felt 600 years later with rioting that led to the destruction of the modern poll tax, known euphemistically as a community charge, introduced by Margaret Thatcher's government in 1989 and dealt with in a later chapter. The stirring theme of this sweeping and vivid struggle of the fourteenth century peasants and others has struck a long lasting heroic note and is deeply rooted in the English psyche. The names Wat Tyler, John Ball and Jack Straw remain familiar in the country's popular culture.

CHAPTER 6

CROMWELL'S COMMONWEALTH AND PROTECTORATE

The seventeenth century witnessed momentous struggles between the crown and Parliament that resulted in the English Civil War; the execution of Charles I; the rule of Oliver Cromwell and the restoration of the monarchy. The Civil War was in part a constitutional and religious revolution. But it was also a struggle of merchants, farmers and a newly rising industrial class seeking to seize power from the feudal aristocracy, the established church and the monarchy. The period witnessed dramatic events that changed the political face of Britain and sowed the seeds for the future rise of democracy in its modern interpretation.

It was also a time in which there was incessant demand for the reform of the medieval criminal law that was so arbitrary and cruel to dissenters.[1] That demand was an integral part in the pamphlet literature of the 1640s and 1650s which was staggering in its quantity and range. It expressed the often inarticulate feelings of the common people who gave their support to the many groups and sects—made up of dissenters and radicals–that thrived in those exciting decades. And although only a few of their aspirations were achieved at the time many of them have been won by subsequent generations, often by the actions of dissenters.

Undermining the Traditional Ethos

Dissent and popular revolt have a long history in England, not least at the time of the English Revolution in the mid-seventeenth century. This period saw an extraordinary ferment of disturbance with Levellers, Diggers, Ranters,

---

1. See Donald Veall. (1970) *The Popular Movement for Law Reform 1640-1660*. Oxford, The Clarendon Press.

Quakers and Muggletonians consistently challenging the sacred ethos underlying the traditional political, religious, economic and educational beliefs. Radical political ideas and new religious sects proliferated. There was, as Christopher Hill put it, a "glorious flux and intellectual excitement" in the air. As part of it the bible and religion were used for political purposes by dissenters in their opposition to kings and tyrants. The people who participated in this agitation were largely drawn from "the hobnails and clouted shoes, the private soldiers, the leather and woollen aprons and the laborious and industrious people in England". They also included "the oppressed friends, the commoners of England, the inferior tenants and poor labourers' who had to beg work for day wages".[2] They were people who found hope and voice in the upheavals of the time and some of their demands are surprisingly close to those of modern dissenters. Not surprisingly, they roused bitter opposition among both wealthy royalists and rich parliamentarians. The critical years 1640-60 had a decisive impact on British history and truly saw "the world turned upside down" with England as the "Island Bedlam".[3] The Church courts became largely defunct, censorship broke down and the judges ceased to go on circuit. As Gerard Wynstanley wrote:

> All men have stood for freedom...and those of the richer sort of you that see it are ashamed and afraid to own it, because it comes clothed in a clownish garment...Freedom is the man that will turn the world upside down, therefore no wonder he hath enemies...True freedom lies in the community in spirit and community in the earthly treasure...[4]

To put the Civil War in perspective, one historian has written that it "has often been romanticised as a chivalrous 'war without an enemy' [but] was, in fact, the bloodiest civil conflict that the British Isles has ever known. As a proportion of the adult population, more men died during England's Civil Wars than during the First World War". Indeed, "it has been estimated that

---

2. *Ibid.* pp. ix-x.
3. Christopher Hill. (1972) *The World Turned Upside Down: Radical Ideas During the English Revolution.* London, Temple Smith, p. 223.
4. Gerard Winstanley. (1649) *A Watch-Word to the City of London and the Armie: wherein you may see that England's freedome which should be the result of all our victories is sinking deeper under the Norman power.* London, pp. 316-7.

some 85,000 men fell in the fighting itself, with a further 100,000 dying from wounds or disease".[5]

John Lilburne and the Levellers

At the heart of the dissenters was John Lilburne. He was born at Greenwich, London in about 1616 his father being Richard Lilburne, an English gentleman. The son was remarkable for his democratic instinct and first came to prominence in 1636 when, at the age of twenty, he was called before the Star Chamber for allegedly bringing into the country religious literature from Holland. He was instructed by the judges to take the ex officio oath which required a prisoner to confess to an unspecified crime levelled by an undisclosed informer.

Knowing little fear and being of undaunted courage, Lilburne refused to obey the judges and asserted that no freeborn Englishman should be required to take the oath, thus giving birth to the accused's right to silence. For his pains the judges had him savagely whipped along the entire route from the Fleet Prison, where he was being held, to Westminster where, bloody but unbowed, he was forced into the pillory. Here he was garlanded with flowers by a large crowd who had gathered and demanded a speech from their hero. Defiantly, and in great physical distress with open weals on his back said to be "bigger than tobacco pipes" he managed to address the crowd. Nevertheless he was returned to the Fleet where he was kept in appalling conditions for five years until released by the Long Parliament on 4 May 1641.

Of all the groups of agitators, pamphleteers and libertarian sects of the time the Levellers were the most prominent. Alongside Lilburne were other influential Leveller writers including Richard Overton, John Wildman and William Walwyn. The word "Leveller" was, in fact, at first a term of abuse, used by their enemies to denigrate them and their beliefs, and falsely suggest that they wished to abolish all property rights. In reality, some of their demands were democratic but they were not democrats and in their struggle to extend the franchise they excluded servants, paupers and even

---
5. Edward Vallance. (2010) *A Radical History of Britain*. London, Abacus, p. 148.

wage-earners. They wanted increased power for the jury to ensure that the common people took part in the administration of justice. And as far as the criminal law was concerned they also demanded freedom from arbitrary arrest, trial by witnesses, no lengthy imprisonment, the right to bail, humane treatment of prisoners, abolition of capital punishment for theft and a number of other demands that are reminiscent of Beccaria's great work on crimes and punishments in the next century. At the time they were totally unacceptable to the ruling power, whether king or Cromwell.

In 1649 when Lilburne, a Leveller leader and former lieutenant-colonel in the republican army, was being held in the Tower of London with others for declaring that Cromwell had betrayed the revolution in favour of the men of property, they managed to smuggle out a manifesto for constitutional reform. This set out the Leveller programme and, among other things, called for:

- a reformed franchise;

- equality of all before the law;

- jury trial in all cases where life, liberty or property was threatened;

- increased power to the jury to ensure that the poorer classes participated in the administration of justice;

- a right against self-incrimination;

- abolition of capital punishment in most cases;

- freedom of religion and the press;

- punishments to fit the crime; and

- no imprisonment for debt.

This manifesto was unmatched in English history until that time and amounted to a clarion call for wider elections, justice and the rule of law.

The Putney Debates

These were debates the like of which have never been seen before or since. The rank and file soldiers of Cromwell's New Model Army had set out their grievances in a pamphlet entitled, "The Case of the Armie Truly Stated" which was presented to General Fairfax on 18 October 1647. This was as a consequence of the discontent in the army. The pamphlet revealed that the senior officers, known as Grandees, called together Agitators (i.e. delegates) and officers from the army together with some prominent Levellers to discuss both "The Case" and the newly published Levellers' Agreement of the People. The debates took place in the parish church in Putney on the edge of the river Thames from 28 October to 11 November 1647. The church, which still exists, is a living memorial to English liberty. The background to the meeting was the Civil War and it was called in response to the dissent inspired by the Levellers among the soldiers of the army and the urban poor. Those attending allowed Cromwell to take the chair and,

> its outcome, against his more conservative instincts, was a resounding victory for what in those days was pejoratively described as 'democracy', a revolutionary idea that most Parliamentarians of the time believed would lead to anarchy. From its first ascendancy in that Putney church there may be traced the acceptance — centuries later in the Universal Declaration of Human Rights and now in two thirds of the nations of the world — of the idea that government requires the consent of freely and fairly elected representatives of all adult citizens, irrespective of class or caste or status or wealth. Today's single most important political principle, the right to live in a participatory democracy, comes down to us not from the slave-owning societies of Athens and Rome...but from buff-coated and blood-stained English soldiers and tradesmen.[6]

The Agreement was amended to extend the franchise to all soldiers and all other males except servants and beggars and for some of those taking part in the English Commonwealth. It amounted to an adaption to a form of democracy. Colonel Thomas Rainsborough MP, for Droitwich and a radical

---

6. Geoffrey Robertson. (2007) *The Levellers: The Putney Debates*. London, Verso. pp. vii-viii.

army officer, put the case for democracy. In words that have echoed down through the centuries he declared: "I think that the poorest he that is in England hath a life to live, as the greatest he; the poorest man in England is not at all bound in a strict sense to that government that he hath not had a voice to put himself under".

But Cromwell and his lawyer son-in-law, Henry Ireton, counter-attacked. Ireton insisted that the franchise be limited to men with a "fixed proprietary interest" in the nation. He said that universal suffrage would give the vote to persons with no stake at all in the kingdom. Rainsborough responded, "I would fain to know what the soldier hath fought for all this while? Hath he fought to enslave himself, to give power to men of riches, men of estates, to make him a perpetual slave".[7]

To which Edward Sexby, representing the ordinary soldiers, added that the soldiers had, "ventured our lives, and it was all for this: to recover our birthrights and privileges as Englishmen... I wonder we were so much deceived. If we had not right in this kingdom we were mere mercenary soldiers".[8]

However, there had been another momentous development. For the first time in British history, the "Agreement of the People" had enumerated a number of rights that could not be abrogated by government. "This marked an evolutionary leap forward from earlier charters and petitions, which could claim only the (often temporary) acquiescence of the monarch as their source of authority. Here were freedoms, liberty of conscience and equality before the law, that no power in the land could encroach upon".[9] Should Parliament become tyrannical the reserved rights would be protected from infringement. They also included, "the right to freedom of worship, freedom from conscription, indemnity from prosecution and a commitment that the content of the law itself must be fair and equal".[10] Thus did the Levellers come close to securing important constitutional change in England.

But it was not to be. At the time the Agitators, who were representatives of the rank and file of the army, and the Levellers lost the initiative to Cromwell and the officers. Saying he feared anarchy, Cromwell successfully

---

7. *Ibid*. pp. 69, 81, 86.
8. Andrew, Sharp. (1998) *English Levellers*. Cambridge, Cambridge University Press, p. 120.
9. Edward Vallance. *A Radical History of Britain. Op. cit.* p. 165.
10. *Ibid*.

insisted that the vote be tied to the right to property and in doing so isolated the Levellers. And, not for much longer did the government consider it politic to allow Lilburne opportunities to express his opinions in public.

Trials of "Freeborn John"

Accordingly, on 24 October 1649 the Lord Mayor of London was one of 40 dignitaries who attended the Guildhall to constitute an extraordinary commission of oyez and terminer (to hear and determine). They were to try, with a jury, this outspoken Leveller leader. Born a gentleman, but popularly known as "Freeborn John", Lilburne was a complex character who had a passion for liberty. Held in the Tower, he was charged with high treason for publishing sundry "scandalous, poisonous and traitorous books asserting that Cromwell's government was tyrannical, usurped and unlawful".[11] At the commencement of the trial Lilburne told the presiding judge, Mr. Justice Keble:

> All the privilege that I shall crave this day at your hands is no more but that which is properly and singly the liberty of every free-born Englishman, namely the benefit of the laws and liberties thereof, which by my birthright and inheritance is due to me and which I have fought for as well as others have done.[12]

Before he would plead, Lilburne asked to see the indictment under which he was charged and to have counsel to assist him on points of law. Both requests were refused and after prolonged argument he pleaded not guilty. Holding in his hand a book by Sir Edward Coke—whom he described as, "that great Oracle of the Laws of England"—he argued that his trial by the special commission of oyez and terminer was contrary to the Petition of Right of 1628 and to the Act of 1641 which abolished all such extraordinary tribunals.[13]

---

11. *A Compleat Collection of State Tryals for High Treason from the reign of Henry IV to the end of the reign of Queen Anne.* (1719) London, T. Goodwin and Others, pp. 580-640.
12. Clement Walker. (1649) *The Trial of Lt. Col. John Lilburne ... Being as Exactly Penned and Taken in Short-hand, as it was Possible to be Done in such a Crowd and Noise.* London, Theodorus Verax.
13. *A Compleat Collection of State Tryals for High Treason. Op. cit.* p. 582. Lilburne excluded ordinary commissions of oyez and terminer. He was attacking only special commissions.

Judges are Ciphers

Lilburne requested to be allowed to speak to the jury who, he asserted, were judges not only of fact but of law. Keble expressed his fury at the suggestion that juries could decide questions of law, upon which Lilburne burst out, "You that call yourselves judges of the law are no more but Norman intruders; and indeed and in truth, if the jury please, are no more but ciphers to pronounce their verdict.[14] This was a direct appeal from the Levellers' belief that the jury had survived from Anglo-Saxon times before the Normans had cast their alien yoke on the country. The concept of what was called the "Norman Yoke" had a patriotic appeal. It was of significance to the Puritans struggling against what they saw as an alien aristocracy[15] and was calculated to be popular with juries. Indeed, the concept of an ideal Anglo-Saxon age of just laws and liberty being overrun by the Norman conquerors who had robbed the common people of England of their birthright was an undercurrent of political thought running through English society for many generations. It had surfaced in the Peasants Revolt, now with the Levellers and the Diggers and was to do so again with many other dissenting groups who came later.

Addressing the jury in a direct and personal manner Lilburne resoundingly declared that they, "by the law of England are the Conservators and sole Judges of my Life, having inherent in you alone the judicial Power of the Law as well as Fact ... I desire you to know your Power and do your Duty".[16] On hearing this, "the spectators who crowded the courtroom cried in a loud voice, "Amen, Amen", and gave an extraordinary great hum which made the judges look something untowardly about them and caused Major-General Skippon to send for three more companies of foot soldiers."[17]

---

14. *Ibid.* p. 627.
15. Donald Veall. *The Popular Movement for Law Reform 1640–1660. Op. cit.* p. 105.
16. *A Compleat Collection of State Tryals for High Treason. Op. cit.* p. 633.
17. *Ibid.* For much of this material about Lilburne see John Hostettler. (2009) *A History of Criminal Justice in England and Wales.* Hook, Hampshire, Waterside Press. pp. 105-8.

"Perverse Verdict"

At the conclusion of Lilburne's address to the jury, Keble instructed them that "You will clearly find that never was the like treason hatched in England".[18] Notwithstanding this direction, the jury found the prisoner not guilty of any of the alleged treasons. "Immediately the whole multitude of people in the hall gave such a loud and unanimous shout as is believed was never heard in Guild Hall, which lasted for about half an hour without intermission".[19] Amidst wild jubilation bonfires were lit and church bells rung throughout London with the army celebrating with the people Lilburne's victory and in support of the supposed ancient rights of the jury to decide law as well as fact.[20]

After the trial, the jurors themselves were taken to the Old Bailey for individual examination on their "perverse verdict". Several of them told their interrogators that they had only discharged their consciences and others vowed that despite what the judges had said they took themselves to be "Judges of Matters of Law" as well as of fact.[21] Cromwell is reported to have looked upon the acquittal of his former friend and ally as a greater defeat than the loss of a battle[22] and, because the press of the Commonwealth avoided all mention of the trial, the Levellers were able to have the last word. They struck a medal with a portrait of their hero on one side and the names of the jurors on the other. Its inscription reads: "John Lilburne, saved by the power of the Lord and the integrity of his jury, who are Judges of law as well as fact. October 26, 1649".[23]

---

18. *A Compleat Collection of State Tryals for High Treason. Op. cit.* p. 633.
19. H. N. Brailsford. (1961) *The Levellers and the English Revolution*. London, The Cresset Press. p. 603.
20. *Ibid.*
21. *A Compleat Collection of State Tryals for High Treason. Op. cit.* pp. 638-40.
22. H. N. Brailsford. *The Levellers and the English Revolution. Op. cit.* p. 603.
23. *Ibid.*

Women Levellers

In this period women played a more important role than the Church had previously been prepared to accept. For instance, according to Christian practice a wife who sat in the same pew in church with her husband was liable to penalties in the ecclesiastical courts.[24] Now, in the marriage ceremony the Quakers abolished the wife's vow to obey her husband and the Ranters refused to regard sex outside of marriage as sinful. Women frequently found a place in these sects, even officiating as preachers in some of them.

Of particular interest here is the leader of Leveller women, Katherine Chidley. As early as 1641 she argued that a husband had no more right to control his wife's conscience than the magistrate had to control his.[25] And whilst Lilburne's trial was proceeding Chidley led several hundred Leveller women in besieging the House of Commons in his support. Although at the end of the trial Lilburne was found not guilty he was kept in custody and it was the tactics of these women that secured his release. A year earlier they had presented a Petition of Women, Affecters and Approvers of the Petition of September 11 1648 in which they justified their political activity. They argued for "our creation in the image of God, and of an interest in Christ equal unto men, as also of a proportional share in the freedoms of this Commonwealth".[26] With Lilburne's second prosecution, in 1653, Chidley again rallied to his defence. She organised a petition to Barebone's Parliament and was said to have collected signatures to it from over 6.000 women. They were told that Parliament could not notice the petition, "they being women and many of them wives, so that the Law took no notice of them";[27] a sentiment frequently echoed in the law until modern times.

Chidley was a religious and political activist who supported Parliament in the Civil War. She was the mother of seven children and was active in the struggle against the backward-looking innovations in the Church initiated by Archbishop Laud. In Parliament the Presbyterian MP Thomas Edwards vehemently opposed the Independents, who were more closely identified

---

24. Thomas Thiselton Dyer. (1891) *Church Lore Gleanings*. London, A. D. Innes and Co. p. 192.
25. E. Rogers. (1867) *An Account of the Life and Opinions of a Fifth-Monarchy-Man*. London, p. 69.
26. Women's Petition (1649). http://www.fordham.edu/halsall/mod/17women.html.
27. *Dictionary of National Biography*. (2004) Oxford, Oxford University Press.

with Cromwell, and argued for compromise between total religious conformity and complete religious freedom. He was put down in no uncertain terms by Chidley who in three works promoted the principle of the separation of Church and state. Little is known about her after 1653, however, and the date of her death is unknown.

Second Prosecution of Lilburne

Lilburne continued to dissent and in 1653, just prior to Cromwell being proclaimed Lord Protector for Life, he was subjected to a second prosecution by the Commonwealth. This produced an argument about the jury that was to re-appear with embellishments when adopted by the Whigs during the events leading to the Glorious Revolution at the end of 1689. Having, under Statute, been banished abroad on pain of death if he returned, Lilburne decided he was free to return when Cromwell dissolved the Rump Parliament. As a consequence he was brought to trial at the Old Bailey on 13 July 1653 for breaching his banishment. At this trial he once again appealed to the jury to decide the law as well as fact and acquit him on the ground that the Statute under which he was banished was null and void under the true fundamental law of England.[28] At the end of the trial the jury found him not guilty of any crime worthy of death. Although acquitted for a second time, Lilburne was imprisoned for two years following this trial and died a few years later. He had, however, planted the seeds of the dream of the jury's right to decide the law which was later to dominate Whig literature on the trial jury. Although this was not to be achieved his strong stand for more freedom from judicial restraint for juries was to bear fruit in the future. It has been said that:

> Trial rights established by Leveller and Quaker activists were, later in the century, mobilised by the Whigs in their own power struggle with the Stuart monarchy. Within just a few decades, demands for free jury trial were to make the significant

---

28. 5 *Howell's State Trials*. (1886) col. 444.

transition from the manifestos of Radical libertarian Puritanism to the mainstream ideology of the dominant political class.[29]

Prophecy

Lilburne declared at the bar of Parliament in "England's New Chains Discovered" on 26 February 1649 that, "Our cause and principles do through their own natural truth and lustre get ground in men's understandings ... so that though we fail, our truths prosper. And posterity we doubt not shall reap the benefit of our endeavours whatever shall become of us".[30] A prophecy that was, indeed, fulfilled.

Lilburne died on 29 August 1657. His body was conveyed to London and caused dispute between his old partisans, the Levellers, and his new friends, the Quakers. The former wished to bury him in the customary manner with a pall over the bier, the latter according to their custom in a plain coffin. Of the crowd outside the house of mourning the Quakers were in a majority and gained their point.[31]

It has well been said that the Levellers considered that all men,

> have potentiality and this can only be realised to the full in the free type of society envisaged in the Agreement of the People ... Only when all unnecessary restrictions — for example, inequality before the law, trading privileges, press censorship and conscription — have been abolished, will the fulfilment of the individual become possible ... This inherent optimism, constantly seeking an improving society, ... is the basis of modern democracy.[32]

---

29. Richard Vogler. (2005) *A World View of Criminal Justice*. Aldershot, Ashgate Publishing Limited. p. 204.
30. Text of England's New Chains Discovered. (Published in March 1649) Included in Geoffrey Robertson. (2007) *The Levellers: The Putney Debates. Op. cit.* London, Verso. p. 114.
31. Eduard Bernstein. (193) *Cromwell and Communism: Socialism and Democracy in the Great English Revolution*. London, George Allen & Unwin Ltd. p. 158.
32. J. Frank. (1955) *The Levellers*. Cambridge, Harvard University Press. Cited by Howard Shaw. (1973) *The Levellers*. London, Longman Group Ltd. p. 101.

The Diggers or True Levellers

In addition to the disruption of life caused by the Civil War, the late 1640s saw a series of disastrous harvests leading to widespread hunger and unemployment, particularly among the many disabled soldiers. Moreover, large numbers of agricultural workers had been dispossessed of their lands by enclosures and as a result food prices had soared. One consequence was that on Sunday 1 April 1649 a group of 20 or 30 poor men arrived at St. George's Hill in Walton-on-Thames in Surrey and began to cultivate the barren and untilled waste common land. It was reported that they had invited all to come in and help them, with a promise of meat, drink and clothes. What they wanted, they said, was to spearhead local colonies across the country that would cultivate all land communally.

But in addition to being more concerned with economic issues than the Levellers they also sought more radical changes in society. Community cultivation was to be carried out on a voluntary basis with the abolition of private property in land as the ultimate goal. What they wanted was to call into being a new social order based on an agrarian lifestyle built around small egalitarian rural communities. It was a utopian form of primitive Communism.

Gerard Wynstanley

Wynstanley, the leader of the Diggers, was one of the most original political thinkers and writers of the period. He was a social critic with a passionate sense of justice and a social theory that anticipates much modern thought. However, stung by the use of the law by landowners against the Diggers he attacked the law without having a viable alternative—merely general sentiments of justice.

Denouncing the Common Law Wynstanley claimed that the, "binding and restraining laws that have been made from one age to another since the [Norman] Conquest were the cords, bands manacles and yokes that the enslaved English, like Newgate prisoners, wear upon their hands and legs as they walk the streets".[33] Unlike the Levellers, the Diggers were hostile to trial by jury altogether since, Wynstanley complained, its property composition meant that it was biased in favour of the landowners. It was as a consequence of that bias, he believed, that caused jurors to dispossess them from their settlement at St. George's Hill. They were composed, he said, of "rich freeholders and such as stood strongly for the Norman power".[34] But he not only proposed no alternative and endeavoured to opt out of the English legal system, he also failed to recognise the positive side of the Common Law and trial by jury, as well as their adaptability as society became less authoritarian in the future.

Wynstanley, who curiously described himself as a servant, said he was never brought up to beg or work for day wages. However, he spoke for those to whom the Levellers would not have granted the franchise, namely servants, labourers, paupers and the economically unfree.[35] In reality, Wynstanley was a well connected cloth merchant who, after his business had failed in the early days of the Civil War, took to the land. "Describing himself as a man of little education and quoting little else but the Bible, he nevertheless wrote in simple lucid prose, born of the urgency and intensity of his beliefs and the need to appeal to the ordinary reader".[36] He believed that heaven and hell were not real places and that heaven meant living on earth with a spirit of love and charity.

Although believing in the theory of the Norman Yoke he transcended it with a theory of natural rights. "The best laws that England hath", he declared, "are yokes and manacles, tying one sort of people to another... All laws that are not grounded upon equity and reason, not giving a universal freedom to all but respecting persons, ought... to be cut off with the king's head".[37] Royal power, clergy, lawyers and buying and selling were all

---

33. Gerard Wynstanley. (April 1649) *The Levellers' Standard Advanced.* In G. H. Sabine (ed.) (1941) *The Works of Gerard Wynstanley.* New York, Cornell University Press. p. 259.
34. *Ibid.* p. 37.
35. Christopher Hill. *The World Turned Upside Down: Radical Ideas during the English Revolution. Op. cit.* p. 97.
36. Donald Veall. *The Popular Movement for Law Reform 1640-1660. Op. cit.* p. 106.
37. G. H. Sabine. (ed.) *The Works of Gerard Wynstanley. Op. cit.* pp. 303, 390.

linked together; "if one truly fall, all must fall".[38] A sentiment similar to that expressed by James I in his well-known aphorism, "No bishop, no king".

St George's Hill and Cobham

The Diggers challenged the rights of two lords of the manor at St. George's Hill and at Cobham, not merely by squatting on the commons and planting beans, parsnips and carrots, but also by defiantly felling timber. In consequence, the lords had the Diggers' settlements destroyed. Soldiers stood by whilst the lords' men burnt furniture and huts and turned cattle into the growing corn.[39] Men were also beaten and imprisoned. Landowners in the area round St. George's Hill were more disturbed by the digging than were the Council of State or General Fairfax, commander of the New Model Army, who, at the request of local landowners, had arrived at the site with his troops and had a series of amicable conversations with Wynstanley—despite the latter's refusal to remove his hat to a "fellow-creature".[40] The Diggers were also harassed with legal actions in the assize court at Kingston-upon-Thames where in one case a court official said, "If the Digger's cause was good he would pick out such a jury as should overthrow him".[41] It is little wonder that, unlike the Levellers, the Diggers had no faith in local justice.

Wynstanley believed that from a half to two-thirds of the land of England was not properly cultivated. The other third of England was barren waste, which lords of manors would not permit the poor to cultivate.[42] He said that, "If the waste land of England were manured by her children, it would become in a few years the richest, the strongest and [most] flourishing land in the world".[43] There was land enough to maintain ten times the present population, abolish begging and crime, and make England "first of the nations".[44]

---

38. *Ibid.* pp. 381-2.
39. H. N. Brailsford. *The Levellers and the English Revolution. Op. cit.* p. 657.
40. Christopher Hill. *The World Turned Upside Down: Radical Ideas during the English Revolution. Op. cit.* p. 90.
41. *Ibid.* p. 91.
42. G. H. Sabine. *The Works of Gerard Wynstanley. Op. cit.* pp. 200, 304, 356.
43. *Ibid.* p. 408.
44. *Ibid.* p. 414.

When he was arrested, he declared, "And is this not slavery that though there be land enough in England to maintain ten times as many people as are in it, yet some must beg of their brethren, or work in hard drudgery for day wages, or starve, or steal, and so be hanged as men not fit to live on earth"?

Political Programme

Wynstanley set out the Digger political programme for a new society in a publication addressed to Cromwell and all Englishmen entitled, "The Law of Freedom in a Platform: or, True Magistracy Restored" (1651-2). In it he indicated that neither Cromwell nor his officers had conquered the king alone but only with the aid of the common people who should share in the fruits of victory. The land should be made over to the people. The grievances, he said, from which the people suffered were:

1. The influence of the clergy on the people was continuing.

2. Many priests were enemies of liberty and supported the king.

3. Tithes still continued in force and pressed heavily on the people.

4. Justice was still administered by the judges with the old severity.

5. The laws were still the old anti-popular ones.

6. Economic evils were very great with the lords of the manor still oppressing the people with fines and other legal dues.

Indeed, he continued, "the main work of reformation lies in this, to reform the clergy, lawyers and law". Otherwise all monarchical members will, "laugh in their sleeves, to see the government of our commonwealth built upon kingly laws and principles".[45] Wynstanley always insisted that

---
45. Gerrard Wynstanley. (1973) *The Law of Freedom and Other Writings*. London, Penguin Books. p. 280.

political freedom was impossible without economic equality, which meant abolishing private property and wage labour.

Digger influence spread across southern and central England and may have contributed to the development of the early Quakers.[46] Their communities were started near Wellingborough in Northamptonshire, Iver in Buckinghamshire, Enfield, Dunstable, Barnet, Bosworth in Gloucestershire and one in Nottinghamshire. By 1651 they were all finally crushed, however, as a result of attacks by local landowners supported by troops deployed by the Council of State. Their dissent was essentially defeated by a government using the full power of the law and the army.

Like Bunyan later, Wynstanley sympathized deeply with the plight of the landless poor. Private property, he complained, "hath made laws to hang those that did steal: it tempts people to do an evil action and then kills them for doing of it. If they beg, they whip them by their laws for vagrants; if they steal they hang them".[47] His solution was a democratic assembly, elected by manhood suffrage, when property belonged to all and not just a rich minority. This meant a profound social revolution and is a theme that runs through most of the dissent dealt with in this book.[48]

---

46. See W. S. Hudson. "Gerard Winstanley and the Early Quakers". *Church History*. vol. xii, pp. 191-4.
47. Christopher Hill. (1996) *Liberty Against the Law: Some Seventeenth-Century Controversies*. London, Allen Lane, The Penguin Press. p. 275.
48. *Ibid*. p. 276.

CHAPTER 7

THE ISLAND BEDLAM

It would be easy today to consider that some of the people and sects dealt with in this chapter were foolhardy if not unbalanced. However, they were taking part in the great tumult of ideas that burst upon England and flourished in the crisis caused by the Civil War, the execution of the king, the Commonwealth and, ultimately, the Restoration. All this gave England in the time of those upheavals the appearance of being an island bedlam.

But who are we to pass judgment with our modern conspiracy theories and the terrible world wars and dictatorships of the last hundred years? In their own way those dissenters and heretics were seeking a better world than the one in which they lived and which had been truly turned upside down. Many of them certainly provoked governments to clamp down on them because they had a serious and extensive following that threatened to upset the established order of things. But in reality, they played their part in bringing about the constitutional settlement that followed the Glorious Revolution at the end of the century and brought England into the modern world. Who then were they?

The Seekers and Ranters

Seekers formed a Protestant Dissenting Society who believed that the Roman Catholic Church was corrupt and by descent and common heritage the Church of England equally so. They considered that only a new Church to be established by Christ could possess his grace. This would have no clergy or hierarchy. They rejected all forms of a visible Church and denied that baptism, the sacraments or the scriptures could lead to salvation. Since their following was small, however, they posed little threat to the established order and were largely ignored.

The Ranters were a radical group or sect who from 1649 to 1654 were more prominent that the Seekers and had a more powerful impact. Their opponents called them "high professors", apparently as an insult. Their beliefs led them into conflict with the law and authority and they were characterised as heretical by the established church. According to their primary historian, A. L. Morton, they had,

> A deep concern for the poor, a denunciation of the rich and a primitive biblical communism that is more menacing and urban than that of Winstanley and the Diggers. Like the Diggers, and unlike Lilburne and his followers, they were ready to accept the name of Leveller in its most radical implications...It is hardly accidental that the Ranters began to come into prominence after the Leveller defeat at Burford and would seem to have attracted a number of embittered and disappointed former Levellers. Where Levelling by sword and by spade had both failed what seemed called for was a Levelling by miracle, in which God himself would confound the mighty by means of the poorest, lowest and most despised of the earth.[1]

Believing that God is in every creature the Ranters denied the authority of the Church and of scripture and called upon men to listen to the Jesus within them. This meant that they rejected the very concept of obedience and they were perceived to be a great threat to the social order and the exercise of power by the government. Even Wynstanley thought their principles led to a lack of moral values and restraint in worldly pleasures. They believed in nudity in public as a means of social and religious protest and as a symbol of abandoning worldly goods. Man, they said was free of both sin and the law. And they were firm advocates of blasphemy and engaged in public swearing and open sexual activity. As a consequence, they were accused of immorality and often imprisoned. The Blasphemy Act 1650 was directed at the Ranters and it may seem surprising today but many of their values were also shared by early Quakers.

---

1. A. L. Morton. (1970) *The World of the Ranters: Religious Radicalism in the English Revolution.* London, Lawrence & Wishart Ltd. p. 71.

Scourges of the Wealthy

Prominent among the Ranters was Laurence Clarkson, born at Preston, Lancashire in 1615. He became a Ranter leader in Cambridge having served in Cromwell's New Model Army as an army preacher. He believed there was no such thing as theft and, pre-dating Karl Marx, that the expropriators should be expropriated. "Taxes", he said, "rob the poor to pay the rich, and men that have no more religion than a horse act as censors of other men's writings".[2] He rejected all restraints, believed that sin was a product of the imagination and that private ownership of property was immoral. He considered that the individual could only become free from sin by acting out the vices. As Christopher Hill has written:

> At one Ranter meeting of which we have a (hostile) report, the mixed company met at a tavern, sang blasphemous songs to the well-known tunes of metrical psalms and partook of a communal feast. One of them tore off a piece of beef, saying "This is the flesh of Christ, take and eat". Another threw a cup of ale into the chimney corner, saying "there is the blood of Christ". Clarkson called a tavern the house of God; sack was divinity. Even a puritan enemy expresses what is almost a grudging admiration for the high spirits of the Ranters' dionysiac orgies: "they are the merriest of all devils for extempore lascivious songs,...for healths, music, downright bawdry and dancing".[3]

In 1650 Clarkson published a tract called *A Single Eye All Light, no Darkness; or Light and Darkness One* in which he set out the Ranters' ideals. These included his teaching that,

> There is no such act as drunkenness, adultery and theft in God...Sin hath its conception only in the imagination...What act soever is done by thee in light and love, is light and lovely, though it be that act called adultery...No matter

---

2. Christopher Hill. *The World Turned Upside Down: Radical Ideas during the English Revolution.* Op. cit. p. 172.
3. Ibid. p. 161.

what Scripture, saints or churches say, if that within thee do not condemn thee, thou shalt not be condemned.[4]

It is significant that the work indicates that it was published by Gilles Calvert, "in the yeer that the powers of heaven and earth was, is, and shall be shaken, yea damned, till they be no more for ever". In the event, the pamphlet was seized and burned and Clarkson was sentenced to banishment for his efforts. The sentence was never carried out, however, and after a month in prison he was released and he returned to his wife in Suffolk, finally ending up with the Muggletonians for about a year before he died.

Another prominent Ranter was Abiezer Coppe, an Oxford undergraduate from Warwick who had also served as an army preacher. As a scourge of the wealthy, he wrote in highly charged words,

> For this Honour, Nobility, Gentility, Propriety, Superfluity etc. hath (without contradiction) been the Father of hellish horrid pride, arrogance, haughtinesse, loftinesse, murder, malice, of all manner of wickedness and impiety, yea, the cause of all the blood that ever hath been shed, from the blood of the righteous Abell, to the blood of the last Levellers that were shot to death. And now as I live (saith the Lord) I am come to make inquisition for blood.[5]

Coppe believed the world was about to come to an end, yet he wanted to see far greater political changes than did the Levellers and Wynstanley and he disavowed both "sword-levelling" and "digging levelling".[6] He was passionate in denouncing the rich and followed the communistic teachings of John Ball. He called upon the rich, "Hide not thyself from thine own flesh, from a cripple, a rogue, a beggar, … a whoremonger, a thief, etc, he's thine own flesh".[7] He depicted God as a highwayman warning a rich man, "Thou hast many bags of gold, and behold, now I come as a thief in the night, with my sword drawn in my hand, and like a thief as I am — I say 'deliver

---

4. Laurence Clarkson. (1650) *A Single Eye All Light, no Darkness; or Light and Darkness One.* London, Gilles Calvert. pp. 8-12, 16.
5. A. L. Morton. *The World of the Ranters: Religious Radicalism in the English Revolution.* Op. cit. p. 86.
6. Abiezer Coppe. (1649) *A Fiery Flying Roll.* (1973 edn.) Exeter, University of Exeter. pp. 1-5.
7. Ibid.

your purse ... or I'll cut thy throat'". In 1650 his books were condemned by Parliament to be publicly burnt and he suffered a long period of imprisonment. He died in 1672 and was buried in the parish church near the Thames at Barnes in Surrey.

Abominable Practices

Unlike the Seekers the Ranters grew in influence and Parliament set up a committee to inquire into their activities. It reported on, "the several abominable Practices of a Sect called Ranters" and as a consequence an Act was passed in August 1650 for the Punishment of Atheistical, Blasphemous and Execrable Opinions. These included maintaining that God "dwells in the creature and nowhere else", that "the acts of uncleanness, Prophane Swearing, Drunkenness and the like Filfthiness and Brutishness, are not unholy and forbidden in the Word of God". Such heresies were punishable by six months' imprisonment, with banishment for a second offence. Police raids followed and leading Ranters were examined by a parliamentary committee but they stood on their rights and refused to answer questions that would incriminate them. Nonetheless, this did not save them and many Ranters were imprisoned and some tortured.[8]

Because they asserted that God existed in all things they argued that whatever men did naturally and spontaneously could only be good. This led to the rejection of moral codes although Morton considers that their enemies may have exaggerated their "immoral" conduct. On the other hand we have the writings of Clarkson and Coppe to help us decide. In any event, following the enactment of the 1650 Statute as a sect they were quickly destroyed and ceased to exist. According to George Fox most of the Ranters who survived the persecution became Quakers by the time of the Restoration.

---

8. *A. L. Morton. The World of the Ranters: Religious Radicalism in the English Revolution. Op. cit.* pp. 103-4.

Muggletonians

The Muggletonians were named after Lodowicke Muggleton. They were a small Protestant Christian movement that began in 1651 after the Ranters were suppressed. A London tailor, John Reeve, who was a cousin of Muggleton, believed he had received a commission from God who was Jesus to oversee the Second Coming of Christ. The sect believed that Heaven was six miles above the earth, that God was between five and six feet tall and that religious ceremony was unnecessary. They grew out of the Ranters but were opposed to the Quakers who were also an offshoot of the Ranters. The Muggletonians rejected all forms of worship and met only for discussion, often in public houses. Their core belief was the doctrine of the two seeds. They held that the rich, powerful and wicked were descended from Cain and the poor, oppressed and godly were descended from Abel. Bunyan, among many others, also held this view:

> The Holy Ghost, as Bunyan and every reputable Baptist, Fifth Monarchy Man and Quaker knew, had intended Cain and Nimrod as the types of all kings and tyrants... "It is the lot of Cain's brood to be lords and rulers first, while Abel and his generation have their necks under oppression".[9]

The Muggletonians linked this idea with their doctrine of the Fall, in which Cain was not the son of Adam but of Eve and the devil. Consequently, the inhabitants of the earth are divided into the Seed of Adam (through Abel) who are to be saved, and the Seed of Cain who are not only automatically damned but are in fact devils, for the "right devil" had no existence except in the seed of Cain.[10]

Reeve saw Cain's seed as "serpent-wise prudent men and women that mind earthly things... Their spirits lick up the gold and the silver, and put it into a bag... feeding upon riches and honours".[11] He dealt more fully with

---

9. William York Tindell. *John Bunyan, Mechanick Preacher.* p. 141. Cited by A.L. Morton. *The World of the Ranters: Religious Radicalism in the English Revolution. Op. cit.* p. 139.
10. A. L. Morton. *Ibid.* pp. 139-40.
11. John Reeve and Lolowick Muggleton. (1711 edn.) *A transcendent Spiritual Treatise upon several heavenly Doctrines.* London, pp. 34-5.

the doctrine of the two seeds in *Chapter 21* of his *A Divine Looking-Glass*, in 1656, explaining that, "The curse denounced against Cain and his seed, runs in the line of persons of maturity, not of minority, those dying young not necessarily damned". He declared, "Woe unto all learned men, especially if they be rich." Although not so radical socially as their bitter rivals the Quakers, after the Restoration the Muggletonians were persecuted and they insisted that all persecuting men were Cain's children. Curiously in the light of their views, they survived until 1979 when their last member Philip Noakes died in Kent.

Fifth Monarchists

Another dissenting group, the Fifth Monarchists, who were active from 1649 to 1661, took their name from the promise in the Book of Daniel that after four kingdoms of man (the Assyrian, Persian, Greek and Roman) there would be a kingdom of Jesus on earth. From 1666 "King Jesus" would reign with his saints for a thousand years. The Fifth Monarchists considered themselves to be those saints. After Cromwell had dissolved the Rump Parliament in April 1653, he still needed a Parliament to give his rule legitimacy but believed that the electorate might vote to restore the monarchy. Major-General Thomas Harrison, a Fifth Monarchist suggested to him that instead of an election there should be a ruling body of 70 selected "saints" who would usher in the forthcoming reign of Christ on earth.

Barebone's Parliament

Cromwell accepted a modified version of this proposal. He abandoned the idea of elections and he sought advice on the composition of a new Parliament from the Church and his army officers. In the event, the Army Council wrote to congregational churches throughout the country asking them to nominate persons they considered fit to form a government. Altogether, 140 Members were appointed to a new "Little Parliament", or "Barebones

Parliament"[12] as it was frequently called. As a consequence, on 4 July 1653 a fresh but limited Assembly was brought together in the Council Chamber at Whitehall, before proceeding to the House of Commons the following day.[13] Cromwell frankly informed the Members that they were there because the majority of the electorate had not yet been brought to acknowledge Jesus Christ and were not yet fit to be called. Addressing the Members as if he believed they were saints appointed by God and not himself, he told them that he resigned his power into their hands. Although Cromwell told the Assembly that it had been chosen by the Almighty it bore no resemblance to the "Parliament of Saints" by which name it was also sometimes referred to at the time. Nonetheless, it did set aside a whole day's sitting on 21 January 1652 for "seeking God" and provided for a day of public fasting.[14]

Made up as it was of irreconcilable moderate reformers on the one hand and radical religious zealots including the Fifth Monarchists on the other it is not surprising that in the end it was to prove an ineffective body. Finally, on 2 December, the conservatives in the Assembly surrendered their authority back to Cromwell although a small group of radical "saints" continued to sit. When a colonel came to clear the House and asked what they were doing they replied, "We are seeking the Lord". "Then you may go elsewhere", he said, "for to my certain knowledge he has not been here these twelve years".[15]

After the Restoration of 1660 Harrison was the first person to be found guilty of the regicide of Charles I. Approaching death with bravado and no regrets he was hanged, drawn and quartered looking, in a curious remark of Samuel Pepys, "as cheerfully as any man could in that condition".[16] A descendant of his later became the 23rd President of the United States in 1888. Inflamed by the barbaric execution of the regicides, on 6 January 1661, the anniversary of the Ordinance for the king's trial, some sixty Fifth Monarchists, led by a London wine-cooper named Thomas Venner, attempted

---

12. For its religious fervour the Assembly was named after Praise-God Barebone, a London leather-seller and Anabaptist preacher who was Member for the City of London and was noted for his long prayers, sermons and harangues which greatly amused the people.
13. *Parliamentary History*. vol. iii. col. 1391.
14. *Journals of the House of Commons*. vol. vii. 251.
15. Ivan Roots. (1966) *The Great Rebellion 1642–1660*. London, B. T. Batsford Ltd.
16. Robert Latham and William Matthews. (eds.) (1970) *The Diary of Samuel Pepys*. London, G. Bell & Sons Ltd., vol. i. (1660). p.265.

to take possession of the city in the name of "King Jesus" and establish a government based on the bible. On 10 January Samuel Pepys wrote of them in his *Diary*:

> Of all these Fanatiques that have done all this, viz., routed all the train-bands that they met with—put the King's lifeguard to the run—killed about 20 men—broke through the City gates twice—and all this in the daytime, when all the City was in armes—are not in all above 31. Whereas we did believe them (because they were seen up and down in every place almost in the City, and have been about Highgate two or three days, and in several other places) to be at least 500. A thing that never was heard of, that so few men should dare and do so much mischief.[17]

Most of the "fanatics" were killed or taken prisoner and on 19 and 21 January, Venner and ten others were hanged, drawn and quartered for high treason. Repressive legislation followed to suppress non-conformist sects and Fifth Monarchy came to an end.

In the seventeenth century religion and the Church occupied a central place in everybody's lives. Yet there was a new secularism arising which had both religious and democratic implications that revealed themselves in the writings and practices of the sects portrayed in this chapter. In spite of their ideas being cloaked in religious images there emerges clear radical and heretical yearnings for a better, more egalitarian, society.

---

17. Robert Latham and William Matthews. (eds.) *The Diary of Samuel Pepys, Op. cit.* vol. ii,(1661). p. 10.

CHAPTER 8

THE SOCIETY OF FRIENDS

Quakers

The Society of Friends was founded in 1644 by George Fox who was described by Macaulay as, "too much disordered for liberty and not sufficiently disordered for Bedlam". At the age of 19, after some heavy drinking followed by a night of religious exercises, he claimed to have received a "divine call" to forsake all his existing associations. Later, on impulse, he began his ministry by brawling in a church in Nottingham. After being imprisoned for that offence he was soon giving impressive sermons and quickly acquired a large following. His experiences led him to promote the idea that all men were equal in the sight of God. With the "inner light" as the central idea of his teaching his converts were first called "Children of the Light", then "Truth's Friends" and finally, in 1650, Quakers. The last arose when Fox and another preacher were before a bench of magistrates at Derby. He presumptuously told the justices that they should "tremble at the word of the Lord". In response the chairman abused them as "quakers" and the name took hold.

Before the Restoration of 1660 the Quakers formed a political, social and religious movement and had an important impact on English society. As Christians they chose not to rely upon the traditional "word of God" in the Bible but on the living word, the "inner light", by which they meant God's presence within every person since God speaks to all. Like the Levellers, Diggers and Ranters before them, early Quakers rejected the privileged structure of English society and sought to build a new society based on their religious views that all godly men possessed the same internal Light of Christ and that all men were equal. They denounced what they considered to be ungodly and corrupting influences within society. As with the Ranters, with whom the early Quaker movement had a great deal in common, some early Quakers practised a form of "holy nudism" as a rejection of worldly values. Nonetheless, their sect expanded rapidly and gave cause for alarm to the country's rulers who branded them as seditious.

Blasphemy

The treatment of James Naylor illustrates the harshness with which Quakers could be treated even under Puritan rule. Naylor had served in the parliamentary army for nine years under Major-General Lambert, and subsequently became a prominent Quaker and an eloquent preacher who attracted audiences of many thousands. He was the leader of a movement which included many former Levellers and Ranters. Then, in October 1656, shortly after Cromwell's major-generals were appointed, he was persuaded to symbolically re-enact at Bristol Christ's entry into Jerusalem seated on an ass. This he did with women supporters strewing palms before him. An outraged House of Commons decided to investigate what it called "this blasphemy". One MP recalled that he had, "often been troubled in my thoughts to think of this toleration".[1] Other MPs expressed the view that Naylor was insane. Against the wishes of Cromwell, the Commons hysterically denounced Quakers and sentenced the harmless and bewildered Naylor to branding on the forehead with the letter "B" (for blasphemer). He also suffered mutilation of his tongue with a hot iron, was made to stand in the pillory, was flogged twice and sentenced to indefinite imprisonment. The last continued for three years before he was finally released.[2] His resistance was broken in prison, however, and he died shortly after gaining his freedom.

It is surely unlikely that even then such a savage punishment would have been imposed upon a man considered insane. More likely, the truth is that at the time the Quakers were considered to be a threat to the state and this would explain why Naylor was prohibited from using a pen during his imprisonment. It also indicates why, despite Cromwell's displeasure, Parliament

---

1. J. T. Rutt, (ed.) (1828) *The Diary of Thomas Burton*. M. P. London, Colburn. vol. i. p. 24.
2. *A Compleat Collection of State Tryals from the reign of Henry IV to the end of the reign of Queen Anne*. London, T. Goodwin and Others. vol. iv. col. 796.

spent six months denouncing Naylor in their firm belief that he was part of, or even leader of, a movement that undermined the government.

William Penn

Born in the Liberty (a residential area) of the Tower of London on 14 October 1644, William Penn, the son of Admiral Sir William Penn, was brought up in a stronghold of Puritanism in Essex. Inclined to mysticism he was sent down from Christ Church, Oxford for nonconformity in 1661. After some exploits in the Dutch war and in Ireland he became a Quaker in creed, costume and conduct. This included refusing to take off his hat in the presence of his father or the king. True reverence, he argued, was due to God alone. After another visit to Ireland, he returned to London in 1670 where he found that the Friends' Meeting-house at Gracechurch Street had been closed under the Conventicle Act 1670 which restricted attendance at non-Anglican forms of worship. Undeterred, he proceeded to preach to an impromptu congregation in the open air. Alleged to be present, but not known to Penn, was Captain William Mead, a former soldier but also now a Quaker. They were arrested and taken to Newgate Prison.

Alleged Conspiracy

Both of them were brought to trial at the Old Bailey on 1 September 1670.[3] The trial lasted for four days and was to have startling and lasting repercussions. The judges were Samuel Sterling, the Lord Mayor of London and Thomas Howell, the recorder of London, sitting with four aldermen and two sheriffs. The charge was that, by "preaching in London's Gracechurch Street, they had conspired to assemble tumultuously a large concourse of people to the great terror and disturbance of many of the king's subjects. The essential elements of the indictment were the alleged conspiracy and the resulting unlawful assembly. As to the alleged conspiracy no evidence was

---

3. *6 State Trials*. cols. 951-69.

given that Mead knew Penn or, indeed, had spoken at the meeting at all so that a conspiracy to act in concert was, to say the least, unlikely.

When the prisoners were brought to the bar of the court they were not wearing their hats. The Lord Mayor asked who had taken their hats off and ordered an officer of the court to place them on their heads so that they might show respect to the court by uncovering in the presence of the judges. This he did. The mayor then demanded of the prisoners that they take their hats off and when they declined to do so he fined them 40 marks each for disrespect and contempt of court. Penn responded that, as they had entered the court with their hats off and they were put on by order of the bench, it was not they but the bench who should be fined.

After both the prisoners had pleaded not guilty, two witnesses for the prosecution gave evidence that they were called to disperse the meeting in Gracechurch Street where some four to five hundred people had gathered. Penn was preaching, they said, but due to the noise from the crowd they could not hear what he was saying. At this point, Mead turned to the jury and observed that the witnesses were testifying that they heard Penn preach despite the fact that they could not hear what was said. Further, he complained, the last witness was now swearing on oath that he had seen Mead at the meeting whereas at the committal proceedings before the mayor he had sworn that he had not seen Mead there.

Common Law

Penn indicated that he wanted to declare to all the world that it was his duty to meet incessantly in reverence to the God who made them. Told that he was not in court for worshipping God but for breaking the law, he asked by what law he was being prosecuted? The recorder did not mention the Statute but replied that it was the Common Law, at which Penn asked where that Common Law was. The recorder replied, "You must not think that I am able to run up so many years, and over so many adjudged cases, which we call Common Law, to answer your curiosity". To which Penn rejoined that if it was common it should not be so hard to produce. Continuing to argue his rights Penn was roughly handled out of the courtroom by order of the judges.

Mead then explained to the jury that he and Penn relied upon the liberties of the Common Law as propounded by Lord Coke. At this the mayor began to shout, "You deserve to have your tongue cut out". Mead too was then manhandled out of the courtroom and the recorder virtually instructed the jury to find the prisoners guilty and to ignore what had been sworn against them at what he said would be "your peril".

Incredible Scenes in Court

At the time prisoners were not allowed to give evidence on oath and when the jury returned from their retirement the foreman told the court that they found Penn guilty of speaking in Gracechurch Street. "Is that all", asked one of the judges? On their refusal to find that there was a tumultuous assembly, without which the indictment would fail, the judges abused and vilified the jurors and told them they could not be released until they had given a proper verdict. After asking for pen and paper the jury then retired again only to produce the same verdict on Penn and to find Mead not guilty.

The foreman of the jury was Edward Bushell. The mayor addressing the jury again now said "What, will you be led by such a silly fellow as Bushell, an impudent, canting fellow"? He was followed by the recorder who could hardly contain himself and told them that they would not be dismissed until the court had a verdict it could accept. "You shall be locked up", he growled, "without meat, drink fire and tobacco ... we shall have a verdict, by the help of God, or you shall starve for it". Their request for a chamber-pot was refused.

The following day the jury were called back to court and again returned the same verdicts. Addressing Bushell the mayor complained, "That conscience of yours would cut my throat". "No, my Lord", replied Bushell, "it never shall". Not to be placated the angry mayor retorted in ire, "But I will cut yours as soon as I can", and added that he would cut off his nose also!

On Penn claiming that justice demanded that the verdict of the jury be recorded, the mayor shouted, "Stop his mouth gaoler, bring fetters and stake him to the ground". To which the recorder, not to be outdone, added that it would never be well with the country until the Spanish Inquisition, which he praised at some length, was introduced into England.

On the following day the jury, now freezing with cold and near to starvation but still unbowed, said that they found Penn also to be not guilty. For not taking the advice the court had given them, said the recorder, they would be fined 40 marks each and imprisoned until it was paid. Penn and Mead were also taken to Newgate Prison where they were also to remain until they paid their fines for not removing their hats in court.

Bushell's Case

On 9 November 1670 a writ of *habeas corpus* was taken out in the Court of Common Pleas to show cause why Edward Bushell should not be released from prison. This is a landmark case in English history in securing unfettered jury trial. And Bushell and his co-jurors are still commemorated for their fight against tyranny by a plaque in the great hall of the Old Bailey which reads:

> Near this Site
> WILLIAM PENN and WILLIAM MEAD
> were tried in 1670
> for preaching to an unlawful assembly
> in Grace Church Street
> This tablet Commemorates
> The courage and endurance of the Jury Thos Vere Edward Bushell
> and ten others who refused to give a verdict against them although
> locked up without food for two nights, and were fined for their final
> Verdict of Not Guilty
> The case of these Jurymen was reviewed on a writ of Habeas Corpus
> and Chief Justice Vaughan delivered the opinion of the Court
> which established "The Right of Juries" to give their Verdict
> according to their Convictions

In the seventeenth century juries could be chosen only from male owners of freehold land valued at £20 or more. Moreover, they were selected by royal officials. Despite these considerable restrictions their members were also liable to suffer from direct judicial coercion since, as is shown in this trial, they could be fined and imprisoned if they refused to convict when directed to do so by the judges. At last, after centuries of judicial abuse, Bushell's case was to change the law.

The *habeas corpus* writ came before Chief Justice Vaughan sitting in the Court of Common Pleas. He was no friend of dissenters but he was keenly aware of the meaning of justice and the rule of law. First, he dismissed the contention that the jury had acquitted the prisoners against the direction of the court on a point of law. Take away the veil, he said, and we find that no evidence can be given to a jury of what is law. Therefore they cannot try a matter in law and any such direction is invalid. The jury, he continued, find on questions of fact and their full reasons may not be known to the judge since they might have personal knowledge beyond the evidence given in court which is all the judge could learn.

The chief justice then proceeded to draw, more clearly than ever before, the distinction between two types of misconduct of which jurors might be guilty. One was ministerial. For example, refusing to give a verdict or receiving evidence privately from a party to proceedings. For these, he said, they could be fined. However, the verdict itself was not a ministerial act but a judicial one and given according to the best of their judgment. For this, he said, they could not be fined and any other conclusion would be absurd.

The verdict of a jury on questions of fact was, he declared, unassailable — as it remains today. He continued, with unassailable logic, to ask what use was the jury if a judge could order it on pain of punishment to take his view of the facts? They might as well be abolished, which he said would be "a strange new-found conclusion after a [form of] trial so celebrated for many hundreds of years".

Such reasoning by the judge was to become conclusive. In the meantime the judgment that juries could not be fined or imprisoned for their verdict was reversed, on the technical ground that a criminal case could not be heard by the court of common pleas when in reality it was sitting on a writ of habeas corpus. Notwithstanding that judgment, Vaughan's arguments and reasoning were so obviously correct and in accord with legal and public opinion that they have been accepted as good law to this day.

Here we have with Penn, Mead, Edward Bushell and his co-jurors prime examples of dissenters fighting tyranny and changing the law despite threats and hardship.

Changing Image

Such was the perception of the Quakers as dissenters and blasphemers that even in 1684-5, some 1,400 of them were to be found in prisons and many of them died from their sufferings. There were perhaps 40,000 of them altogether at that time, an inspired and intractable community. They had in fact become a powerful force in English dissent and had accepted into their ranks many Ranters and some Levellers including John Lilburne.

Later, however, they prospered and became more respectable and their hostility to authority diminished to formal symbols like the refusal to swear an oath or to bare the head. And, owing to the persecution many of their most energetic spirits had emigrated to the plantations of North America where William Penn was to give his name to the colony of Pennsylvania.[4]

Quakers today, who number some 25,000 worshippers in the United Kingdom, cannot be regarded as dissenters in the sense that Fox, Penn and the early quakers were. They are less vehement but they still believe it is possible for every individual to have a real and direct experience of God, without the need for priests and rituals. And, in their desire to help make the world a better place they are active in helping slaves, the mentally ill, prisoners, refugees and war casualties among others.

---

4. E. P. Thompson. (1968) *The Making of the English Working Class*. London, Pelican Books. p. 33.

CHAPTER 9

JOHN COOKE

Barrister-at-Law

John Cooke's date of birth is not known but he was baptised in All Saints Church in Husbands Bosworth, just south of Leicester, on 18 September 1608. He was born into a poor Puritan family, his father, Isaac, and mother, Elizabeth, being tenant farmers. Nevertheless, they managed to have him educated at Wadham College, Oxford and he was called to the Bar by Gray's Inn in 1631 at the age of 23.

Until the publication of Geoffrey Robertson's biography in 2005[1] little was known about Cooke apart from the bare fact that he prosecuted Charles I at his trial in 1649. In fact, however, as a radical lawyer he had before that trial already advocated a whole series of reforms of the law, some of which were achieved in his lifetime whilst others were introduced over succeeding centuries. Acting for John Lilburne he had helped to establish the right to silence. He had advocated the fusion of law and equity and the abolition of imprisonment for debt. He forcefully argued that poverty was a cause of crime. And, he was a conscientious lawyer in his professional work but not always trusted by contemporaries because of his independence of mind and outspokenness.

Not having the money or status to make his way with ease at the English bar Cooke joined the Irish bar in 1634 and took employment with Thomas Wentworth, the Lord Deputy. Cooke had been influenced by Wentworth's leadership of the struggle in the House of Commons for a Bill of Rights. In Ireland Wentworth removed judges who took bribes and insisted upon fair

---

1. Geoffrey Robertson, QC (2005) *The Tyrannicide Brief: The Story of the Man who sent Charles I to the Scaffold*. London, Chatto and Windus.

trials. It was Cooke's task to carry this into effect and introduce measure of law reform, although he left Wentworth's service after only two years. Later, Wentworth reneged to the side of the king who eventually left him to his fate when he was attained by Parliament and executed.

Cooke's greatest testing time came when he was instructed to prosecute the king for war crimes. When the Civil War between king and Parliament broke out in 1642 the death of Charles was no part of Parliament's purpose. His enemies wanted to change his policies and the style of his rule, not to end that rule. But once his armies were defeated this was to change when he continued not only to hold to the doctrine of the divine right of kings but to intrigue with the Scots to plot the overthrow of his victorious parliamentary opponents.

Solicitor-General

It was on Christmas Day in the year 1648 that, with Charles their prisoner, the House of Commons appointed a committee to arrange for his trial. Less than two weeks later, on 6 January 1649, they decided to appoint a High Court to try the king. The House of Lords refused to participate and the vote in the Commons was a mere 26 to 20. Not surprisingly, most lawyers, including Bulstrode Whitelocke, the Lord Chancellor, and the Lord Chief Justice, retreated rapidly from London to their houses in the country. Some pleaded sudden illness. Cooke remained, however, and at the age of 40 and fairly lowly in the profession of barrister, he was chosen to prosecute the charge against the king. It was a momentous task since kings were widely believed to be above the law and God's representatives on earth and many asked where was the precedent in Common Law? The arraignment had all the appearance of blasphemy and Europe's heads of state looked on aghast. Who was powerful enough to try sovereigns? Well, it was what Cromwell and the army wanted and they had parliamentary backing. So, Cooke drafted the Act which abolished the monarchy on the ground that, "the office of a king in this country is unnecessary, burdensome, and dangerous to the liberty, safety and public interest of the people".

The new *ad hoc* High Court of Justice established by the Commons consisted of 135 commissioners presided over by the lawyer John Bradshaw. For the trial Cooke was appointed Solicitor-General. It was intended that he would be junior counsel to the Attorney-General, William Steele, but Steele sent a message to the court to say that he was seriously ill. So with all the legal luminaries now avoiding the trial it fell to Cooke to lead the prosecution. Success would depend on him and he vigorously undertook the task of persuading the court that a sovereign should not enjoy impunity after oppressing his people. It was an example that led ultimately to the case of the former Chilean head of state, General Pinochet, in 1989 when he was denied impunity as a former sovereign for torture and other crimes against humanity.

Prosecuting the King

On Saturday, 20 January 1649 Charles I was brought by river in the king's barge to the court sitting in the Painted Chamber of Westminster Hall. There he was charged with high treason. When the court was convened Bradshaw sat in the centre on a chair draped in crimson velvet. The commissioners sat around him on benches hung with scarlet. Before them was a table bearing the sword and mace. Beyond that was the dock containing a chair and writing desk for the royal prisoner. Galleries were provided for well-connected spectators.[2]

Proceedings commenced with the crier reading the names of the commissioners. A number of soldiers were then sent to bring in the king. Charles entered dressed in black and round his neck wore his blue ribbon and jewelled George. On his cloak was the silver star of the Garter. He carried a white cane with a silver head and was attended by 32 armed officers and his own servants. Seating himself, he left his hat on as a mark of disrespect to the court—an affront they chose to ignore.

After Bradshaw told the king they would proceed to do justice John Cooke stepped forward but before he could speak Charles tapped him on

---

2. John Hostettler. (1998) *At the Mercy of the State: A Study in Judicial Tyranny*. Chichester, Barry Rose Law Publishers, pp. 68-9.

the arm several times with his cane and said, "Hold"! At this moment the silver head of the cane fell off and this was widely held to be an ominous omen as to the king's fate. Despite the king's sign that Cooke should pick up the silver head he declined to do so and the king had to degrade himself by picking it up instead. Charles then endeavoured to speak but Bradshaw silenced him and commanded Cooke to read the charges. These had been prepared by Cooke and accused the king of levying war, causing many thousands to be slain, exhausting the public treasury and destroying trade. They concluded that Charles was being impeached, on behalf of the people of England, as a tyrant, a traitor, a murderer and a public and implacable enemy of the Commonwealth. Charles betrayed no emotion during the recital until Cooke read the words, "tyrant and traitor" at which point he laughed in the face of the court.

Asked by Bradshaw for his answer to the charges, Charles replied that he had a trust from God and would not betray it by answering to an unlawful authority. Bradshaw responded that their authority was "that of the Commons of England assembled in Parliament, in the name of the people of England, of which you are elected king". Charles denied he had been elected and again and again he demanded to be told by what authority he was there. The king and Bradshaw continued to skirmish in this fashion for some time until, in exasperation, Bradshaw had Charles removed from the court and ended the sitting. By the following Monday, when the court resumed, the commissioners and Cooke had decided what to do if the king continued to refuse to recognise the jurisdiction of the court.

"Refusal to Plead is a Confession"

Cooke accordingly opened by asking the judges to consider, contrary to law except in cases of treason, the king's denial as a confession of guilt. Without indulging in histrionics, he said,

> My Lord, to put an end to this great delay of justice, I shall now humbly move your Lordship for speedy judgment against him. I might press your Lordships, because according to the known rules of the law of the land, if a prisoner shall

stand mute or contumacious and shall not put in an effective plea — guilty or not guilty — to the charge against him whereby he may come to a fair trial, that operates as an implicit confession — it may be taken pro confesso. The House of Commons has declared that the charge is true — and its truth, my Lord, is as clear as crystal and as clear as the sun that shines at noon day. But if your Lordship and the court is not satisfied about that, then on the people of England's behalf, I have several witnesses to produce. And therefore I do humbly pray — and yet it is not so much I who pray, but the innocent blood that has been shed, the cry whereof is very great for justice and judgment — that speedy judgment be pronounced against the prisoner at the bar, according to justice.[3]

Cooke then put before the court the written evidence of witnesses who established that the king had started the Civil War and had taken part in it in person. After three days of such evidence, which was not challenged since Charles did not recognise the court, 45 of the commissioners resolved that the king should be sentenced to death as a tyrant, traitor, murderer and public enemy of the Commonwealth. Without delay, on the morning of 30 January he took his last journey to Whitehall surrounded by infantry and with banners flying and drums beating.

Told by a bishop that the executioner's axe would carry him from earth to heaven where he would find a great deal of cordial joy and comfort, he replied, "I go from a corruptible crown to an incorruptible crown, where I shall have no disturbance to fear". Outside the Banqueting Hall in Whitehall his head was struck off with one blow of the axe amidst what was officially described as a long deep groan from the vast crowd. The executioner held up the severed head and cried: "Behold the head of a traitor"! And with that the sovereignty of Parliament was established. The Commons ordered that the king's body be buried in St. George's Chapel at Windsor Castle where they forbade the use of the burial service of the Church of England.

---

3. Geoffrey Robertson, QC. *The Tyrannicide Brief: The Story of the Man who sent Charles I to the Scaffold. Op. cit.* pp. 169-70.

Trial of John Cooke

On the Restoration of Charles II in 1660, the new king's revenge against those involved in his father's death was bloody. Cromwell and Bradshaw were already dead and buried in Westminster Abbey but their coffins were removed and their remains hung on the gallows as Tyburn. Afterwards they were cut down and buried in a pit, after their heads had been removed and exposed on top of Westminster Hall until they were blown down by the great storm of 1703.

Some regicides had fled to the Puritan colonies of Virginia and Massachusetts, others to Geneva and the Low Countries. But 33, including Cooke, were arrested for trial at the Old Bailey. They were denied the benefit of the Indemnity and Oblivion Act which had excused some from crimes committed during the Interregnum and Cooke took his place at the bar of the court for a rigged trial on Saturday, 13 October 1660. His defence was to be the cab-rank rule that he had a duty to accept any brief to appear in a court in which he was entitled to practise.

Orlando Bridgeman was appointed as the presiding judge and Sir John Finch, who had replaced Cooke as Solicitor-General, opened the case for the prosecution. He said that the 1648 court was a "shambles of justice" which had proceeded to try—"I had almost said crucify"—the king. It was treason and murder. He continued that the prisoner was a wicked instrument who had written the charge of high treason against Charles I. He would not allow the king to speak in his own defence and had pressed hard for judgment. Slaying the Lord's anointed, he urged, was so great a crime that the news of it, he claimed in all seriousness, had caused many subjects at home and abroad to fall down dead. Witnesses gave evidence that Cooke had drafted the charge and had presented the case against the king, as his brief required him to do.

But, one prosecution witness, James Nutley who knew the accused, surprisingly assisted the defence by testifying that Cooke had told him there had been no intention to put the king to death. In response, a surprise witness called by Finch, a George Starkey, negatived the benefit to Cooke of Nutley's testimony by claiming that Cooke had said to him that, "He [the king] must die and monarchy must die with him". This alone was claimed to show malice and to prove the "overt act" required in treason trials. It was denied by Cooke and, indeed, the law required two witnesses to an overt act although no other was produced.

At the termination of the prosecution case, in accordance with the practice of the time, Cooke was not allowed to testify in his own defence but was permitted to address the court. He declared that he merely did his duty as a barrister and did not act maliciously. A barrister, he said, could not be held responsible for what happens to a prisoner he prosecutes. It had been for the court to pronounce the verdict.

Vitriol

Towards the end of the trial Bridgeman addressed the jury. For an hour and a half he poured forth vitriol to ensure there was no acquittal. He insinuated that Cooke was much more involved in the death of the king than the evidence had revealed. He had, he said, positively demanded judgment against the "blessed King". And in this case he held, contrary to the law of treason, that one witness to an overt act was sufficient. The evidence, he told the jury, was clear for compassing and imagining the death of the king. After his vehement and biased speech it came as no surprise when the jury found Cooke guilty. He was then sentenced to the horrendous death of being hanged, drawn and quartered and this was carried out on 16 October.

This penalty was merciless. A man found guilty of treason was drawn behind a cart to the place of execution where he was hanged and cut down whilst still alive, to be disembowelled and castrated with his intestines burnt before his eyes and finally decapitated with the remainder of his body cut into quarters.

Yet Cooke, and the others suffering the same fate, died loudly glorying in their fidelity to the "Good Old Cause" of republicanism until drums beat under the scaffold to silence them. Shortly before his death, Cooke wrote a letter in which he said, "We fought for the public good and would have enfranchised the people and secured the welfare of the whole groaning creation, if the nation had not more delighted in servitude than in freedom".

One of those executed was Major Thomas Harrison, a descendent of whose, as we have seen, became the 23rd president of the United States in 1888. Cooke also suffered the gruesome experience of having Harrison's bloody head placed in front of him during his journey to the gallows. He remains, however, a brave reforming barrister who gave his life in an endeavour to make tyranny a crime. His place in history has long been hidden but his inspiration has finally borne fruit with the prosecutions of Pinochet, Miloševic and Saddam Hussein for war crimes against their own people.

CHAPTER 10

JOHN MILTON

Revolutionary Ardour

John Milton, an outstanding poet, polemicist and young radical, was born in Bread Street, Cheapside, London on 9 December 1608 the son of John Milton, a scrivener and composer of some distinction, and Sarah Jeffrey. After study with a private tutor he went to St. Paul's School in London where according to his brother Christopher Milton, "when he went to Schoole, when he was very young, he studied very hard, and sate-up very late, commonly till twelve or one a clock at night and his father ordered the mayde to sit up for him".[1] At St.Paul's he studied Latin and Greek following which he went up to Christ's College, Cambridge where he graduated B.A. in 1629 and M.A. in 1632. He also became proficient in Hebrew, Spanish, French, Italian and Old English.

Whilst he was on a tour of France and Italy in 1638-9 he heard, he said, of "sad tidings of approaching Civil War in England".[2] On his return to this country he joined the struggle and with revolutionary ardour began to write prose tracts for the parliamentarians against episcopacy, i.e. government of the Church by bishops. In doing so he erupted with unrestrained fervour against the high-church group within the Church of England and in particular their leader the Archbishop of Canterbury, William Laud for his closeness to Rome and his emphasis on ritual and ceremony. In *Areopagitica* he was to denounce the wealthy man who resolved, "to find himself out some factor, to whose care and credit he might commit the whole management

---

1. Oliver Lawson Dick. (ed.) (1972) *Aubrey's Brief Lives*. London, Penguin Books. pp. 360-61.
2. John Milton. (1959) *Complete Prose Works*. (ed.) Don M. Wolfe. New Haven, Yale University Press. vol. iv. part i. pp. 618-19.

of his religious affairs" and resign "the whole warehouse of his religion". At the same time, he used his pen to great effect in linking episcopacy with the monarchy. In his *Of Reformation*, when working as a schoolmaster to the children of a London tailor, he described episcopacy as the "Huge and Monstrous Wen little lesse than the Head [monarchy] itself". Radical surgery was required upon the body politic to support the "floating carcase of a crazy and diseased Monarchy".[3]

He also coined the maxim that "new presbyter is but old priest writ large".[4] He vigorously denied that the state should involve itself with matters of religion and argued that magistrates should not seek to enforce religion but should simply defend the Church. If they did so, he said, the Commonwealth would be better served. He hated priests and deplored Sunday service which if it conflicted with a man's faith was a sin and violation of the law. A faith was worthwhile only if it resulted in charitable works. In fact, all his writings about contemporary issues at the time of political and religious strife in Stuart England reflect his deeply held convictions about them.

Divorce Pamphlets

In 1642, at the age of 35, Milton married 17-year-old Mary Powell the daughter of a royalist. Although they had four children they appeared to have little else in common and she refused to return to him after a visit to her parents' home. This caused him to write his controversial divorce pamphlets arguing both for the morality and the legality of divorce in which his emphasis was on God within us. In his defence of divorce he wrote that a man might put away his wife if he did it in accordance with his conscience. The elect, he believed, were free from all restraints including the marriage bond.[5] Nevertheless, he continued to believe in the importance of monogamy and that marriage should be based on love. On 5 May 1652 Mary died and Milton married Katherine Woodcock in 1656 and on the death of Katherine he

---

3. Edward Vallance. (2010) *A Radical History of Britain*. London, Abacus. p. 144.
4. Sir Charles Firth. (1900) *Oliver Cromwell and the Rule of the Puritans in England*. London, Oxford University Press, p. 140.
5. *Ibid.* vol. ii. pp. 366-7.

married for a third time on 24 February 1662. His wife on this occasion was Elizabeth Mynshull and this marriage, which lasted over eleven years until his death, was apparently the most successful.

Secretary for Foreign Tongues

Once the parliamentary forces were victorious in the Civil War Milton defended the republican principles of the Commonwealth. In *The Tenure of King's and Magistrates*,[6] as the full title indicates, he supported both the trial and the execution of Charles I. He said that though it was for God to punish wicked princes, yet God might choose to act through human agents: as He had done on 30 January 1649[7]–the date of the execution of the king. He further asserted that all men were born free, being the image and resemblance of God Himself.

His political stand secured his appointment by the Council of State in the same year as Secretary for Foreign Tongues. This involved his use of Latin in producing propaganda and serving as censor for the Commonwealth. Ten days after the execution of the king the royalists published a highly successful best-seller entitled *Eikon Basilike* which portrayed Charles I as an innocent Christian martyr in his solitude and suffering. The work clearly had an influence in glorifying the king so that in response, Milton wrote, *Eikonoklastes* (the image breakers) a clear defence of the regicides. In it he complained that the people, "with a besotted and degenerate baseness of spirit, except some few who yet retain in them the old English fortitude and love of freedom, are ready to fall, down flat and give adoration to the image and memory of this man, who hath offered at more cunning fetches to undermine our liberties and put tyranny into an art, than any British king before him".[8] Adding that "liberty hath a sharp and double edge, fit only to be handled by just and virtuous men".

---

6. John Milton. (1649) *The Tenure of Kings and Magistrates: proving that it is lawfull, and hath been so held through all ages, for any, who have the power, to call to account a tyrant or wicked king, and after due conviction to depose, and put him to death*. London, M. Simmons.
7. Christopher Hill. (1965) *Intellectual Origins of the English Revolution*. Oxford, The Clarendon Press. p. 185.
8. Sir Charles Firth. *Oliver Cromwell and the Rule of the Puritans in England. Op. cit.* p. 236.

The war of words continued when Charles II had published a defence of monarchy entitled, *Defensio Regia Pro Carolo Primo*. The Commonwealth Council of State then asked Milton to write a defence of the English people to help establish diplomatic and cultural ties in Europe. In 1652 this became, in Latin prose, *Defensio Pro Populo Anglicano* (the First Defence) which ran to many editions.

This brought royalist attacks on Milton himself and in response, in 1654, he published another defence of the English people, *Defensio Secunda*, in which he praised the Lord Protector, Oliver Cromwell, whilst calling upon him to remain true to the principles of the Republic. He also said that the Bible ought to be "so in proportion as may be wielded and managed by the life of man, without penning him up from the duties of human society".[9] This was written despite the fact that by this time Milton was completely blind and had to dictate his writings to helpers who included the poet Andrew Marvell.

Freedom of Speech

From the time of his conflict with Archbishop Laud, Milton had stood entirely apart from the Church of England and argued for its disestablishment. He believed in the right of weavers, carpenters and smiths to have a voice in the elections of Church ministers. He also kept his distance from most of the sects that proliferated at the time, except the Quakers. In fact, according to Christopher Hill he was a precursor of the Ranters[10] and he adds that Milton shared the millenarian hopes of the radicals. In the *Aeropagitica, A Speech for the Liberty of Unlicensed Printing,* Milton called for religious tolerance but this was to include only the Protestant sects and not extend to Catholics or Jews.

Nonetheless, failing as a man of his time to see his inconsistency, in *Aeropagitica*, he also declared, "give me the liberty to know, to utter and to argue

---

9. John Milton. (1959) *Complete Prose Works*. (ed.) Don M. Wolfe. New Haven, Yale University Press, vol. i. p. 699.
10. Christopher Hill. (1972) *The World Turned Upside Down: Radical Ideas during the English Revolution*. London, Temple Smith Ltd. p. 320.

freely according to conscience above all liberties. Truth is strong next to the Almighty; she needs no policies, no stratagems nor licensings to make her victorious... Give her but room, and do not bind her when she sleeps". It is a famous attack on censorship and a plea for freedom of the press which is still quoted when that freedom is in danger. In fact, it is often claimed to be the basis for the First Amendment of the United States Constitution and quotations from it appear in many public libraries in that country. It is interesting, and unforgivable, that in 1683 the University of Oxford officially condemned Milton's works on political theory and had them burnt.[11]

The Restoration

On the death of Cromwell on 3 September 1658, his son Richard, known as "Tumbledown Dick", became protector in accordance with his father's wishes, but he was unambitious and lacked the support of the army. After nominally ruling for only eight months he resigned. In his place, the landed gentry, the merchants and the professional classes were prepared to compromise with Charles II provided he would work with Parliament to preserve their interests. Milton remained true to his beliefs, however, and wrote several letters advocating the retention of the Republic. At the same time he returned to his attacks on the idea of a state-dominated church and the inevitable corruption within it. He saw the country slowly sliding away from the cause of liberty but his views became unpopular as the people came to support the restoration of the monarchy.

Paradise Lost

At this time Milton went into hiding following the issue of a warrant for his arrest and the burning of his books and poems, which were considered dangerous to the state. He returned when a general pardon was issued but was still arrested and served a short term in prison before Andrew Marvell, now

---

[11]. Christopher Hill. (1961) *The Century of Revolution: 1603-1714*. London, Thomas Nelson and Sons Ltd. p. 249.

an MP, and other friends secured his release. After the death of Cromwell he started writing his greatest work, the blank-verse epic poem *Paradise Lost*,[12] and completed it four years after the Restoration of Charles II. Since he was blind he dictated it to helpers and it was published in 1667 when he received for it the princely sum of £10! It reveals his despair at the failure of the Revolution with the Garden of Eden reflecting England's fall from republicanism and an earthly paradise. Eden is a Utopia with many traditional features of the earthly paradise he had described earlier and the revolution he had striven for. But he also re-affirms his optimism about the future of mankind with Adam sacrificing paradise for love of Eve. Adam's fall was not a consequence of curiosity as indicated in the Bible but of his love of a woman. *Paradise Lost* was described by Christopher Hill as a great hymn to wedded love. The poem also contains numerous references in code to his continuing support for the "Good Old Cause".

Optimism

Milton followed *Paradise Lost* with a sequel, *Paradise Regained* which he published along with a tragedy, *Samson Agonistes,* in 1671. In the first, which shows the reviving spirit of rebellion,

> The insistence that Christ's kingdom is not of this world is also a continuation of the lifelong battle of Milton (and the radicals) against the union of church and state, coercion of consciences by the civil power…The confidence that despite the political catastrophe of 1660 Christ's kingdom will still come—"but what the means Is not for thee to know nor me to tell'"—also recalls the Quaker analysis of the Restoration.[13]

It also reveals some resignation on Milton's part and despair at the failure of the Revolution. But *Samson Agonistes,* exhibiting echoes of his own life, shows that Milton still had confidence in ultimate political victory, even if

---

12. John Milton. (1788 edn.) *Paradise Lost*. Belfast, James Magee.
13. Christopher Hill. *The World Turned Upside Down: Radical Ideas during the English Revolution. Op. cit.* p. 323.

he could not envisage the means by which it would be achieved.[14] It emphasises man's integrity and the ultimate victory of his cause.

In 1666 the house in which Milton had lived in Bread Street was destroyed in the Great Fire of London. After his third marriage he had lived a quiet life in some comfort in what is now Bunhill Row in London before moving to Chalfont St. Giles to escape the Great Plague of London. Here he lived in a cottage known as "Milton's Cottage" which is now a museum holding many of his works. He died of kidney failure on 8 November 1674 and was buried next to his father in St. Giles's Church, Cripplegate.

---

14. *Ibid.*

CHAPTER 11

JOHN BUNYAN

From Tinker to Christian

John Bunyan, writer and preacher, is best known for his allegorical work, *The Pilgrim's Progress*. He was a radical whose dissent inspired William Blake and Tom Paine and helped lead to Methodism as a religion of the poor. Yet his position as a dissenter has been largely obscured.

For centuries the wealth and power of the Catholic Church, and its monopoly grip on the economy, had been used, in conjunction with the monarchy, to preserve feudalism against the rise of a merchant class. The Church wanted, therefore, to preserve the medieval form of hierarchy but Charles I shattered the alliance when he sought to rule by divine right. It was in this context that the Civil War erupted with its profound outburst of new thinking and violence that led to the Commonwealth and to Bunyan's dissent. Then afterwards, in the late seventeenth century, the merchants, and rising capitalists, were to join forces with the crown to strip the Church of both its wealth and its power.

He was born to Thomas Bunyan and Margaret Bentley in November 1628 at Bunyan's End, in the parish of Elstow, not far from Bedford. An entry in the Elstow parish register shows him to have been baptised on 30 November 1628. For his first employment he followed the example of his father and became a "braseyer" or tinker. This was a fairly skilled but lowly occupation which meant travelling the countryside by road repairing the holes in poor people's old pots and pans. He was largely uneducated, never having gone to school, and was virtually illiterate until he grew up. He was also burdened by the fact that his family had lost their lands and were close to destitution.

Serious family discord and social strife tormented him to distraction and that torment found expression later in his writings.

Soldier in the New Model Army

After his sixteenth birthday, during the English Civil War, the young Bunyan enlisted in the parliamentary army and from 1644 to 1647 served in the Newport Pagnell garrison in Buckinghamshire under the command of Sir Samuel Luke. In the New Model Army he was likely to have come across words and ideas that would have stirred him into an understanding of the larger issues then at stake in the strife-ridden country. We may conjecture that he would have heard from the politically-minded soldiers sentiments similar to those voiced by Edward Sexby in the Putney Debates of 1647 when he said,

> We have engaged in this kingdom and ventured our lives, and it was all for this: to recover our birthright and privileges as Englishmen...We had little property in this kingdom as to our estates, yet we have had a birthright. But it seems now, except a man has a fixed estate in this kingdom, he has no right in this kingdom.
>
> I wonder we were so much deceived. If we had not a right to the kingdom, we were mere mercenary soldiers...I am resolved to give my birthright to none. Whatsoever may come in the way and whatsoever may be thought, I will give it to none. I think the poor and meaner of this kingdom—I speak as in the relation to the condition of soldiers in which we are—have been the means of this preservation of the kingdom.[1]

Here, the common birthright means the law of liberty in contrast to the rule of imposed law, a concept that Bunyan readily accepted.

Bunyan always had difficult relations with his father and he stayed in the army as long as possible after the war was over but eventually left and returned to his trade of tinker. About 1649 he married a poor girl who gave him two

---

1. Geoffrey Robertson, Q.C. (2007) *The Levellers: The Putney Debates*. London, Verso. pp. 84-5.

religious books which had some influence on him and he started attending church. Struggling also with a sense of guilt and self-doubt arising from the troubled relationship within his family, he soon turned to Christianity and in 1655 he started preaching at which, filled with fire, he soon excelled. Indeed, people came in their hundreds to hear him. However, in the social upheaval of the times and with his denunciations of the rich, he incurred the hatred of the orthodox clergy who were outraged to see a working man in the pulpit. It was at this time that he moved to Bedford where he came into contact with a dissenting group.

Nonetheless, it was not long before he was in vigorous conflict with the Quakers and what he considered to be their anarchic approach. In consequence, it was against the Quakers that he published his first writing, *Some Gospel Truths Opened* (1656). Edward Burrough, a leading Quaker responded and Bunyan replied with *A Vindication of Gospel Truths Opened* in the following year. He declared the ideas of the Quakers were hardly better than those of the Ranters although the latter had made them "threadbare at an alehouse".[2] Even at this early date, however, he questioned whether there was in truth a God or Christ. Were the holy scriptures, he asked, a fable and cunning story written by politicians to make poor ignorant people submit to some religion and government?

As a Puritan, Bunyan had little difficulty in preaching during the Commonwealth but after the Restoration, the Cavalier Parliament with a zeal for king and Church passed, on 19 May 1662, the sectarian Act of Uniformity. Under this Statute, on St. Bartholomew's Day, Sunday 24 August, some 2,000 clergymen were driven from their parishes as nonconformists. The following year saw the passing of the Conventicle Act which made it illegal to attend a service conducted outside the Church of England with more than five persons present. Although many economic and political changes brought about by the Civil War could not be reversed the opportunity to secure religious moderation, as promised by Charles II at Breda in the Netherlands before his return to England, was destroyed by his change of heart.

---

2. John Bunyan. (1859 edn.) *Works*. London, Henry Stebbing. vol. ii.

Imprisonment

This caused problems for Bunyan who preached regularly outside his parish church and as his notoriety grew he was described by enemies variously as a witch, a Jesuit and, grotesquely, as a highwayman with several wives and mistresses. He was first arrested for preaching without a licence in 1658. Then, in January 1660 he was imprisoned for three months after preaching near Bedford and declaring to the court, "If you release me today, I will preach tomorrow". He was told that if he preached again he would be banished abroad and if he returned he would be hanged. After serving his sentence of three months, instead of being released he was kept in gaol for another six years! Efforts were made to persuade Judge Matthew Hale to endeavour to secure his release but although Hale was sympathetic there proved to be nothing he could do to help.

In 1666, when the persecution of dissenters became more acute, Bunyan was again incarcerated in Bedford Gaol in appalling conditions, this time for another six years for preaching at "unlawful meetings". More to the point was the hostility to his teaching when he said such things as "I am apt to think sometimes that more servants than masters, that more tenants than landlords, will inherit the kingdom of heaven". Yet, despite so many years in terrible conditions in prison he never wavered in his belief in the ordinary people from whom he was drawn. And all the while in the periods when he was out of prison and preaching he continued to work as a tinker.

In 1672 Bunyan was released from prison after the king's Declaration of Religious Indulgence. He immediately formed a dissenting nonconformist sect and established a church in a barn in Mill Street, Bedford where today stands the Bunyan Meeting Free Church. In spite of the Declaration he was again imprisoned in March 1675 under the Conventicle Act and secured his release six months later only with the help of his former enemies, the Quakers. It was whilst he was in prison on this occasion that he wrote the first part of *The Pilgrim's Progress* which had in its day a revolutionary significance as a manifesto of Protestantism. Although he was never arrested again he feared he would be and when visiting parish churches to preach he dressed as a waggoner complete with whip in hand.

The Pilgrim's Progress

Bunyan's major work is an allegory taking place in a world of symbolism and myth and yet with a realism based on actual problems faced by people.[3]

> The idea of the Christian life as a pilgrimage would have reached him through various channels; and the trick of personifying sins and virtues and states of mind was common to the period.[4]

And further, says Jack Lindsay, the great capacity the work had to affect his generation and the following generations of dissenters, lay in the fact that it concentrated the ideas and images of a whole vast body of popular literature which had for centuries been close to the living needs of men and women.[5] In it life is seen as a series of trials and conflicts, from pain to bliss, from which the hero at last emerges victorious into a future of fellowship.

And the living reality is there. As Lindsay wrote:

> The impression conveyed by the allegory is the exact opposite of what it literally professes. The phantasms of good and evil become the real world; and in encountering them the Pilgrim lives through the life that Bunyan had known in definite place and time. The pattern of his experience, the fall and the resolute rising-up, the loss and the finding, the resistance and the overcoming, the despair and the joy, the dark moaning valleys and the singing in the places of the flowers—it is the pattern of Bunyan's strenuous life. There are comrades and enemies, stout-hearts and cravens, men who care only for the goal of fellowship and men of greed and fear; and these are the men of contemporary England.
>
> The Celestial City is the dream of all England, all the world, united in Fellowship.[6]

In the book Christian's aristocratic enemies are the "Lord Carnal Delight", the "Lord Luxurious", the "Lord Desire of Vain Glory", "my old Lord

---

3. Jack Lindsay. (1969) *John Bunyan: Maker of Myths*. Port Washington, Kennikat Press. p. vii.
4. *Ibid.* p. 165.
5. *Ibid.* p. 167.
6. *Ibid.* p. 194.

Lechery", "Sir Having Greedy", with "all the rest of our nobility". By contrast the poor were to be found in the Valley of Humiliation of which "Great-Heart" says "It is true ... I have gone through this Valley many a time, and never was better than when here". Indeed, Bunyan's dissent was later to foster John Wesley's religion of the poor.

Milton, Bunyan, Defoe

According to Hill, the hero of John Bunyan's *The Pilgrim's Progress* is

> ...one of the people: the law and its courts, he knows, will not give him justice. The spiritual autobiography itself becomes subversive when its hero is a lower-class itinerant whose major temptations occur when playing tipcat.

There could be no more banal villain than Bunyan's petty-bourgeois Mr Badman, though like Satan in *Paradise Lost* he is often very much livelier than the virtuous characters. "Episodes like his courtship and second marriage look forward to Daniel Defoe in theme as well as in style".[7]

> In fact, Bunyan, with his vivid characterisation, his psychological insight, and his perfect ear for spoken prose, links the pamphlet literature of the forties with the novels of Defoe.[8]

Affinity with the Ranters

Of some interest is the connection of Bunyan with the Ranters. His approach to social and political issues was similar to theirs but he differed from them on theology. In his autobiography, *Grace Abounding to the Chief of Sinners*,[9]

---

7. Christopher Hill. (1972) *The World Turned Upside Down: Radical Ideas during the English Revolution*. London, Maurice Temple Smith Ltd. p. 330.
8. Christopher Hill. (1966) *The Century of Revolution, 1603-1714*. London, Thomas Nelson and Sons Ltd. p. 252.
9. John Bunyan. (1827 edn.) *Grace Abounding to the Chief of Sinners*. London, J.F. Dove. par. 44-5.

written after he experienced deep religious experiences, he claimed to have encountered Ranters before his conversion to Baptism. And, one of Bunyan's intimate companions had, "turned a most devilish Ranter, and gave himself up to all manner of filfiness".

Bunyan denied the existence of God and angels, and laughed at exhortations to sobriety.[10] He observed that many think to swear is gentleman-like.[11] Blasphemy, the taking of God's name in vain, was a form of defiance to the established order. It was an act of defiance and release that would have appealed at least to the young Bunyan.

Some other religious groups were swept away by the Ranters who, for a time, obtained a substantial following. They claimed that they had, "attained to perfection that could do what they would and not sin" — a doctrine which Bunyan found very seductive–"I being but a young man". He was especially tempted to believe there was no judgment or resurrection, and therefore that sin was not such a grievous thing — "the conclusion that atheists and Ranters do use to help themselves withal" turning the grace of God into licentiousness. Nevertheless, ultimately his answer to the Ranters became the orthodox one that they lacked a conviction of sin.[12]

He cared about "the old laws, which are the Magna Carta, the sole basis of the government of a kingdom". Adding that they "may not be cast away for the pet that is taken by every little gentleman against them".[13] He also wrote, "More servants than masters, more tenants than landlords, will inherit the kingdom of heaven. God's own are most commonly of the poorer sort".[14] Whereas most rich men suffered what he called a "sad condition".

Bunyan's death came after he caught a cold when riding from Reading to London in heavy rain. He managed to preach in Whitechapel before the cold developed into a fever but after ten days ill in bed he died at the house of his friend John Strudwick, a grocer, on Snow Hill in Holborn on 31 August 1688. Like Defoe, when he died he was buried in what is now Bunhill Fields

---

10. *Ibid.* p. 164.
11. John Bunyan. *Works, Op. cit.* vol. 3. p. 601.
12. John Bunyan. *Grace Abounding to the Chief of Sinners. Op. cit.*
13. John Bunyan. *Works, Op. cit.* vol. i.
14. *Ibid.* vol. iii.

but was then the dissenters' burial ground at Islington in London. As with Milton, his works have a striking influence in the modern world.

CHAPTER 12

DANIEL DEFOE

Political Leanings

The prolific writer Daniel Defoe is believed to have been born in 1661 in the St. Giles district of London. The exact date is unknown. His original name was Daniel Foe after his father who was a Presbyterian fallow-chandler and butcher, but he later added the aristocratic-sounding "De" and sometimes claimed descent from the family of De Beau Faux. Nevertheless, his writing was in the tradition of anti-feudal realism. His parents were Protestant dissenters and they intended him for the ministry. For this purpose he received an excellent education in the Dissenters Academy at Newington Green in London run by Charles Morton where Charles Wesley was also later to be a pupil. Education was important for dissenters who were prevented for religious reasons from attending the universities of Oxford and Cambridge. At this time a census in London revealed that seven per cent or more of the population of the metropolis were dissenters. However, when of age Defoe decided not to become a minister of the Church and became instead a general merchant dealing in hosiery, woollen goods and wine.

Nevertheless, his political leanings became clear when, in 1685, he joined the cause of liberty and Protestantism in the Monmouth Rebellion in southwest England, the last military campaign in this country. He was arrested after Monmouth's defeat but, fortunately for him, he gained a pardon which enabled him to escape the Bloody Assizes of the hanging Judge Jeffreys. In 1698 he wrote *The Poor Man's Plea* in which he indicated the direction in which his thinking was going. He wrote that, "The man with a gold ring and gay clothes may swear before the justices or at the justices; may reel home through the open streets and no man take any notice of him; but if a poor man gets drunk or swears an oath, he must to the stocks without remedy".[1]

The True-born Englishman

One of his early writings for the public was a satire in verse published in 1701 and called *The True-born Englishman*.[2] His immediate purpose was to present Englishmen as a mixed race and to satirise their claim to racial purity. The book was severely criticised but widely read, selling 80,000 copies.

A few extracts from the poem will illustrate the direction in which the mind of the young Defoe was moving:

> Wherever God erects a house of prayer,
> The Devil always builds a chapel there:
> And 'twill be found, upon examination,
> The latter has the largest congregation.

Then as part of the belief in the Norman Yoke and the origins of the nobility of his day:

> The great invading Norman let us know
> What conquerors in after-times might do;
> To ev'ry Musqueteer he brought to town,
> He gave the lands which never were his own.
> The rascals thus enrich'd, he call'd them lords,
> To please their upstart pride with new-made words;
> And Doomsday-Book his tyranny records.
>
> And here begins our ancient pedigree
> That so exalts our poor nobility:
> 'Tis that from some French trooper they derive,
> Who with the Norman Bastard did arrive:

---

1. Daniel Defoe. (1698) *The Poor Man's Plea*. London, A. Baldwin.
2. Daniel Defoe. (1836 edn.) *The True-born Englishman: a Satire*. Leeds, Alice Mann.

> The trophies of the families did appear;
> Some show the sword, the bow, and some the spear,
> Which their great ancestor, forsooth, did wear.

His attitude to wealth is clear:

> Wealth, howsoever got, in England makes
> Lords of merchants,- gentlemen of rakes!
> Antiquity and birth are needless here;
> 'Tis impudence and money makes a peer.

As is his perception of the clergy:

> As wise men say, they are both dang'rous things,
> The ruling priesthoods and priest-ridden kings;
> And of all plagues with which mankind are curst,
> Ecclesiastic tyranny's the worst.

And law is supreme:

> The voice of nations, and the course of things,
> Allow that laws superior are to kings.

A year after the publication of *The True-born Englishman* Defoe wrote another book called *Reformation of Manners, a Satyr* which contained a strong invective against the slave trade.

Defending Dissenters

Another year later, in 1703, in the reign of Queen Anne, in response to proposals to act against dissenters, he followed with another satire entitled, *The Shortest Way with the Dissenters, or Proposals for the Establishment of the Church*. In this he purported to argue for their extermination in order to show the absurdity of ecclesiastical intolerance. He advocated that the

Dissenters' poison was such as to, "make it a charity to our neighbours to destroy these creatures". He proposed with mock seriousness that anyone attending a nonconformist chapel should for the first offence be fined, for the second offence, flogged and for the third, executed. The irony was not always appreciated, however, and produced a number of works describing the satire as scandalous and malicious.

The House of Commons took a similar squinted view, voted that the pamphlet was a seditious libel and ordered that it be burnt by the public hangman. It was also decreed that the publishers be prosecuted. Once they were arrested Defoe came forward to assist them and stood trial with them. He was convicted, sentenced to be fined, imprisoned in Newgate and to stand in the pillory for three days. In prison he wrote a number of pamphlets and a mock poem called *A Hymn to the Pillory*. So strong was the feeling that he had been treated too severely that Queen Anne sent money to his wife and family. It was this experience that caused Defoe to write:

> Knowledge of things would teach them every hour
> That Law is but a heathen word for Power.

He was also to write, in 1722, the novel, *The Fortunes and Misfortunes of the Famous Moll Flanders,* which is a serious study of crime and the criminal justice system in the late seventeenth and early eighteenth centuries.

Robinson Crusoe

In 1719 Defoe wrote *Robinson Crusoe,* the novel for which he is most famous. It was an instant success with its first print selling out within two weeks. In this and his other novels of creative writing he portrays a vivid realism about life in Restoration Britain. He follows the maxim of Alexander Pope that "the proper study of mankind is man". Life, he says, is today what man makes it as distinct from the uncertainty of feudal times. As one eminent Marxist academic has written:

Shows why we should never give up on the capacity of people to change
Jim Hopkinson, Bradford Children's Services

YOUR HONOUR
CAN I TELL YOU MY STORY?
Andi Brierley

WATERSIDE PRESS

NEW

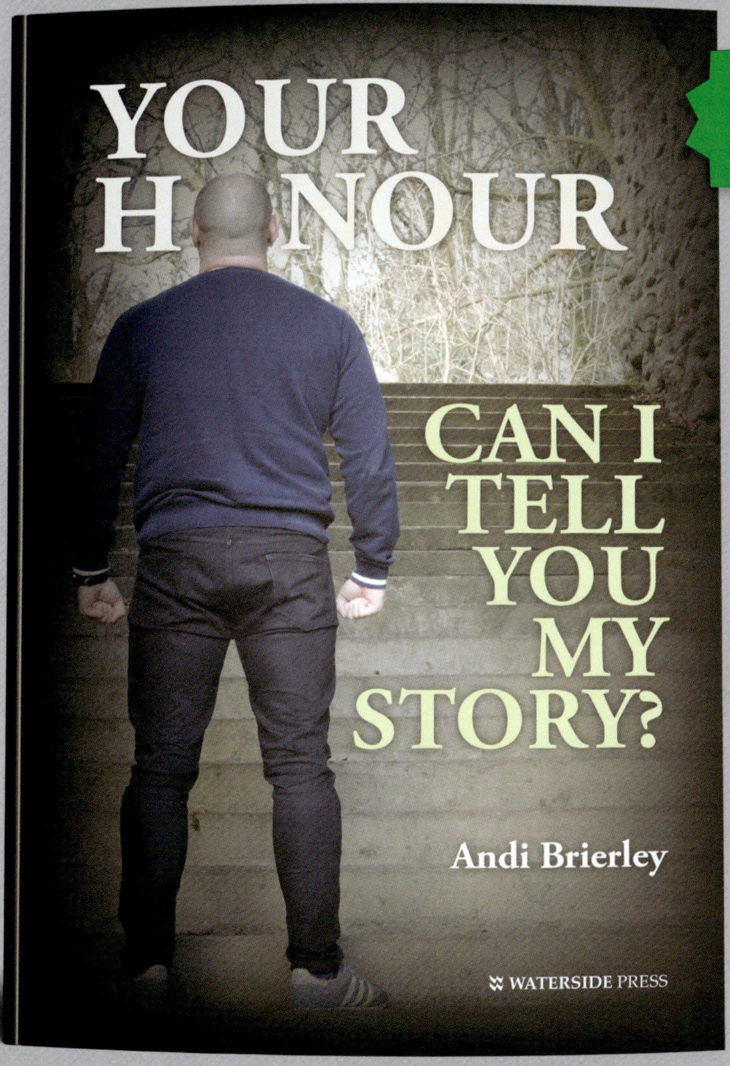

Free UK Delivery

WatersidePress.co.uk

Your Honour Can I Tell You My Story?
by Andi Brierley

Andi Brierley's story of his progress through care, prison and social rejection to youth justice manager in Leeds contains countless clues for those who work with troubled young people. It begins with failures to deal with his chaotic early life moving from place to place, fragmented parenting and poor role models. In a family home encircled by criminality, drugs, violence and baffling adults he ended up first in a young offender institution then in prison.

There he learned how to act and think as a prisoner for his own survival, something that only made matters worse when trying to re-adapt to the world outside on his release. Caught in a downward spiral, hooked on drugs, partying, not strong enough to resist negative influences and his well-being deteriorating, the book shows how small things made a difference.

Until he regained self-worth and rescued his life. Important for the messages it contains for professionals and young people in trouble with whom he has forged a remarkable connection.

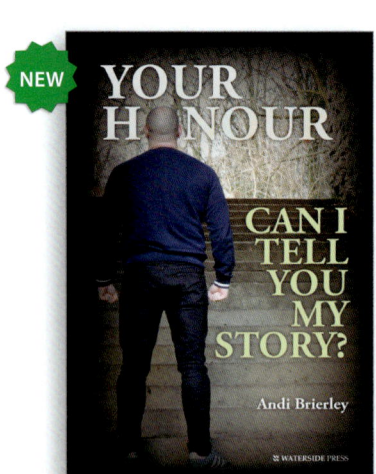

As featured in the *Yorkshire Post* and the Association of YOT Managers *Bulletin*

Available in paperback & ebook
(inc Kindle, Apple and Google)
258 pages | Published in April 2019
ISBN 978-1-909976-64-1
Price £19.95

More details at www.WatersidePress.co.uk

WATERSIDE PRESS

Turn around stories
Writing as a route out of crime and towards a better life

Prison writing is a valuable two-way process. Education aside many prisoners have changed their lives using writing as a bridge to a new life and career. Our first book in this genre was Bob Turney's acclaimed *I'm Still Standing* back in 2002. Recommended personally by Lord Longford, Bob the one-time prolific burglar turned author actually went on to become a probation officer! Ex-offenders who followed his lead include Alan Weaver (who became a social worker, *So You Think You Know Me?*), Ben Ashcroft (young offender to youth worker, *Fifty-one Moves*) who tells of his constant changes whilst in care and Justin Rollins (ex-graffiti artist and now motivational speaker, *The Lost Boyz* and *Street Crhymes*) whose books have been adopted as set texts on degree courses in Birmingham and elsewhere.

Another ex-prisoner turned author whose book has been widely used in education is Frankie Owens whose *Little Book of Prison* also made the final of the People's Book Prize. There is also a book, *Recovery Stories*, about those who have survived addiction.

Actor Stephen Fry's turn around story was included in a collection called *Going Straight* along with that of the train robber Bruce Reynolds whose life changed after being released from his 25 year sentence. Andi Brierley (opposite) who went from prisoner and heroin addict to manager of a youth justice unit in Leeds is the latest in this considerable line-up. Each of these books centres on identifying the changes, choices and threads that led from being an offender to law-abiding citizen.

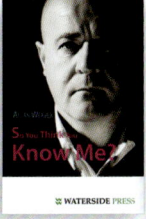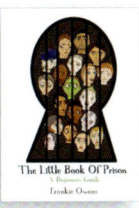

Further details, information and reviews of these and other key texts are available at our website.

WatersidePress.co.uk

Free UK Standard Delivery on Every Order

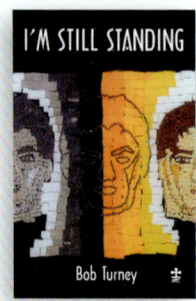 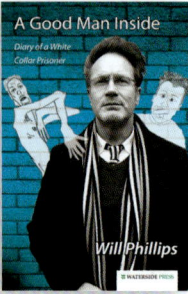

Bob Turney's *I'm Still Standing* is the book that established the turn around genre with Waterside Press. Will Phillip's *A Good Man Inside* is a diary of the impact of imprisonment on a white collar offender telling how he survived it before returning to normal life.

Order Online
WatersidePress.co.uk
Call +44 (0)1256 882250
or ask at all good bookshops

Payment by invoice — for multiple copy orders only, we may invoice your firm/institution (at our discretion). Please place an order via our website and select "Invoice With Order" as your payment method.

Free UK Delivery
- UK Standard Delivery is **FREE** for all orders and takes 2–5 working days.
- First Class starts at £2.00 rising by £1 per additional book to a maximum of £5.95 for 5+ books.
- **In stock items are typically despatched within 24 hours.**

International Delivery
- For rates see www.WatersidePress.co.uk/delivery

   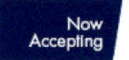 

Ebooks
Most Waterside Press titles are also available as ebooks. These can be read on a variety of devices, including **Kindle**, **iPhone/iPad**, **Android**, **Nook** (and many more). You can buy them through online retailers, including **Amazon**, **Apple** and **Google Play**. Search the web, or see our website for details and links. Our ebooks are also available to institutions via **library agreements** — ask your supplier or contact us for more details.

Available on

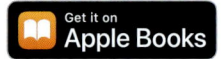

Amazon, Kindle and all related logos are trademarks of Amazon.com, Inc. or its affiliates. The Apple logo is a trademark of Apple Inc., registered in the U.S. and other countries. Apple Books is a service mark of Apple Inc. Google Play and the Google Play logo are trademarks of Google LLC.

Waterside Press
Sherfield Gables, Sherfield-on-Loddon,
Hook, Hampshire, RG27 0JG. Tel. 01256 882 250

Robinson Crusoe is in one sense a story in praise of the bourgeois virtues of individualism and private enterprise. But in another, and more important sense, it celebrates the necessity of social living and the struggle of mankind through work to master nature, a struggle in which the bourgeois virtues are sands upon the Red Sea shore. For where would Crusoe have been without the products of social living which he could salvage from the wreck? And what seekers after "the blessings attending the middle station of life...not embarrassed with the labours of the hands or of the head..." could cry out with Crusoe: "No joy at a thing of so mean a nature was ever equal to mine, when I found that I had made an earthen pot that would bear the fire"?[3]

Defoe was a writer of astonishing versatility. He wrote more than 250 works, including *Moll Flanders, Roxanna, Colonel Jack* and *Captain Singleton* and is regarded as the founder of British journalism from his work with 26 periodicals. He died in his lodgings at Ropemaker's Alley Moorfields on 24 April 1731 and was interred as a dissenter, as was Bunyan, in Bunhill Fields in Islington, London where his grave can still be seen.

---

3. Arnold Kettle. (1951) *An Introduction to the English Novel.* London, Hutchinson's University Library, vol.i. p. 61.

CHAPTER 13

JOHN WILKES

The Hellfire Club

John Wilkes, one of the most astonishing men of the eighteenth century, was born in Clerkenwell, London on 17 October 1725 the son of Israel Wilkes, a malt distiller and his wife Sarah. He was educated at an academy in Hertford before going to the University of Leyden in the Dutch Republic. He was elected a Fellow of the Royal Society in 1749 and appointed High Sheriff of Buckinghamshire in 1754. Clearly he was not born to be a radical or a blasphemer although he became both.

In 1747 Wilkes had married Mary Meade but they separated in 1756. He then plunged into a life of debauchery. He was a member of the so-called Order of Medmenham Monks which met at Medmenham Abbey, the home of Sir Francis Dashwood on the Thames near Marlow. This obscene "Order" soon became known as the Hellfire Club on account of its nightly orgies and mock Devil worship. After a time it moved to the excavated caves at West Wycombe where members of the club could indulge their sexual fantasies with women brought in from the local area. The club had many distinguished members including not only Wilkes but the Earl of Sandwich and Sir Francis Dashwood, the colonel of the Buckinghamshire militia. It was said that on one occasion Wilkes brought into the club a baboon dressed in a cape and with horns and caused considerable mayhem among the drunken "knights".

The *North Briton*

When George III ascended to the throne in 1760 he set about attempting to retrieve the royal power which he believed had been so carelessly allowed to lapse by his two predecessors. George Grenville accepted office as prime minister precisely in order to help free the king from the restraints of the powerful oligarchies formerly in control of the government. The Opposition, however, received advance notice of the Ministry's new policy to be set out in the King's Speech of the Grenville government and to combat it with the maximum of publicity sought the help of Wilkes. He was the editor of the radical *North Briton* journal and, prompted by the elder Pitt, published his famous, or, to some, infamous, issue No. 45 on 23 April 1763 in which he branded the speech as dishonest.[1]

The government decided to prosecute Wilkes for sedition and, as part of their preparations, they sought to undermine his character. To this end they published a private poem to which he had contributed called *An Essay on Woman*, an obscene and blasphemous parody of Pope's *Essay on Man*. The former "monk of Medmenham", the Earl of Sandwich, was delighted by the opportunity to read the *Essay* to the House of Lords and their Lordships unanimously condemned it as "a most scandalous, obscene, and impious libel". In fact, Wilkes was responsible for very little of the *Essay* and there was a good deal of duplicity in the government's action. As a consequence it had little impact upon his followers. Instead, it rebounded on those pursuing Wilkes with the Earl of Sandwich henceforth known as "Jeremy Twitcher". Others involved with Sandwich lost their jobs and were widely known as "informers".

In the meantime, Grenville chose to treat Wilkes's article in the *North Briton* as a personal attack on the king and secured a general warrant to be issued, not against a named person, but for the arrest of all those concerned in the production of that issue of the journal. Their papers were also to be seized. True to its name the warrant permitted arrests indiscriminately and 49 people were detained under it. Wilkes was among those arrested and the authorities had him concealed in the Tower of London in an attempt

---

1. *19 Cobbett's State Trials*. cols. 1075-1138.

to evade a writ of *habeas corpus*. This ruse did not succeed, however, and the liberal-minded Charles Pratt (later Earl Camden) released him. Wilkes appeared in the Court of Common Pleas on 3-6 May 1763 and was set free under privilege of a Member of Parliament.[2]

Wilkes and Liberty!

When he later sued under-secretary Robert Wood for trespass in entering his house and seizing his papers the case also came before Charles Pratt, this time as Lord Chief Justice of the Court of Common Pleas, sitting with a special jury (i.e. a jury specially chosen by the crown from among wealthy landowners). At one point, in the case in Westminster Hall, Wilkes cried out, "My Lords, the liberty of all peers and gentlemen, and, what touches me more sensibly, that of all the middling and inferior set of people, who stand most in need of protection, is in my case this day to be finally decided upon a question of such importance as to determine at once whether English Liberty shall be a reality or a shadow".[3]

Large crowds invaded the court sitting at Westminster Hall crying, "Wilkes and Liberty!" and the jury may have been influenced by them. Whether they were or not they found a general verdict in Wilkes' favour and awarded him the surprisingly large damages of £1,000. More importantly, the judge ruled that general warrants, which did not name the person to be arrested, were illegal, as they have remained ever since.[4] After his release Wilkes defiantly reissued No. 45 and the House of Commons again voted that the publication was a seditious libel. They ordered that it be burned by the public hangman in front of the Royal Exchange where he and the Sheriff of London suffered gross indignities at the hands of the crowd who prevented the burning from taking place.

---

2. J. Steven Watson. (1960) *The Reign of George III, 1760-1815*. Oxford, The Clarendon Press. p. 99.
3. George Rudé. (1962) *Wilkes & Liberty: A Social Study of 1763 to 1774*. Oxford, Clarendon Press. pp. 26-7.
4. *19 State Trials. Op. cit.* cols. 1154-1176. And see Raymond Postgate. (1956) *That Devil Wilkes*. London, Dennis Dobson, pp. 51-58.

Absurd Ruling

Before Wilkes could be re-arrested, however, his friends managed to get him away to Paris. After five years in France he returned in 1768, to an England suffering considerable economic distress, in order to plead to be allowed to stay. Whilst here he stood as a Radical candidate for Parliament and received enthusiastic support on a "Wilkes and Liberty" ticket. In a boisterous campaign involving thousands of people he won election to the House of Commons as the member for Middlesex. At the same time he presented himself at the Court of King's Bench to surrender as an outlaw. Crowds escorted him to the door of the court and troops guarded every approach. Lord Mansfield presided over the case and at the end surprised everyone present by declaring that he could take no notice of the matter as Wilkes was not in fact before the court at all. The Attorney-General had not arrested him by a writ of *capias utlegatum* so the court, said Mansfield, could not see him![5]

But this absurdity did not prevent an alarmed government continuing his confinement as an outlaw and he was imprisoned in the King's Bench Prison. Riots followed and they continued for a fortnight. During this time crowds frequently gathered at the gaol and one evening the prison lobby was demolished amid more shouts of "Wilkes and Liberty"! Other slogans which had a republican or revolutionary character included: "Damn the King, damn the Government, damn the Justices"! And, "This is the most glorious opportunity for a Revolution that ever offered".

Massacre of St. George's Fields

The next day, 10 May 1768, witnessed a violent affray known to history as the "Massacre of St George's Fields". Some 15,000 or 20,000 supporters of Wilkes gathered in the fields and a fearful government called out a troop of horses and 100 men of the third regiment of Foot Guards.[6] Justice Gillam read the Riot Act and was met with jeers and a volley of stones. Shortly afterwards the soldiers were ordered to fire into the crowd killing eleven

---

5. *Annual Register.* (1768) pp. 93-95.
6. *Ibid.* p. 49.

people and creating the first martyrs of the Wilkite cause.⁷ That evening the houses of two Southwark magistrates were pulled down and the riots spread to other parts of the capital. Incendiarism was widespread.

A few weeks later Wilkes published, with his own comments, the instructions sent by Lord Weymouth to magistrates in April, enjoining them to make full use of the military in the event of riots. This, he told the public, revealed that there had been deliberate killings by a tyrannical government prepared to trample on Englishmen's liberties with the muskets of an alien soldiery.⁸

Unconstitutional Ploy

On 8 June Lord Mansfield, in the Court of King's Bench, reversed Wilkes's outlawry but ten days later he was fined £1,000 and sentenced to a further 22 months imprisonment. The government now expelled him from the House of Commons which he had first entered in 1757. They continued to deny him his seat when he was re-elected on three subsequent occasions. In the end they not only declared that his election was null and void but the House of Commons proclaimed as duly elected Colonel Luttrell whom Wilkes had defeated at the last poll by a majority of 1,143 votes to 296.

King George III was delighted with the House of Commons and wrote to thank Lord North for his spirit and good conduct in the affair. There was no statutory authority for such a move, however, which could involve the dangerous threat of MPs being appointed instead of elected. It also made a resolution of the Commons equal in its effect to a law made by both Houses of Parliament and the king. That made the ploy unconstitutional. Such blatant interference with the will of the electorate gave Wilkes great popular support and triggered a widespread interest in the franchise in both Britain and the American colonies. He finally secured re-election to Parliament for Middlesex unopposed in 1774. But it took another 13 years before the motion first declaring Wilkes incapable of taking his seat was expunged from the *Journals of the House of Commons*. Notwithstanding these unsavoury manoeu-

---

7. *Ibid.* pp 49 and 51.
8. *Ibid.* p. 56.

vres, the distinguished historian W. E. H. Lecky considered that the "Wilkes affair" gave birth to the movement for parliamentary reform in England.[9]

Unreformed Parliament

On 21 March 1776 Wilkes introduced a Bill in the House of Commons for "a just and equal representation of the people of England in Parliament". He told the House that the existing representation was insufficient, partial and unjust. Some decayed boroughs had in the distant past been disenfranchised but "what a happy fate", he said, remained with the boroughs of Gatton and Old Sarum (which had no residents) where "four respectable gentlemen represent their departed greatness as the knights at a coronation represent Aquitaine and Normandy".[10]

To this can be added the words of historian E. P. Thompson:

> Wilkes had known well how to strike this chord—the champion defending his individual rights passed imperceptibly into the free-born citizen challenging King and Ministers and claiming rights for which there was no precedent. In 1776 Wilkes went so far as to plead in the House of Commons for the political rights of the "meanest mechanic, the poorest peasant and day labourer", who [in the words of Wilkes] "has important rights respecting his personal liberty, that of his wife and children his property however inconsiderable, his wages...which are in many trades and manufactures regulated by the power of Parliament...Some share therefore in the power of making those laws which deeply interest them...should be reserved even to this inferior but most useful set of men".[11]

Wilkes' Bill was defeated but, as a small recompense, in 1771 he secured the right of printers to publish verbatim accounts of Parliamentary debates.

In 1770 he was appointed a sheriff in London and he became Lord Mayor of the city in 1774. However, he subsequently lost his interest in public affairs

---

9. W. E. H. Lecky. (1882) *A History of England in the Eighteenth Century London*. Longmans, Green & Co. vol. iii. p. 174.
10. *Parliamentary History*. [18] (1288)
11. E. P. Thompson. (1968) *The Making of the English Working Class*. London, Pelican Books, p. 91.

although he remained an MP until 1790. His popularity declined after his role in defending the Bank of England in the Gordon Riots in June 1780 when, using troops, he took the offensive against the rioters two of whom were killed. The former man of the people was now seen as having given up his radicalism—he had become, in his own words, an extinct volcano. He died on 26 December 1797 having recently presented the freedom of the City of London to Sir Horatio Nelson as the hero of the Battle of Trafalgar then was.

Despite his dissolute youth, Wilkes had four great achievements to his name. Never again were general warrants used by government. The right of printers to publish verbatim accounts of Parliamentary debates was established. Members of Parliament could not be denied their seat once elected by a majority of the voters. And he played a large part in bringing to life the movement for parliamentary electoral reform and the right of the poor to take part in the franchise.

He was, in the words of George Rudé "one of the principal founders of a mass radical movement in Britain". And, "the various currents of the Wilkite movement revived in new forms to flow into the main stream of British radicalism and nineteenth-century movements for parliamentary reform".[12] In the end it is summed up by the engraving upon the plate of his coffin. The epitaph he had chosen himself reads simply: "The remains of John Wilkes, a Friend of Liberty".

---

12. George Rudé. *Wilkes & Liberty: A Social Study of 1763 to 1774. Op. cit.* pp. 196,198.

CHAPTER 14

TOM PAINE

Common Sense

The outstanding radical Tom Paine was born in Thetford, a flourishing market town in Norfolk, on 29 January 1737. His father, Joseph, was a Quaker and a maker of stays. After being apprenticed to his father, young Tom established himself as a master stay-maker in Sandwich, Kent in 1759 but eventually worked for the Excise Service in Lewes in Sussex where he remained for six years. He led an agitation by the excisemen for an increase in salary (they had not had an increase for a century) and as a consequence was dismissed from the service. Later, in 1774, being in London without work and looking rather dishevelled, he happened to meet Benjamin Franklin to whom he said he wanted to do something useful. Franklin told him to stop pitying himself, to wash and shave off his beard and to stop thinking the world had knocked him harder than anyone else. He then gave him a letter of introduction to his son-in-law in America.

Paine emigrated to the American colonies, which were in ferment, that same year. His pamphlet "Common Sense", written two years later, sold 100,000 copies in six months and made a powerful contribution to the colonists' struggle for American independence from Great Britain. He refused to take any money for it and the effect "Common Sense" had on many thousands of colonists led to a close friendship with Washington and Thomas Jefferson. He is also considered to be one of the Founding Fathers of the United States, a term which he first coined. John Adams, himself a United States President, wrote that without the pen of the author of "Common Sense", the sword of Washington would have been raised in vain. However, it is his contribution to English history as a radical and revolutionary that concerns us here.

The Rights of Man

The years leading up to 1792 presented one disaster after another for the British government. It had suffered a severe reverse with the victory of the American colonists in 1782. This was followed by "Grattan's Revolution" in Ireland in 1782-83 which achieved independence and an Irish Parliament, although for only 19 years. Then came the shock of the French Revolution which struck into Pitt's government alarm that the contagion might spread across the Channel to Britain. This fear was enflamed by the radical writings of Paine and in response they set agents to harass him as well as instigating mobs to burn him in effigy in an effort to force him to go abroad.

It comes as no surprise, therefore, that in 1792 the government decided to prosecute Paine for alleged seditious libel in Part II of his *The Rights of Man*. He was denounced as a traitor and dangerous agitator and, indeed, this prosecution marked the commencement of the serious targeted repression of radical opinion at the time. When Pitt's niece mentioned the book to him, the prime minister revealingly replied, "Paine is no fool, he is perhaps right; but if I did what he wants, I should have thousands of bandits on my hands tomorrow and London burnt".

Part I of *The Rights of Man*, dedicated to George Washington as President of the United States, had been published a year earlier as a defence of the French Revolution and a biting response to Burke's *Reflections of the French Revolution*. In his book, Burke, ignoring the unrepresentative nature of the franchise, had written that, "our representation has been found perfectly adequate to all the purposes for which a representation of the people can be desired or devised".[1] He further argued that the English Settlement of 1689 had established the form of the English Constitution "for ever". Paine pointedly retorted that the legislators might as well pass an Act to enable

---

1. Edmund Burke. (1969) *Reflections on the Revolution in France and on the Proceedings in Certain Societies in London Relative to that Event*. London, Penguin Books. p. 146.

themselves to live forever. The idea, he said, of hereditary legislators is as inconsistent as that of hereditary judges, or hereditary juries.

Burke also contended that the people as a whole, the nation, had no right to choose their government and that the English would resist the assertion of this right "with their lives and fortunes". Paine poured scorn upon the sentiment. "That men should take up arms", he retorted, "and spend their lives and fortunes, not to maintain their rights, but to maintain they have not rights, is an entirely new species of discovery, and suited to the paradoxical genius of Mr. Burke".[2]

Part 1 enjoyed a wide sale and became in its day the most widely read book of all time selling some four to five hundred thousand copies. It is estimated that about one in ten literate people in England owned a copy and there were many pirated editions also in circulation.[3] Yet, it attracted no attention whatever from the government, perhaps because it was thought the high price of three shillings would ensure it did not reach the poorer people.

Social Reform

Part II, on the other hand, was considered dangerous by the government, in part because it was critical of the monarchy and the aristocracy. More importantly it not only set out the rights of the poor but also set forth a radical programme of social reform. In doing so the book made history since it was the first of its kind to appear in England and it also has the ring of modernity. It proclaimed the need for universal public education, for children's allowances, for old age pensions (beginning at 50 and rising at 60) and for a graduated income tax.[4]

"When it can be said", Paine declared, "by any country in the world, 'My poor are happy: neither ignorance nor distress is to be found among them; my jails are empty of prisoners, my streets of beggars: the aged are

---

2. Tom Paine. (1937 edition) *Rights of Man: Being an Answer to Mr. Burke's Attack on the French Revolution*. London, Watts & Co. pp. 2-7.
3. John Keane. (1995) *Tom Paine: A Political Life*. London, Bloomsbury. p. 307.
4. Thomas Paine. (1792) *Rights of Man: Part II–combining Principle and Practice*. London, J. S. Jordan.

not in want: the taxes are not oppressive: the rational world is my friend, because I am the friend of happiness'. When these things can be said, then may that country boast its constitution and its government".[5] For this, he added, society had to be based upon human freedom and representational democracy. By which he meant political democracy, he was not yet ready for economic democracy.

Part II alone sold over a million and a half copies—a colossal figure for the time. And many of those copies were read aloud to groups of people. With the French Revolution uppermost in their minds the government was galvanised into action and decided to prosecute Paine for seditious libel as the commencement of a serious targeted repression of radical opinion. The militias were mobilised, justices were instructed to seek out all distributors of seditious writings and the Attorney-General, Sir Archibald Macdonald, instituted the proceedings against Paine.

The accusation of seditious libel was meant to be preliminary to a charge of high treason and Paine's friend, the poet William Blake, convinced him that he was as good as dead if he did not go at once to Paris where he had been elected to the National Convention as a partisan of liberty. Paine thereupon removed himself to France and the trial was held *in absentia* in the King's Bench before Lord Chief Justice Kenyon and a special jury on 18 December 1792.[6] It is of interest to note that during the trial the judge did indeed mistakenly assert that the prisoner was charged with treason.

Trial for Seditious Libel

Thomas Erskine received a brief to act in the defence of Paine. Thinking he might soon be appointed to the Woolsack, several of Erskine's friends urged him to refuse the brief. And when he was walking on Hampstead Heath one dark November evening he was sought out by Lord Loughborough who is said to have ominously exclaimed, "Erskine, you must not take Paine's brief", to which Erskine replied, "But I have been retained, and I will take it, by

---

5. *Ibid.*
6. *State Trials. Op. cit.* col. 358.

God". He received a similar message from the Prince of Wales but would not change his mind despite a threat of dismissal as legal adviser to the prince.

The Attorney-General, in opening the case for the prosecution, explicitly evoked treason, which was not the charge, and made the preposterous claim that to write that the people did not already have all the rights they needed was in effect levying war upon the king and the constitution. On the contrary, replied Erskine, a published work genuinely written with the object of benefiting mankind could never be a libel, let alone treason. He referred to the "caluminous clamour" raised against himself "only for not having shrunk from the discharge of a duty with no personal advantage, only a thousand difficulties". It was in this trial that he set out the "cab-rank" rule that a barrister should not refuse to defend any client and adopt the role of judge—a principle now said to be the "glory of the Bar".[7]

Erskine urged upon the jury that the book was part of the tradition of free speech that included the writings of John Milton, John Locke and David Hume. Furthermore, when the press was free, he said, the government was secure. Paine's opinions, he declared, were adverse to the system but "I maintain that opinion is free and that conduct alone is amenable to the law".

Notwithstanding the power of Erskine's pleas in a lengthy speech, the special jury, selected by the crown lawyers from among men of wealth, in an astonishing scene found Paine guilty before the attorney-general had made his reply or the judge had had an opportunity to address them. *The Rights of Man* was accordingly condemned as a seditious libel and Paine was sentenced to the medieval punishment of outlawry by which his property was forfeit and he was to be executed if he returned to England.

Alleged Spy in France

For the time being Paine remained in Paris as a member of the National Convention and sat on the committee which prepared a new French constitution. When it was proposed to execute the king, Paine courageously opposed the death penalty suggesting instead that the king and his family

---

7. The rule is set out in full in section 602 of the 8th edition of *Code of Conduct of the Bar of England and Wales*. (31 October 2004) London, General Council of the Bar.

should be banished to the United States. Then, in December 1793, after quarrelling with Robespierre, who considered him an enemy, he was expelled from the Convention as an alleged English spy and imprisoned. He spent ten months in the dungeons of the Luxembourg where he contracted gaol fever and nearly died.

The night before he was due to be taken to the guillotine for execution a chalk mark which should have been made on the outside of his cell door was placed on the inside instead. This arose from his door having been left open to let in air because of his fever. That night the prisoners who shared his cell closed the door and the mark was overlooked the next morning. Owing to this chance (if it was not a deliberate act by a warder) he remained alive until, when Robespierre fell a few days later in July 1794, James Monroe became United States ambassador to France and secured his release in November of that year.

The Age of Reason

In 1795 Paine published Part I of *The Age of Reason* which had been written under the shadow of the guillotine when he was imprisoned in France.[8] It was a sustained attack on state religion and all forms of priesthood and promoted reason and freethinking. In Part II, published a year later, he referred to Christ as a virtuous and amiable man but denied the immaculate conception. He argued that the bible was not the word of God but mere story-telling which piled hearsay upon hearsay. Yet, as a Deist, he believed in God and natural religion and hoped for an after-life. He further considered that Christianity contained good moral precepts. But it also had a bloody history of bigotry with its crusade against Islam, its persecution of Jews and its enslavement of Africans. What he said he was opposed to was organized religion and he saw the bible as a "history of wickedness that had served to corrupt and brutalize mankind".

Once again a work of Paine's was prosecuted, this time for blasphemous libel. Not by the government, however, after they had witnessed a vast

---

8. Tom Paine. (1795) *The Age of Reason: Being an Investigation of True and of Fabulous Theology.* London, H. D. Symonds.

increase in sales of *The Rights of Man* following its earlier prosecution. Instead, the Society for the Suppression of Vice and Immorality considered the book to be a profane and blasphemous attack on the Christian religion and, with Paine still in France, indicted a bookseller named Thomas Williams at whose shop it had been sold. They also decided to instruct Erskine as prosecuting counsel. Surprisingly Erskine accepted the brief. But he had a deep belief in the Bible and he told the jury that he was deeply devoted to the truths of Christianity. In any event, he was bound by his own "cab-rank" rule. It is curious, however, to see him prosecuting Paine's book, and he lived to regret it.

Ironically, counsel for the defence was Stewart Kyd who had been a co-defendant with Thomas Hardy and Horne Tooke in the 1794 treason trials in which Erskine had so ably succeeded.[9] Kyd, in fact, adopted many of the arguments used by Erskine in the earlier treason trials. For instance, he told the jury that the real question was not whether they or the judge approved the book, or shared the author's opinion. It was whether the author believed in what he wrote and meant seriously to examine an important subject without a malevolent intention to do mischief. If the Christian religion was founded in truth, he said, the more it was examined the more it would be firmly established in the minds of men. To punish for disputing its truth was to admit it would not bear the test of rigid scrutiny.

As prosecutor, Erskine accepted the sincerity of Kyd but considered that public renunciation of the truths of religion upon which the government and the constitution rested must be a serious crime. In summing up the judge called the book a nefarious publication with malignant purposes and the special jury needed no time to find the bookseller guilty and he was sent to prison.

Paine wrote to Erskine to deplore the very existence of special juries nominated by the crown. They were comprised, he said, of London merchants who if spoken to about scripture would understand it to mean scrip, and tell how much it was worth at the Stock Exchange. As for theology, they would say that they knew of no such gentleman on the 'Change. "Tell them", he said, "it is in the Bible and they will lay a bowl of punch it is not, and leave it to the parson of the parish to decide".[10]

---

9. See the following chapter.
10. John Keane. *Tom Paine: A Political Life. Op. cit.* p. 394.

As was not unusual at the time, Williams was allowed to be at liberty for seven months before being brought back to the court to have the term of his imprisonment determined. During that period Erskine came across the bookseller in a small hovel in Holborn sitting with his wife emaciated with disease and his three children all suffering from smallpox. He concluded that Williams' dire poverty and not his will had led him to sell the book. He was so affected that he urged the Society for the Suppression of Vice and Immorality to exercise leniency but it declined to do so. Erskine immediately refused to continue to act for them and returned their retainer.

When Williams finally stood before Mr. Justice Ashurst for sentence the judge said the court would not pass so severe a sentence as perhaps it should only on account of Mr. Erskine's pleas. In the event, the sentence pronounced was one year's hard labour and a recognizance for good behaviour of £1,000.

Return to America

Paine remained in France during the early part of Napoleon's rule but in 1802 he returned to America at the invitation of Thomas Jefferson. By 1809, however, he had become a bedridden and feeble old man and he died in his sleep in Greenwich Village, New York at the age of 72 on the morning of 8 June. Even at the last he refused to acknowledge that Jesus Christ was the son of God.

No church, including the Quakers, would receive his body for burial and his remains were buried under a walnut tree on his farm in New Rochelle. Then, in 1819, his bones were dug up by his former enemy, but now a radical himself, William Cobbett and brought back to England for an heroic re-burial. This never happened, however, and after Cobbett's death they disappeared. Today there stands a fine statue of this extraordinary Englishman, a great champion of democracy and human rights, with quill pen and a copy of *The Rights of Man* in hand in King Street, Thetford, his place of birth.

CHAPTER 15

WILLIAM WILBERFORCE

The Clapham Sect

In many respects William Wilberforce was himself an establishment figure. He was independently wealthy after the death of his grandfather in 1776 and conservative both by instinct and background. But his dissent on the slave trade was real enough. His crusade took place over many long years and met with enormous and unprincipled enmity. However, he never wavered until he had secured victory. We shall discuss his dissent and also his general conservative approach to the issues of his time in what follows.

Wilberforce was born on 24 August 1759 in Kingston upon Hull, in the then East Riding of Yorkshire, the only son of Robert Wilberforce, a wealthy merchant, and his wife Elizabeth Bird. His grandfather, William, had made a fortune in trade with Baltic countries and was twice elected mayor of Hull. William started his education at Hull Grammar School and went on to study at St John's College, Cambridge where he met and formed a lasting friendship with the future prime minster, William Pitt the Younger. At the age of 21 and, unusually while still a student, he was elected to be MP for Hull in September 1780, at a cost in election expenses of £8,000. Later, in 1784, he was to represent Yorkshire. His lifestyle when first an MP was dissolute, he being largely engaged in gambling and late night drinking. But all that changed completely, however, when he became an evangelical Christian.

It was not until he was in his late thirties that he married, his bride being 20-year-old Barbara Spooner. The wedding took place on 30 May 1797.[1] The

---

1. *Dictionary of National Biography*. (1975) Oxford, Oxford University Press.

couple had six children and his wife was of great assistance in looking after him in times of his ill-health but took little interest in his parliamentary work.

He helped found the influential Bible Society as well as the Church Missionary Society and in 1784 joined the evangelical "Clapham Sect"—a title first given to them by Sydney Smith. Known also as the "Saints of Clapham", this remarkable group was centred around the Rev. Joseph Venn's church in what was then the south London village of Clapham. It comprised, in addition to Wilberforce, Henry Thornton of the Bank of England, Granville Sharp, a radical philanthropist, Lord Teignmouth, Zachary Macaulay, James Stephen and others. Stephen was counsel to the colonial office and drew the Slavery Emancipation Act 1833 that, so far as Britain was concerned, abolished slavery itself. The spiritual fervour of these men was fed by a vision of the fatherhood of God and the brotherhood of man. A religious revival for the moral reform of the nation was their stated purpose.

Despite this, and although they condemned and vigorously campaigned against the slave trade, they failed for a long time to attack the institution of slavery itself. Eventually, they supported the campaign for complete abolition of slavery but, in the meantime, they were so steeped in the sublimity of the Christian religion that Wilberforce, and most of the others except James Stephen, whilst opposing the pillage of Africa and the torment of slaves, optimistically believed that the slave owners could be persuaded to act as gentlemen towards their "chattels". It was of a piece with their unwillingness to accept the need for trade unions, flowing from an equally benevolent but misguided view of the moral sensibilities of the employers of the time.

Crusade Against the Slave Trade

Nonetheless, Wilberforce's greatest claim to fame comes from his persistent crusade against the massive and monstrous traffic in African slaves who were carried in frightful conditions in British ships to be sold and bought as goods in the West Indies. In order to provide additional profits to the slave owners and ship owners, the ships were then returned to Britain with products such as sugar, cotton and tobacco grown by the slaves. During the course of the slave trade carried on by Portugal, Britain, France and Spain from the sixteenth to the nineteenth century, it is estimated that some 2.2 million men, women and children died in transport across the Atlantic. Many more were killed in the slave raids in Africa and, of those who survived the raids and the transatlantic crossing, untold numbers died from diseases such as dysentry once they had landed in the West Indies and America. And they died not only from disease. Many slaves were tortured to "break them in" and it is estimated that 5 million were killed in the process.

In his crusade Wilberforce was joined by the Whig leaders, Charles James Fox and Henry Brougham, and was ably assisted by Macaulay and James Stephen. In particular, however, he worked in tandem with Thomas Clarkson, a fellow graduate at Cambridge, whose research and activity provided the basis for a fruitful collaboration of almost 50 years.[2] It is not possible to overestimate the help and encouragement Wilberforce received from his friend.

Wilberforce lobbied for the abolition of the slave trade for 18 years by regularly introducing anti-slavery motions in the House of Commons. After understanding its wickedness, altogether he headed the parliamentary campaign against the British slave trade for 26 years.

That wickedness has been described by William Hague:

> The human consequences of the trade were unspeakable. The methods by which slaves were captured by traders or rival tribes were bad enough, but that was only the beginning: they were then flogged into the ships and chained in tiny spaces for a three-month voyage. Slave ships were famous for their unbearable stench, with many of the slaves dying in epidemics or driven mad. Whips were used without limit, those who became unfit for work were often killed, with many deaths soon after arrival, and those who survived spent the rest of their lives without property, freedom or hope.[3]

It is estimated that some 15 million slaves were transported across the seas, and, as we have seen as many as 2.2 million died or were thrown overboard during the voyage.

Speaking to the House of Commons on 18 April 1791 Wilberforce declared:

---

2. Adam Hochschild. (2005) *Bury the Chains: The British Struggle to Abolish Slavery*. London, Macmillan. pp. 123-4.
3. William Hague. (2004) *William Pitt the Younger*. London, Harper Perennial. p. 293.

Let us not despair; it is a blessed cause, and success, ere long, will crown our exertions. Already we have gained one victory; we have obtained, for these poor creatures, the recognition of their human nature, which, for a while was shamelessly denied. This is the first fruits of our efforts; let us persevere and our triumph will be complete. Never, never will we desist till we have wiled away this scandal from the Christian name, released ourselves from the load of guilt, under which we at present labour, and extinguished every trace of this bloody traffic, of which our posterity, looking back to the history of these enlightened times, will scarce believe that it has been suffered to exist so long a disgrace and dishonour to this country.[4]

But Wilberforce's dissent led to establishment criticism that he was ignoring injustices at home while campaigning for slaves abroad and he was never offered a ministerial post even by his friend Pitt. He was regarded by many with suspicion as a radical out to overthrow church and state. And, all the while, in an attempt to justify the unjustifiable commercial interests produced "evidence" to suggest not only alleged economic advantage to the nation from this atrocity but even the "humanity" of such a trade in human beings exchanged in barter for sugar, spices and dyes. Wilberforce exploded in anger saying, "As soon as I had arrived thus far in my investigation of the Slave Trade, I confess to you, so enormous, so dreadful, so irremediable did its wickedness appear that my own mind was completely made up for Abolition".[5] And, Pitt responded by exclaiming, "Necessity is the plea for every infringement of human freedom. It is the argument of tyrants".[6]

In the House of Commons Fox derided both the distorted economics and the false "altruism" of the merchants. He asserted that to consider the matter on any principles other than those of compassion and justice was both idle and absurd. It was an odious and immoral evil. So powerful was his passion that it swept over to the West Indies themselves where slave compounds in Grenada resounded with the cry, Mr Wilberforce for Negro! Mr Fox for Negro! God Almighty for Negro!"[7]

---

4. Hansard. (1817) and William Hague (2007) *William Wilberforce: The Life of the Great Anti-Slave Trade Campaigner*. London, Harper Press. p. 193.
5. *Ibid.* p. 291.
6. Speech. (18 November 1783).
7. *Parliamentary History*. vol. xxvii. pp. 495-506.

In 1807, after both Pitt and Fox had died, Parliament by a large majority passed a Bill to abolish the slave trade, with Wilberforce present with tears streaming down his face. In the House of Commons the Bill was carried by 114 votes to 15 and in the House of Lords by 41 votes to 20. The size of the majorities persuaded supporters to urge the abolition of slavery itself but Wilberforce made it clear that total emancipation was not the aim, only the slave trade.

The Statute provided that if British sailors boarded a ship and found it was still carrying slaves, the captain was to be fined £100 for each slave found aboard. This led some captains who tried to continue the trade to avoid fines by having the slaves thrown alive into the sea. Nevertheless, despite this continuing but declining horror, the campaign was the first grassroots human rights undertaking in the world in which men and women from different social classes and backgrounds fought to end the injustices caused by the slave trade.[8]

Morality

In most respect Wilberforce was against change. He spoke in the Commons in favour of the Combination Acts of 1799 and 1800 which made trade unions illegal. He opposed an inquiry into the Peterloo Massacre and approved repressive legislation. He also opposed women working in the anti-slave trade movement and he introduced into the Commons a Bill to permit the dissection after execution of criminals such as arsonists, rapists and even thieves. Considering society to be degenerate Wilberforce founded the Society for the Suppression of Vice and Immorality in 1802 which, as we saw in *Chapter 14*, to the disgust of Erskine insisted that the bookseller Thomas Williams be imprisoned for selling Tom Paine's *The Age of Reason*.

On the other hand, he did speak in favour of some limited reform of the franchise such as the abolition of rotten boroughs. He advocated legislation to improve the working conditions of chimney sweeps and textile workers and supported efforts to restrict capital punishment and the severe penalties

---

8. Adam, Hochschild. *Bury the Chains, The British Struggle to Abolish Slavery. Op. cit.* pp. 5-6.

imposed under the Game Laws. And he did advocate lower sentences than burning at the stake for women convicted of treason, which included the murder of a husband. The Bill to provide for this passed in the Commons but was defeated in the House of Lords. He also believed in prison reform.[9] And, in 1813 he was critical of the racial prejudice of the British in India whilst also condemning the Hindu caste system and the practices of infanticide, polygamy and suttee — the burning of women alive with their husband's corpses. But he could not help adding, "Our religion is sublime, pure beneficent, theirs is mean, licentious and cruel".[10] He encouraged Christian missionaries to go to India and he was also closely involved with the Royal Society for the Prevention of Cruelty to Animals.

The End

Wilberforce resigned from Parliament in 1826 through ill-health but continued his interest in the campaign of his friends, including James Stephen, for the complete abolition of slavery. On 26 July he heard of government concessions that guaranteed that the Bill for the Abolition of Slavery would pass. He died three days later, on 29 July 1833, in Cadogan Place, London and was buried in the north transept of Westminster Abbey, close to William Pitt. Also in the Abbey a seated statue of Wilberforce by Samuel Joseph was erected in 1840 and in the grounds of Hull College there is a 31 metre Greek Doric column with a statue of him at the summit.

Finally, as a result of the 26-page Statute, the Emancipation of Slavery Act, drawn up in a single week-end by James Stephen, some 800,000 slaves were freed in 1833 at a cost of £20 million paid in compensation to the slave owners.

---

9. William Hague. *William Wilberforce: The Life of the Great Anti-Slave Trade Campaigner. Op. cit.* p. 447.
10. Stephen Tomkins. (2007) *William Wilberforce: A Biography*. Oxford, Lion; and John Keay (2000) *India: A History*. New York, Grove Press. p. 428.

CHAPTER 16

THOMAS HARDY AND THE TREASON TRIALS OF 1794

Government Repression

The notorious treason trials of 1794 took place against a backcloth of political and social turmoil. On the one hand there was widespread pressure at all levels of society for reform of the grossly unrepresentative electoral system. Generally, the demand was to take the franchise away from rotten boroughs and enfranchise the large and growing conurbations like Manchester, Liverpool, Birmingham and Leeds. Alongside this pressure there was a strong popular demand for universal manhood suffrage. On the other hand there was the revolution in France which provoked serious alarm in government circles at Westminster whose resolve to deny reform was merely strengthened. Together, these currents encouraged the growth of a radical movement of Corresponding Societies devoted to electoral reform and so named because they corresponded with similar societies in France. One consequence was that an alarmist government mounted over 100 prosecutions for sedition in the 1790s alone. It was in this situation that Tom Paine published *The Rights of Man* in May 1792. And it was now that the French Revolution and the oncoming Terror struck new fear deep in the hearts of the members of the government and with that fear turning to panic they set out to destroy the influence of the radicals.

Rehearsal in Scotland

In August 1793 the government charged with sedition for recommending the works of Tom Paine, a young barrister in Scotland named Thomas Muir.

He was brought to trial before the High Court of Justiciary in Edinburgh. Lord Braxfield was the presiding judge and Muir conducted his own defence. Evidence was given that he had praised the French financial system and had even visited France. This severely displeased the judge who said, "I never was an admirer of the French but now I can only consider them as monsters in human form". Ironically, Braxfield was himself described by Lord Cockburn, a future Lord Chief Justice of the Queen's Bench, who was present in court, as "a little, dark creature, dressed in black, with silk stockings and white metal buttons, something like one's idea of a puny Frenchman, a most impudent and provoking body".[1]

In his summing up at the end of the trial, Lord Braxfield indulged in a number of observations. There were two things, he said, which the jury had to attend to that required no proof. The first, echoing Burke, was that the British constitution was the best that ever was since the creation of the world, and it was not possible to make it better. Secondly, there was a spirit of sedition in the country which made every good man uneasy, yet the prisoner had gone among ignorant country people making them forget their work, and telling them that a reform of the franchise was absolutely necessary for preserving their liberty.

What right, he asked, had they to representation? A government in every country should be just like a corporation, and in Britain it was made up of the landed interests who alone had a right to be represented. The uncouth Braxfield also whispered to a juror who passed behind the Bench, "come awa', Master Horner, come awa' and help us hang ane o' thae damned scoundrels". At the end of the trial the pliant jury quickly found Muir guilty whereupon, despite widespread protests, he was sentenced to transportation to Botany Bay for 14 years.[2] Fortune smiled on him, however, and he was rescued on the journey by a United States ship and eventually died in France.

Three others, who had travelled from London to a Scottish convention to advocate electoral reform were then tried before the same presiding judge on

---

1. Henry, Lord Cockburn. (1888) *An Examination of the Trials for Sedition which have hitherto occurred in Scotland*. Edinburgh, David Douglas.
2. John Hostettler. (2010) *Thomas Erskine and Trial by Jury*. Hook, Hampshire, Waterside Press Ltd. p. 107.

similar charges. One prisoner, Maurice Margarot, who had been educated at the University of Geneva, questioned the judge.

> Q. Did you dine at Mr. Rochead's at Inverleith in the course of last week?
> A. And what have you to do with that, Sir?
> Q. Did any conversation take place with regard to my trial?
> A. Go on, Sir.
> Q. Did you use these words: "What should you think of giving him an hundred lashes, together with Botany Bay"? or words to that purpose?
> A. Go on: put your questions, if you have any more.
> Q. Did any person, did a lady, say to you that the mob would not allow you to whip me? And, my Lord, did you not say that the mob would be better off for a little blood? These are the questions, my Lord, that I wish to put to you.
> Braxfield: (Turning to a brother judge) Do you think I should answer questions of that sort my Lord Henderland?
> Lord Henderland: No, my Lord.
> Lord Esgrove: What may have been said in a private company cannot in any way affect this case.
> Lord Swinton: My Lord, not one of them are proper.[3]

It occasioned no surprise when Braxfield refused to deal with Margarot's questions and continued to preside at the trial. Nor when after another prisoner, Joseph Gerrald, proudly suggested that Jesus Christ was himself a reformer, Braxfield chuckled, "Muckle he made o' that: he was hangit"! Each of the three prisoners was unceremoniously found guilty and duly sentenced to 14 years transportation.[4] In Westminster prime minister Pitt spoke approvingly of the judges punishing "such daring delinquents" and "suppressing doctrines so dangerous to the country". He conveniently forgot that only a few years before he had himself been advocating electoral reform.

---

3. G. D. H. Cole and Raymond Postgate. (1938) *The Common People 1746-1938*. London, Methuen & Co. Ltd., pp. 152-3.
4. *Ibid.* p. 108.

Reign of Terror

Now came the treason trials at the Old Bailey on 5 November 1794, described by some historians as an integral part of the "English Terror".[5] Some 800 warrants of arrest were prepared and as a first step 12 members of Corresponding Societies were arrested including John Horne Tooke, a well known philologist; Thomas Hardy, a shoemaker; and John Thelwell, an avowed Jacobin. At the same time *habeas corpus* was suspended, the discovery of an alleged revolutionary plot was announced and the House of Commons received a message from the king requiring the enactment of a Special Powers Act. For six months, from May to October, these 12 men were incarcerated in the Tower of London and suffered severely from ill-health and depression: particularly, in Hardy's case when, with her husband still confined in the Tower, his wife suffered an attack on their home by a "Church and King" mob and died in childbirth, leaving an unfinished note to her despairing husband saying, "You are never out of my thoughts, sleeping or waking".[6]

Edmund Burke added to the hysteria when he accused the as yet untried prisoners of being assassins and urged that the disease of the body politic demanded the "critical terrors of the cautery and the knife".[7] Yet, these men, whose moderation was widely known, were charged with high treason in "compassing the death of the king" although it was never suggested that they actually threatened the life of the king or to use any force whatsoever. In fact, they spoke of "preserving the people's love" for the king.[8]

Trial of the Shoemaker

Hardy was to be tried first since the prosecution believed he would be the most easily convicted. In this they underestimated the skills of the defence counsel. The trial commenced at the Old Bailey on 28 October before Lord

---

5. For example, J. R. Green. (1874) *A Short History of the English People*. London, The Folio Society edition (1992) p. 818.
6. John Hostettler. *Thomas Erskine and Trial by Jury. Op. cit.* p. 111.
7. Thomas Hardy. (1882) *Memoir*. London, pp. 42-3.
8. Philip Sheldon Foner. (ed.) (1969) *The Complete Works of Thomas Paine*. 2 vols. New York, Citadel, i. p. 291.

Justice Eyre and several other judges sitting with a jury.[9] Among the numerous prosecuting counsel was William Garrow. For the defence Thomas Erskine appeared without fee despite being at the height of his powers as an advocate. The Attorney-General, Sir John Scott, afterwards the dilatory Lord Chancellor Eldon, opened the case with a speech lasting nine hours.[10] It is noteworthy that until this time there had never been a trial for high treason that had lasted longer than a day. Creating a precedent, this trial was to continue for eight days. Scott contended that the prisoner was guilty of treason as laid down by the Treason Act 1351 in having embarked upon a course of conduct that was likely to lead to the death of the king, that is, he claimed, convening a National Convention to subvert the legislature and government and depose the king.[11]

In defending, Erskine's biting cross-examination of prosecution witnesses whom he exposed as government spies completely demolished their testimony. He then argued that the Radicals' plan for a Convention of delegates to discuss electoral reform was similar to a plan advanced earlier by prime minster Pitt himself. He argued that it was wrong to consider consequences when the law commanded that it was only intentions that were relevant. He called as witnesses the Duke of Richmond and the playwright Richard Brinsley Sheridan who both testified that they supported the aims of the Convention and knew well that Hardy was a law-abiding citizen.

At the conclusion of the evidence Erskine addressed the jury for seven hours and this caused his voice to become hoarse and faint. However, the impact of his words on all those in the courtroom, including the jury, was electric. When the jurymen returned to court after retiring to the jury room for three hours the foreman, a Thomas Buck from Acton in West London, delivered the verdict in a whisper and then fainted on the spot. The verdict was not guilty and was received with rapturous rejoicing by the crowds inside the court and the streets surrounding it outside.

On a more sombre note, after his acquittal, Hardy immediately visited his wife's grave in St. Martin's Churchyard. According to *The Times*:

---
9. *24 Howell's State Trials*. (1818) col. 199.
10. Alan Wharam. (1992) *The Treason Trials, 1794*. Leicester, Leicester University Press. p. 148.
11. Ibid.

> On approaching the grave [he] immediately fell and embraced the cold earth...he was lost in the agony of his grief; it was with difficulty that he could be removed; and such was the effect upon his wounded feelings and dilapidated frame and most "constructively" destroyed prospects, that for a considerable time there were entertained apprehensions regarding his own life.[12]

William Pitt's Testimony

Despite the verdict in Hardy's trial, the government persisted in the prosecution of John Horne Tooke who was nearly 60-years-old. This trial commenced on 17 November and among the witnesses called by Erskine this time were not only the Duke of Richmond and Sheridan but also the Bishop of Gloucester, Earl Stanhope, Earl Camden and Charles James Fox. Then into the witness box came William Pitt himself in response to a subpoena taken out by the defence. The prime minister was forced, reluctantly, to remember that he had once attended and spoken at meetings composed of delegates who wished to work for parliamentary reform. This admission virtually destroyed the prosecution case that such delegate meetings were merely a device to cloak the organizing of treasonable insurrection.

The prosecutor continued undeterred, however, and produced amongst others a William Sharpe, an engraver, who gave formal evidence of Horne Tooke's presence at a meeting of the legal Constitutional Information Society as if that were itself treason. The case against Tooke rested chiefly on a letter sent to him by another prisoner, Jeremiah Joyce, which the government had intercepted and Tooke never received. The short letter gave the news of the arrest of Hardy and concluded with the sentence: "Query: is it possible to get ready by Thursday"? In Parliament, in endeavouring to inflame public feeling against the prisoner, the government had interpreted this sentence to indicate preparations for insurrection which might be got "ready by Thursday".

Sharpe testified that all Tooke had undertaken was to collect from the Court Calendar a list of titles, offices and pensions bestowed by Pitt upon

---

12. *The Times*. 17 October 18 1832, (Obituary of Hardy).

himself, his relatives, friends and dependants. Anxious to receive the list Joyce had asked if it could be ready by Thursday. To make matters more ridiculous the government had sent a troop of Light Dragoons to the neighbourhood of Tooke's home at Wimbledon to look out for whatever was to be ready by Thursday. Nothing incriminating was found.

In his speech to the jury Erskine poured scorn on the government's attempts to link Tooke with an armed rebellion. The prisoner, he declared, was a gentleman who rarely left his home. There was, he said, nothing in *The Arabian Nights* or *The Tales of the Fairies* to compare with the prosecution's fantasies. The address combined powerful reasoning, eloquence and tact and caused intense applause in the courtroom. After the judge had summed up the jury took only eight minutes without leaving the jury box to return a verdict of not guilty. Outside the court Erskine's horses were taken from his carriage amidst bonfires and blazing tableaux and he was drawn by the crowds to his home in the Temple.

The government now blindly continued with the prosecution of John Thelwell against whom they thought the case was particularly strong. However, during the prosecution opening speech the Lord Chief Justice fell fast asleep and Thelwell too was acquitted. The government finally had to scrap the 800 warrants that had been prepared for use following the anticipated convictions.

Victory Tokens

Winston Churchill in *A History of the English-Speaking Peoples* wrote about this moment of history. "In England", he said, "the Government had been forced to take repressive measure of a sternness unknown for generations. Republican lecturers were swept into prison. The Habeas Corpus Act was suspended. Distinguished writers were put on their trial for treason; but juries could not be prevailed to convict".[13] History supports the decision of the juries. There is no evidence that the radicals in England or Scotland were ever planning violent revolution.

---

13. Winston Churchill. (1957) *A History of the English-Speaking Peoples*. London, Cassell & Co., vol. iii, p. 249.

Coin-like tokens were struck to celebrate the stirring victory of the defendants. One in my possession bears an image of Thomas Hardy on one side with the words: "Tried for high treason, T. Hardy 1794" and on the reverse side: "Acquitted by his jury. Counsel Hon T. Erskine and V. Gibbs Esq". Another depicts a man and a woman with banners inscribed: "Magna Carta" and "Bill of Rights". On the same side are the words: "Erskine and Gibbs and Trial Jury". On the reverse side are the names of the first eight prisoners chosen for trial. Both these tokens are featured on the cover of my book *Thomas Erskine and Trial by Jury* published in 2010 by Waterside Press.

Hardy to Lafayette

Thus did Erskine and these three radicals thwart the government and preserve freedom, liberty and the rule of law in those dark days for dissenters. Not without counter measures from a government in panic, however. The following year saw the passing of the Seditious Meetings Act and the Treasonable Practices Act (known as the "Two Acts"). Under them it was exceedingly difficult to hold a public meeting or speak freely at any that might be held. And the law of treason was extended to include inciting hatred of the king, his heirs, his government or his constitution. It was the first time mere speech was made treasonable since a similar, but short lasting, provision had been introduced by Henry VIII.

This situation prevailed for a quarter of a century but the struggles of the treason trial defendants were continued by subsequent generations and bore fruit in the violent passions that led to the passing of the Great Reform Act of 1832 which commenced the progress towards universal suffrage that was finally achieved in England in 1928.

In fact, shortly before the passing of the Reform Act the elderly Hardy in his 80th year wrote in a letter on 11 April 1831 to Lafayette in France in which he said,

> I cannot help mentioning to you how much I am pleased with the Revolution which has taken place in this country, for revolution it is. The King, and his Ministers, are now turned Parliamentary Reformers! They are guilty of the very crime,

if crime it be, with which Parliamentary Reformers, in the year 1794, were charged by the infamous Government of Pitt, Dundas, and Grenville, the greatest crime known in our laws — High Treason. Many were imprisoned, some were banished, and three were tried for it; but an English jury had a very different opinion of the criminality of their conduct and honourably acquitted them.[14]

Hardy died on 11 October 1832 having seen the enactment of the Great Reform Act and was buried like so many other eminent dissenters at Bunhill Fields in Islington, London.

---

14. Alan Wharam. *The Treason Trials, 1794. Op. cit.* p. 265.

CHAPTER 17

MARY WOLLSTONECRAFT

Early Development

Mary Wollstonecraft was born on 27 April 1759 at Spitalfields in London. She was the second child of six children born to Edward Wollstonecraft, a handkerchief weaver, and Elizabeth Dixon. The family had a comfortable income when she was born but her father squandered it and made the family financially unstable. He was also a violent man who beat his wife in drunken rages and as a teenager Mary would lie outside the door of her mother's bedroom in an endeavour to protect her from an entry and assault by her husband.[1]

Clearly unhappy in her family life, Mary left home in 1778 to work as a lady's companion to Sarah Dawson, a widow living in Bath. Dawson was a difficult person to get on with, however, and two years later Mary left her and returned home to care for her mother who was now dying. Then, when her mother passed away, she went to live with her friend Fanny Blood. To make a living Mary, her sisters and Fanny Blood started a school together in Newington Green in south east London, a district which harboured a large dissenting community. She drew upon her experiences in the school to write, *Thoughts on the Education of Daughters: With Reflections on Female Conduct, in the More Important Duties in Life* (1787). In this she attacked traditional teaching methods and suggested new topics for study by girls. This represented the beginning of her career as a writer, an intellectual and a feminist.

Whilst at Newington Green, Mary became a friend of Richard Price a minister at the local dissenting chapel which she soon began attending. Price

---

1. See Claire Tomalin. (1974) *The Life and Death of Mary Wollstonecraft*. London, Weidenfeld & Nicolson.

was a radical and, among other things, supported the cause of American independence which brought him many virulent enemies. Later, he was to preach a sermon in praise of the French Revolution which was the direct cause of Edmund Burke writing his *Reflections on the Revolution in France* as a reply. Burke's book not only brought a response from Tom Paine with his *The Rights of Man* but caused Mary to defend Price in a pamphlet entitled *A Vindication of the Rights of Man*. In it she attacked the aristocracy and advocated republicanism. Apart from supporting Price, she also argued against the slave trade, the game laws and Burke's ignorance of the treatment of the poor in society as well as what she saw as his obsession with the sanctity of private property. "Where", she asked, "is the eye that marks these evils, more gigantic than any infringements of property, which you piously deprecate? Are these remediless evils? And is the human heart satisfied with turning the poor over to another world, to receive the blessings this could afford"? This polemic made her a public figure and something of a celebrity.

With Fanny Blood's health deteriorating Mary now left the school in Newington Green in 1785 and this led to its decline. In its place she took up duties as governess to the daughters of Lord Kingsborough which meant going to live in Ireland. However, two years later she returned to London with a strong desire to pursue her interest in writing. Here she met not only Richard Price again but also other radical activists, including Tom Paine, William Blake, John Horne Tooke and William Godwin, the author of *Political Justice* whom she later married.

A Vindication of the Rights of Woman

In 1792, Mary Wollstonecraft published her important work, *A Vindication of the Rights of Woman*. This advocated equality of the sexes and poured scorn on the prevailing ideas about women as helpless, charming adornments in the household. On women and the franchise she wrote:

> I really think that women ought to have representatives, instead of being arbitrarily governed without having any direct share allowed them in the deliberations of government. But as the whole system of representation is now, in this country, only

a convenient handle for despotism [women] need not complain, for they are as well represented as a numerous class of hard working mechanics, who pay for the support of royalty when they can scarcely stop their children's mouths with bread.

"How many women," she continued, "thus waste life away the prey of discontent, who might have practised as physicians, regulated a farm, managed a shop, and stood erect, supported by their own industry, instead of hanging their heads surcharged with the dew of sensibility, that consumes the beauty to which it at first gave lustre".[2]

She also showed concern about the upbringing and lack of education for gentlewomen. Because they were raised only for marriage, she said, they became unsuited to be wives and mothers. Moreover,

Strength of body and mind are sacrificed to libertine notions of beauty, to the desire of establishing themselves — the only way women can rise in the world,–by marriage. And this desire making mere animals of them, when they marry they act as such children may be expected to act:–they dress, they paint, and nickname God's creatures.— Surely these weak beings are only fit for a seraglio!— Can they be expected to govern a family with judgment, or take care of the poor babes whom they bring into the world.[3]

Society, she claimed, was breeding "gentle domestic brutes". It had transformed these angels of the household into tyrants over children and servants. Education was required to give women a sense of self-respect and self-image that would enable them to exercise their talents to the full. She used her greatest vitriol against writers like Jean Jacques Rousseau who wanted to deny women an education and claimed in his *Émile* in 1762 that women should be educated for the pleasure of men.

On the other hand, she openly addressed herself to the middle class. Rather like William Wilberforce, who led the movement against the slave trade but refused to accept that workers should be allowed to join trade unions, Mary Wollstonecraft held that middle class women could prevent the poor from

---

2. Mary Wollstonecraft. (1996) *A Vindication of the Rights of Woman*. London, Constable, p. 15.
3. *Ibid.* p. 9.

falling into a vicious indolence by employing them as servants.[4] At the same time, working class boys and girls should be removed to separate schools and be taught according to their destination in life. For girls this meant plain work, mantua-making, millinery, and the like.[5] However, she claimed that women were essential to the nation because they educate its children and could be companions to their husbands rather than mere wives.

As part of her feminist stand, Wollstonecraft had nothing but contempt for conventional ideas of feminine beauty. She used no cosmetics and clothed herself in cheap, rough dresses. Nonetheless, judging by the portrait by John Opie of about 1797 she was herself quite beautiful.

Controversy

At the time, *A Vindication of the Rights of Woman* caused intense controversy. One critic described its author as a "hyena in petticoats". Even some fellow radicals were shocked and most of them continued to reject the idea of female suffrage. Hannah More, the philanthropist and socialite famous for her good works, described the title to the book as "fantastic and absurd", and refused to read it. But to Mary the rights of men and the rights of women were the same, but women had to be independent of men. She wrote:

> It is vain to expect virtue from women till they are in some degree independent of men; nay, it is vain to expect that strength of natural affection which would make them good wives and mothers. Whilst they are absolutely dependent on their husbands they will be cunning, mean and selfish. The preposterous distinction of rank, which renders civilization a curse, by dividing the world between voluptuous tyrants and cunning envious dependents, corrupts, almost equally, every class of people.

In *A Vindication* she also wrote that, "A wild wish has just flown from my heart to my head, and I will not stifle it though it may excite a horse-laugh. I do earnestly wish to see the distinction of sex confounded in society, unless

---

4. *Ibid.* pp. 177-78.
5. *Ibid.* p.178.

where love animates the behaviour. For this distinction is, I am firmly persuaded, the foundation of the weakness of character ascribed to woman".

In 1798 her *Maria, or the Wrongs of Woman* was published in Paris. She had been staying in the city from 1792 and thus witnessed Robespierre's Reign of Terror. In the book she asserted that women had strong sexual desires and that it was degrading and immoral to pretend otherwise. The book revolved around the story of a woman imprisoned in an insane asylum by her husband. There she found fulfilment outside of marriage in an affair with a female fellow inmate. This book damned her in the eyes of Victorian society and it was not until the twentieth century that her general philosophy gained some acceptance both inside and outside the feminist movement and she became regarded as one of the founding feminine philosophers.

William Godwin

In March 1797 Mary married William Godwin, a famed anarchist and the author of *Political Justice*, a book which was subversive of both law and marriage. It is quite possible that she decided to woo him for a husband in cool — if not quite cold — blood.[6] However, she gave birth to a daughter also named Mary, later Mary Shelley after her marriage to Percy Bysse Shelley, and is celebrated as the author of *Frankenstein*. Although she and Godwin both believed marriage was a form of tyranny they wed because of her pregnancy. They rented a house at 29 The Polygon, Somers Town in London but Godwin also rented rooms nearby and returned to The Polygon only in the evenings. He said this combined "the novelty and lively sensation of a visit, with the more delicious and heart-felt pleasure of domestic life". Mary responded that, "A husband is a convenient part of the furniture of a house... I wish you, from my soul, to be riveted in my heart, but I do not desire to have you always at my elbow".[7] Unhappily when born the baby was essentially healthy but part of the placenta had been retained in the womb. The doctor's attempt to remove the remaining placenta resulted in blood

---

6. Claire Tomalin. *The Life and Death of Mary Wollstonecraft, Op. cit.* p. 255.
7. Caroline Franklin. (2004) *Mary Wollstonecraft: A Literary Life*. Basingstoke, Palgrave Macmillan, p. 173.

poisoning and Mary Wollstonecraft died at the age of 38 on 10 September 1797. She was buried at Old Saint Pancras Churchyard, and a memorial to her was erected there. Later, her remains and those of Godwin were moved to Bournemouth. There is, however, a plaque commemorating her on the site of her last residence with Godwin at The Polygon, St. Pancras.

Mary Wollstonecraft was a dissenter in her dismissal of eighteenth century society's endorsement of the subservient role of women although her *A Vindication of the Rights of Woman* did not achieve the audience it deserved until modern times. However, she initiated the long struggle for feminism despite not always being consistent, particularly so with regard to her attitude to middle-class women. She was also a radical in that she desired to bridge the gap between present day life and an ultimately perfect society. Having witnessed the French Revolution at first hand she believed in an age of reason and fraternity. Accordingly, she worked tirelessly to help women secure a better life both for themselves and for their families, and that is her lasting epitaph.

CHAPTER 18

THE PETERLOO MASSACRE

"Orator" Hunt

The massacre of Peterloo occurred at St. Peter's Field, Manchester on 16 August 1819 when cavalry charged into a crowd of 70,000 men, women and children gathered to demand the reform of parliamentary representation. It is an important landmark in the radical struggle for a democratic franchise. The background was the end of the Napoleonic Wars in 1815 and the consequent famine and unemployment which were made worse by the Corn Laws. The country was witnessing chronic economic depression, which particularly affected textile workers. Yet, the suffrage barely existed in the new manufacturing towns of the North where like other major urban centres, Manchester had no separate representation. It was a widely held view that an extension of the franchise would give voice to the concerns of the working class and help alleviate their suffering. Accordingly, the Manchester Patriotic Union, which agitated for parliamentary reform, organized a demonstration to be addressed by the well-known radical speaker, Henry "Orator" Hunt in St. Peter's Field which at the time was on the outskirts of Manchester on the site where the Free Trade Hall was later built.

That 16th August was a hot summer's day and huge crowds flocked to the Fields to hear the famous Hunt speak. Flags fluttered bearing the inscriptions — "Parliaments Annual" and "Suffrage Universal". The carnival atmosphere and the presence of many women and children testify to the peaceful nature of the gathering. In fact, the legend "Cleanliness, Sobriety, Order and Peace" on banners exemplified the order of the day. And weapons of all kinds were banned.

It was a feature of the outing that many groups were of female reform societies with the women dressed all in white. The crowd was disciplined, many wore their "Sunday-best" clothes and initially there was no disorder. But the magistrates, concerned at the large numbers expected at the event, had brought in 400 special constables, soldiers and 520 armed yeomen cavalry as well as two six-pounder guns. Either they had panicked or were acting to a pre-conceived plan. Whatever the case, with no provocation but alarmed by the discipline of such a large crowd, they ordered the cavalry to arrest Hunt and disperse the milling multitude. In the main the yeomen were anti-reform manufacturers, merchants, publicans and shopkeepers.

The Yeomen Charge

In attempting to reach Hunt through the dense throng they drew their sabres and slashed at the men, women and children in their way. They were joined by a troop of 600 Hussars, although the soldiers remained far more restrained than the yeomen. However, the ensuing massacre left eleven dead on the field (including two women) and over 400 injured. Of those wounded, 161 received sabre wounds and the remainder were caught by the crush and the horses hooves. More than a hundred of them were women and girls. The massacre was given the name Peterloo in ironic reference to Wellington's victory at the Battle of Waterloo four years earlier. *The Times* immediately condemned what it called,

> the dreadful fact that nearly a hundred of the King's unarmed subjects have been sabred by a body of cavalry in the streets [i.e. people fleeing from the attack] of a town of which most of them were inhabitants, and in the presence of those magistrates whose sworn duty it is to protect and preserve the life of the meanest Englishman.[1]

Women seem to have been particularly subject to brutal treatment by the yeomanry. For instance, one woman, Elizabeth Farren was attacked by

---

1. *The Times*. (18 August 1819).

a yeoman named Tebbutt. She received a deep sabre cut to the forehead and fell to the ground. Tebbutt continued to attack her as she fell, causing her to drop her child, who was also struck by his sword. And Tebbutt was not a stranger to Farren but a close neighbour.[2]

One eye-witness of the massacre was Samuel Bamford, a Lancashire weaver, who recalled that "sabres were plied to hew a way through naked held-up hands, and defenceless heads; and then chopped limbs, and wounded gaping skulls were seen; and groans and cries were mingled with the din of that horrid confusion". He painted a vivid picture of the appalling outcome of the charge:

> In ten minutes...the field was an open and almost deserted place...The hustings remained, with a few broken and hewed flag-staves erect, and a torn and gashed banner or two drooping; whilst over the whole field were strewed caps, bonnets, hats, shawls and shoes, and other parts of male and female dress, trampled, torn and bloody. The yeomanry had dismounted—some were easing their horses' girths, others adjusting their accoutrements, and some were wiping their sabres.[3]

Another witness who was present was Archibald Prentice. He wrote:

> Our company laughed at the fears of the magistrates, and the remark was, that if the men intended mischief they would not have brought their wives, their sisters, or their children with them. I passed round the outskirts of the meeting, and mingled with the groups that stood chatting there. I occasionally asked the women if they were not afraid to be there, and the usual laughing reply was—"What have we to be afraid of".[4]

It was this defining incident of the time that led Percy Bysshe Shelley to write in Italy his famous poem entitled *The Masque of Anarchy: Written on the Occasion of the Massacre at Manchester.*[5]

---

2. M. L. Bush. (2005) *The Casualties of Peterloo*. Lancaster, Carnegie Publishers. p. 31.
3. Samuel Bamford. (1844) *Passages in the Life of a Radical*. London, Simpkin, Marshall & Co. pp. 152 and 157.
4. Archibald Prentice. (1851) *Historical Sketches and Personal Recollections of Manchester*. London and Manchester.
5. Percy Bysshe Shelley. (1969) *Poetical Works*. London, Oxford University Press.

York Assizes

Hunt and nine others were tried at York Assizes on 16 March 1820 on charges of assembling with banners at an unlawful meeting for the purpose of exciting discontent. After a two-week trial five of the ten prisoners were found guilty. Hunt, who in 1830 was to be elected MP for Preston, was sentenced to 30 months in Ilchester Jail whilst three others were imprisoned for one year each and the fifth was jailed for two years. Four members of the Manchester Yeomanry were belatedly brought before the Lancaster Assizes two years later, on 4 April 1822, where all were acquitted when the court ruled that their actions were justified in dispersing an illegal gathering.

Was the carnage pre-meditated? Probably we shall never know. But it was at least reckless to use the ill-disciplined yeomanry when regular disciplined troops were available. And, in any event, why were so many yeomen and soldiers present, or used at all? Lord Sidmouth, the Home Secretary, and the Prince Regent were quick to congratulate the magistrates and yeomanry for, "their prompt, decisive, and efficient measures for the preservation of the public peace", which in reality they destroyed. Shelley's response to Sidmouth in his poem was:

> Clothed with the Bible, as with light,
> And the shadow of the night,
> Like Sidmouth, next, Hypocrisy
> On a crocodile rode by.[6]

Instead of their congratulations, the government should have asked why was any force deployed at a peaceful carnival-type meeting? But it refused out of hand to hold a parliamentary inquiry and Eldon, the Lord Chancellor, declared that the meeting was an overt act of treason. Not to be outdone, two weeks later an outwardly Christian clerical magistrate at Manchester used his position on the bench to tell an accused, "I believe you are a downright blackguard reformer. Some of you reformers ought to be hanged, and some of you are sure to be hanged — the rope is already round your necks".[7] He was

---

6. *Ibid.* p. 338.
7. *The Times.* (27 September 1819).

rewarded with the £2,000 living at Rochdale. By contrast, Lord Fitzwilliam, who protested at the massacre, was dismissed from his Lord-Lieutenancy.

E. P. Thompson has written that, "Confronted by this swelling power, Old Corruption faced the alternatives of meeting the reformers with repression or concession. But concession in 1819", he adds, "would have meant concession to a largely working-class reform movement; the middle-class reformers were not yet strong enough (as they were in 1832) to offer a more moderate line of advance. This is why Peterloo took place".[8]

One thing is certain. Shelley's rousing lines from the *Masque of Anarchy*, had a profound effect on radicals. He exhorted the people to:

> Rise like Lions after slumber
> In unvanquishable number —
> Shake your chains to earth like dew
> Which in sleep had fallen on you —
> Ye are many — they are few.

Eventual Success

Reports of the bloody scenes remained alive in many memories and kept the torch of reform burning despite the continuing repression exemplified by the Savage Parliament's draconian '"Six Acts" passed in November 1819. These gave magistrates fresh powers to convict political opponents of the government summarily without the delays involved in prosecuting at Assizes. They were authorised to secure searches of private houses as well as places of public resort, to confiscate weapons, to suppress all drilling and training in the use of arms and to close any meeting they chose. Penalties against alleged blasphemous and seditious publications were strengthened and the heavy newspaper tax was extended to all periodical journals.

Despite this, more political unions were formed across the country and, in its effect upon public opinion, Peterloo was a moral victory. Hunt made a triumphal entry into London soon after the massacre when *The Times*

---

8. E. P. Thompson. (1968) *The Making of the English Working Class*. London, Pelican Books. p. 749.

estimated that 300,000 people were present in the streets to welcome him. And radicals advocating electoral reform were eventually to succeed with the enactment of the Great Reform Act of 1832 and the revival of further franchise reform radicalism in the Chartist movement. Furthermore, never again would such force be used against a peaceful demonstration in Britain.

Another consequence of Peterloo was that after the Great Reform Act, Manchester became a parliamentary borough and elected its first two MPs, both Whigs. Another was the founding of the *Manchester Guardian* in 1821 as a reforming newspaper. In 2006, the *Guardian* (which that newspaper became) conducted a survey in which Peterloo came second to the *Putney Debates* as the event in British history that most deserved a proper monument or memorial. The memory of the massacre of Peterloo had not dimmed in nearly two centuries. A year later the Lord Mayor of Manchester, in place of an earlier blue plaque, unveiled a new red plaque which under the Manchester City Arms and the heading "St. Peters Fields: The Peterloo Massacre" reads:

> On 16 August 1819 a peaceful rally of 60,000 pro-democracy reformers, men, women and children, was attacked by armed cavalry resulting in 15 deaths and over 600 injuries.

Thus does the memory of dissent live on to inspire following generations.

CHAPTER 19

REFORM OR REVOLUTION

Franchise Anomalies

In the early nineteenth century the Industrial Revolution was producing a growing working class, centred in the main in the large industrial towns, whose members, as we have seen, were almost entirely without representation in Parliament. These included Birmingham, Manchester, Bristol and Leeds. At the same time there was also a great expansion in the numbers of the middle class who, although also largely denied representation, were experiencing a new sense of power.

James Mill, the father of John Stuart Mill, had written an "Essay on Government" for the *Encyclopedia Britannica* in 1818.[1] In it he claimed that the "middling classes", as he called them, had guided the majority of the people throughout history and were the highest product of civilization. This is seen by Harold Perkin as a "blatant attempt to substitute middle class for aristocratic political leadership of society [which] was exactly what increasing numbers of the middle class now wanted to hear."[2] As indeed, it was. Although the demand for franchise reform had been stifled since the treason trials of 1794 and Peterloo it was now ready to burst upon the scene with a new sense of urgency.

Unmoved by this sea-change the Tory government remained adamantly hostile to reform of the franchise. As a consequence the large number of Political Unions which had been formed in many parts of the country continued to grow and spread the gospel of reform. In Birmingham, for instance,

---
1. James Mill. (1818) "Essay on Government". *Encyclopedia Britannica*. London. Supplement.
2. Harold Perkin. (1969) *The Origins of Modern English Society: 1780-1880*. London, Routledge & Kegan Paul. p. 216.

there were, for a time, 25 Political Union debating clubs meeting weekly under the inspiration of banker Thomas Attwood. They encouraged the middle and working classes to join forces in support of the 1831 Reform Bill of the Whig government led by Lord Grey. The representation anomalies are well illustrated in the Duchy of Cornwall, which was subject to considerable crown influence. It returned 44 borough members to the House of Commons, none of whom represented more than 200 voters. This was only one fewer than the number of MPs for the whole of Scotland. Middlesex, with a population estimated at one million people, elected only eight MPs.

The Reform Bill

Towards the end of 1830 Lord Grey, leader of the Whigs, had replaced the Tory Duke of Wellington as prime minister and arranged for Lord John Russell to introduce into the House of Commons a Reform Bill. This provided, among other measures, for 60 small boroughs to be disenfranchised thus abolishing, with some others, the rotten boroughs. On the other hand, many large boroughs were to be entitled to elect MPs for the first time. The Bill received its second reading on 23 March 1831 and was passed on 22 September by just one vote. Later, on 3 October, the second reading in the House of Lords was moved by Lord Grey himself who confidently believed it would prove to be no threat to the aristocracy, as indeed it did not for some decades. The right to send representatives to Parliament, he said, was a trust and not a form of property as was being argued by the Tories. Other lords, however, continued to defend rotten boroughs and the nomination of candidates to them. As a consequence, on 8 October the Lords rejected the Bill by a majority of 41. This defeat resulted in Parliament being dissolved.

Rioting

The rejection by the Lords was received in London as a national calamity. *The Times* could barely get over the enormity of what had happened. It asked, "What have the Lords done"? And answered, "They have done what they can never undo … the four hundred or so Lords have drawn a line between them and 22 million people".[3] On 9 October the Whig *Morning Chronicle*, the *Sun* and Thomas Wakley's Radical newspaper, *The Ballot*, each appeared with black borders and there were many disorderly meetings. The house of the Duke of Newcastle was attacked and the Marquis of Londonderry was almost murdered in his coach. And the police had great difficulty in controlling a large body of supporters of the National Union of Working Classes who marched on Westminster.

In Derby there were riots during the night of 9 October. The house of a surgeon, Mr. Hayden, was partially destroyed and his son was killed by a crowd of hooligans. Shots were fired and a man hit in King Street was not expected to live. Life in the town virtually ceased with all the shops shut the next day. The Riot Act was read and soldiers fired on the people; two more men were shot, one dead and the other seriously wounded.

In Nottingham every house was closed up and all business was at a standstill. The castle was burned down, for which, in the following year, three men were hanged. In Birmingham bells were tolled all night when the news of the Lords' vote reached the city and Thomas Attwood quickly called a meeting which was attended by 100,000 people. In London demonstrations culminated in the windows being smashed for the second time that year of Apsley House, the home of the Duke of Wellington.[4]

Bristol in Flames

Bristol had already seen serious rioting on 30 September 1793 with what became known as "The Bristol Bridge Riot". It began as a protest at the renewal of a Statute levying tolls on Bristol Bridge which included a proposal to demolish several houses to create a new access road. Eleven people were killed and 45 injured in what was one of the most violent riots of the eighteenth century.[5]

---

3. *The Times*. 10 October 1831, p. 4.
4. These details are taken from *The Times* newspaper.
5. Michael Manson. (1997) *Riot! The Bristol Bridge Massacre of 1793*. Bristol, Past and Present.

The worst rioting in the Reform Bill agitation also occurred in Bristol in 1831 where, although the city had been represented in the House of Commons for generations, there were only some 6,000 voters out of an adult population estimated at 104,000. It became the bloodiest battle in Britain since Culloden. Charles Greville, clerk to the Privy Council, recorded in his journal that the Bristol Riots,

> for brutal ferocity and wanton, unprovoked violence may vie with some of the worst scenes of the French Revolution…

Anger was aroused by the complacent inaction of the members of the Tory corporation of the city who were self-appointed and weak-willed. The die-hard opponent of reform Sir Charles Wetherell, who had been Attorney-General in Wellington's government and was recorder of Bristol, went to the city on 29 October for the ordinary gaol delivery. Because of the riots that had occurred in other cities he made his entry in a carriage drawn by four grey horses many hours before he was expected. He was also escorted by a body of special constables and three troops of horses were sent to assist in keeping order. This was seen by the Bristol Political Union, and even some members of the city council, as a serious provocation.

In the event, the precaution was not entirely successful and large numbers of men and women who lined the route early yelled, hissed and groaned when they saw the recorder and threw stones at his carriage. Then, soon afterwards, when Wetherell was in the Assize court, and the town clerk said reform was not relevant to the proceedings, uproar broke out. Wetherell told the members of the public who were present that if anyone caused a disturbance they would be sent to prison. This only provoked the spectators to further fury and the court was quickly adjourned. Being chased by an angry crowd, the recorder managed with difficulty to get to the Mansion House, outside of which a man was killed by a blow on the head from a constable.

Something approaching a riot then ensued and indeed the Riot Act was read. At this the crowds, instead of being cowed, rushed the constables who fled and also took refuge in the Mansion House. This building was soon itself attacked and Wetherell escaped in disguise by ignominiously clambering over the roofs of adjoining houses. He then left the city. More troops now appeared on the scene and order was restored overnight. However, early the next morning of Sunday 30 October several hundred people assembled in the city square. They managed to occupy the Mansion House and then attacked the gaol, to which several arrested men had been taken, and sent it up in flames after releasing all the prisoners.

The troops returned but under the weak command of Colonel Brereton, who was said to support the reformers, they took no action despite the colonel having been authorised by the city's mayor, Charles Pinney, to take such steps to restore order as he thought fit once the Riot Act had been read. Encouraged by the immobility of the soldiers, the crowds set on fire the Mansion House and then fired the Bishop's Palace, the Excise Office, the Custom House, two more prisons, four toll houses and 42 private dwellings and warehouses. *The Times* reported that altogether eight people were killed[6] although in reality the total number of casualties ran into several hundred. After all this destruction the troops received cavalry reinforcements from Gloucester and Colonel Brereton belatedly found the will to restore order.

Aftermath

In early January 1832, just over two months after the riots had broken out, a number of men prominent in the disturbances were tried for various forms of riot by a special commission sitting at Bristol Guildhall with Sir Nicholas Tyndal, Lord Chief Justice of the Court of Common Pleas, as the presiding judge. Most pleaded their innocence but were found guilty amidst scenes of distress among both the defendants and the spectators in court. Of 127 prisoners, 81 were convicted and 21 acquitted. Against 12 no bills were found by the grand jury and on 13 indictments no evidence was offered by the prosecution. Of the prisoners convicted 31 were sentenced to death, one was transported for 14 years, six for seven years and 43 were sentenced to various terms of imprisonment with hard labour.[7]

---

6. *The Times*. 1 November 1831.
7. A Citizen (John Eagles). (1832) *The Bristol Riots, their Causes, Progress and Consequences*. London, Cadell. p. 258. It is perhaps not surprising that the author should have wished to remain anonymous since the book is seriously flawed by anti-reform bias. However, it does contain

On 9 January 1832 Colonel Brereton himself was taken before a court-martial charged with conducting himself so feebly during the riots as to encourage the violence. He pleaded not guilty but after four days of the hearing, and facing disgrace, he took his own life by shooting himself through the heart.

Whilst Bristol was burning, riots had also occurred at Bath, Coventry, Warwick and Worcester. And in London angry crowds manhandled the king's carriage. On Guy Fawkes night effigies of bishops were hanged on many bonfires in place of the usual guy.

In point of fact these extreme outbreaks were an expression of the revival of political life taking place among the middle and working classes after decades of repression. They transformed the battle for reform. There was now to be a fight to the finish with either reform or revolution triumphant. A third way was no longer possible.

Propaganda

Talk of revolution was widespread and Home Office files bear witness to numerous disturbances occurring up and down the country. MPs and peers who opposed the Bill were mobbed and had their houses broken into, indeed often burned down. Pamphlets, leaflets and posters tumbled off the presses in profusion and many are still to be seen in the National Archives at Kew. Examples of propaganda abound. One poster headed, "Reform! or Revolution!!" asked, "The House of Lords have presumed to reject the Bill… Will you submit that 200 individuals shall make slaves of millions?" After calling for the creation of new peers its main message was: "Pay no more Taxes — Pay no more Tithes".[8]

Another poster, under a heading "BLACKLIST", set out in full the names of the Lords who had voted against the Bill with figures of their wealth — described as "Pickings".[9] All were backed by argument in an era

---

useful appendices about the trials which followed the riots and statements by participants including Sir Charles Wetherell.
8. Public Record Office. Home Office Files. 40/29.
9. *Ibid.*

when posters put a case in words rather than by visual image. More succinct was a handbill which simply called for the right to vote and "war to the knife".[10] On 10 December 1831 an unstamped issue of the *Poor Man's Guardian* published a statement by a Macclesfield Radical that, "it matters not to me whether I am governed by a boroughmonger, or a whoremonger, or a cheesemonger if the system of monopoly and corruption is still to be upheld".

For the other side were posters giving details of the arrangements for the enrolment of special constables and a pamphlet by Joseph Sparrow entitled, "Reform not Revolution". Edward Gibbon Wakefield published an undated but eagerly read pamphlet entitled, "Householders in Danger from the Populace". In it he classed radicals and London thieves together as special objects of menace to all householders. "These", he wrote, "will be the fighting men of our revolution, if we must have one". Not to be outdone, both Whig and Tory newspapers denounced the Radicals as revolutionaries, pickpockets and incendiaries contemplating an attack on every possessor of property and the uprooting of all law and order. Thus did the inflammatory war of words rage around this entirely unrevolutionary Bill.

On 6 December 1831 Parliament was recalled and six days later Lord John Russell moved for leave to reintroduce a slightly amended Reform Bill. In March the following year the third reading of the Bill in the House of Commons received a majority of 116 votes. It was then sent to the House of Lords where Lord Grey indicated that what the Bill would achieve was not a revolution. However, Lord Ellenborough, with unusual prescience, still wanted the measure to be rejected since otherwise "it would be impossible to resist demands for further concessions until universal suffrage was established". Precisely, of course, what eventually happened.

Francis Place

After the debate the second reading of the Bill in the Lords received a majority of nine votes. But when, in committee, the House decided to delete the disenfranchising clauses of the Bill the government resigned. The loss of the

---

10. *Ibid.* 44/24.

measure again caused dismay and indignation throughout the land. Wellington and the Tories struggled to form a government but now for the first time the middle class and working class organizations were spurred into joint action, led by Francis Place. Place, a tailor, had already earned his spurs by leading the successful campaign for the repeal of the Combination Act of 1800 and for the statutory legalization of trade unions. Wellington had already said that, "the people of England are very quiet if they are let alone, but if they won't be quiet, there is a way to make them". Now, by May 1832 insurrection was expected as the National Political Unions began to prepare for armed action against the duke and his government.

Place recorded in his journals[11] later that if Wellington had been appointed prime minister there would have been an open civil and military response. He wrote that soldiers of all ranks, as well as naval men of wide experience, were in contact with him and were ready to organise and conduct the operations of the people. Even generals and colonels were involved. And by this time many citizens were armed with swords, pike-heads and muskets. The clouds of revolution threatened.

Victory

On 12 May Place and delegates from many parts of the country held a secret meeting at a tavern in Covent Garden at which they hit upon the cry: "To stop the Duke, Go for Gold". Sufficient cash was raised on the spot to have bill-stickers at work posting fly-bills raising this call in less than four hours. Place wrote to the government warning them that if they allowed the Duke to take office as premier there would be Civil War with the money from the banks "at our command". He added that, "When we obtain the money he cannot get it... we shall then have power to feed and lead the people and in less than five days we shall have the soldiers with us".[12]

The king now appealed to the Lords to end their opposition to the Bill and avoid his having to create new peers, which he let it be known he was at last prepared to do. They accordingly reluctantly voted in favour of the

---

11. Place Papers. British Library. Add. MSS. 27,793, fol. 100 and 27,794, fols. 58, 344 and 347.
12. *Ibid.* Add. MSS. 27,794, fol. 278.

Bill and the Reform Act became law on 7 June—one day after the death of the apostle of reform, Jeremy Bentham.

Place's desperate gamble had paid off because the temper of the times gave him the will to threaten to use arms and cause a run on the pound. Unlikely as it may seem today the threat of revolution was real. "We were within a moment of general rebellion", wrote Place.[13] The Duke of Wellington himself saw the essence of the struggle as a contest between two engaged armies. He regretted he could place no river between them with adequate sentinels and posts on the bridges because "the enemy was installed within his own camp".[14] And John Croker, the influential secretary to the Admiralty, had claimed that the struggle was no longer between two political parties for the ministry but between the mob and the government.

Under the Act, far fewer people secured the vote than had been hoped for, or feared, by different parties. Members of the working class were not given the vote—indeed it was taken from artisans in many of the 59 boroughs that had hitherto enjoyed a "scot and lot" or a "potwalloper" franchise. The qualification for the first depended on paying minor or church rates whilst the potwalloper had to show that he provided his own sustenance and was master of a fireplace at which to cook it.[15] Moreover, the franchise was confined to "male persons" thus excluding women from the franchise in explicit terms for the first time in British history. In fact, those entitled to vote were a smaller proportion of the population than in 1640. Nevertheless, the Act opened the way for considerable advances later in the substantial extension of the right to vote as a result of the hostility and tensions between Gladstone and Disraeli, the prelude to the final achievement of universal adult franchise in 1928 when the gender distinction was finally swept away. All that remained was for the minimum voting age to be reduced to 18 which was achieved in 1969.

The grass-roots radical heroes of this notable battle for franchise reform are largely unknown but they fought a bitter fight that led, in time, directly to the electoral democracy we enjoy today.

---

13. *Ibid.* Add. MSS. 27, 795, fol. 27.
14. PRO. HO. (1878) *Wellington Despatches.* 2nd ser. vii. 353.
15. *House of Commons Journals.* vol. xi. p. 492.

CHAPTER 20

CHARTISM: JOHN FROST AND ERNEST JONES

The Peoples' Charter

The Great Reform Act of 1832 began the slow transition to democracy in Britain. But, as we have seen, the working class who had joined with the middle class in the bitter struggle to achieve its enactment were left without representation in Parliament and the secret ballot had not been achieved. Moreover, within two years the new Poor Law was passed which provided that:

(i) There was to be no poor law relief except within a workhouse,

(ii) Such relief was to be "less eligible" than the most unpleasant means of earning a living outside,

(iii) Man and wife were to be kept separate to prevent child-bearing.

Thus came into being the workhouses known to the poor as the hated "Bastilles" also notoriously called "gaols without guilt". A central authority was set up to enforce a uniform policy under the poor law commissioners known as the "Three Bashaws of Somerset House". The widespread loathing provoked by these provisions ignited a fresh explosion of demands among the working class for its own political representation to alleviate poverty and economic distress.

Such, in brief, was the background to the rise of Chartism with its famous political six points forming the "People's Charter" in the style of a parliamentary Bill aimed at regenerating society. These were:

1. Universal male suffrage,

2. Equal electoral districts,

3. Annual Parliaments,

4. Payment of Members of Parliament,

5. A secret ballot,

6. No property qualification for Members of Parliament.

Women Supporters

None of these was won at the time by the Chartists but, except for number 3 which is not desirable, they were all achieved subsequently. At the time one of the Chartist leaders, William Lovett who drafted the Charter, wished to include women in the franchise demand but the others thought such a claim would not be taken seriously and would be used to laugh the Charter out of court and damage their campaign. As a consequence the idea was abandoned. Nevertheless, a public meeting of women in Birmingham was held at the Town Hall on 2 April 1838 which pledged its support for the already published demands of the Charter.[1] And a leaflet issued in Birmingham on 16 August 1838 over the name of T. Clutton Salt, claimed that "within a fortnight 50,000 women shall have signed that National Petition".[2]

Dorothy Thompson quotes[3] a telling conversation between Mrs. King, a Manchester Chartist, and Richard Webb, a public registrar of the district:

> Mr. Webb — What is the child to be called?

---

1. *Birmingham Journal.* (7 April 1838).
2. The leaflet is reproduced in Constance Rover's (1967) *Women's Suffrage and Party Politics in Britain, 1866-1914.* London, Routledge & Kegan Paul, p. 9.
3. Dorothy Thompson. (1986) *The Chartists: Popular Politics in the Industrial Revolution.* Wildwood House. p. 146.

Mrs. King—James Feargus O'Connor King.
Mr. Webb—Is your husband a Chartist?
Mrs. King—I don't know, but his wife is.

In fact, by the early 1840s there were over a hundred local women's Chartist associations. Mary Savage, secretary of the Nottingham Female Political Union, instructed her members: "Let every shop and shopkeeper be noted in a book kept for the purpose, stating name residence, trade and whether Whig or Tory; also another book containing the names of those friendly to the cause of the people". Those deemed "unfriendly", she said, could expect a sharp decline in their trade in areas where Chartist support was strong.[4]

Divisions within the Movement

The Chartist Movement was formally launched at a vast and enthusiastic meeting in Birmingham on 6 August 1838. But from the start the movement was divided into two factions who differed on the means of obtaining the Charter. One group wanted to rely upon what was called "moral force". This meant petitions, meetings resolutions and education. The other group relied upon "physical force" including insurrection.

Whilst the first group was made up of middle class supporters and better-paid skilled artisans the latter was, in the main, drawn from workers in mines and mills in South Wales and the North of England. The "moral force" group were led by the popular William Lovett and Thomas Attwood. The "physical force" group were headed by James Bronterre O'Brien and the fiery giant of a man, Fergus O'Connor, who had entered Parliament in 1832 as Member for Cork.

Starvation, poverty and distress were rife and the Charter was quickly endorsed at gigantic meetings held by torchlight across the country. In Manchester an estimated 300,000 people joined in such meetings, at Leeds, 250,000, at Glasgow, 200,000 and 80,000 in Newcastle. The Charter soon had 150 supporting societies and the collection of signatures to a mass petition

---

4. Edward Vallance. (2010) *A Radical History of Britain*. London, Abacus, p. 391.

was organised. Nevertheless, the split mentioned above now caused a serious weakening of the movement's unity of purpose and its impact.

The first Chartist Convention, with 53 delegates, held its initial meeting at the British Coffee House in Cockspur Street, London on 4 February 1839 amidst great excitement. However, it dragged on for two months in a fog of acrimonious debate between its two wings. Meanwhile, the "physical force" group were active. Early in 1839 there were reports that Chartists in Norwich were arming, that some 300 men were already armed, mostly with halbards but some with pistols.[5] By April some supporters were drilling illegally and the government began to contemplate the use of troops.

John Frost

John Frost was a respectable justice of the peace and former mayor of Newport in South Wales. He was not expected by the government to support Chartism and the Home Secretary, Lord John Russell, wrote to him on 16 January 1839 asking whether there was any truth in reports that he was a delegate to the Chartist National Convention and had attended meetings at Pontypool and elsewhere at which violent and inflammatory language had been used. If true, he said, Frost's name would be erased from the commission of the peace.

In a lengthy and spirited reply on 19 January, Frost who, despite his official positions, had no political affinity with the middle class, denied the allegations and took the opportunity to deplore Russell's interference with his right to express private views. Moreover, he reminded the Home Secretary that there was a time when the Whig ministry were not so fastidious about violent language at public meetings — as in 1831-32 (in the campaigning for the Reform Bill).[6] But it was to no avail. The Lord Chancellor was in no doubt about what he should do and instructed the mayor of Newport to remove Frost's name from the list of magistrates.

---

5. *The Times*. (8 March 1839) p. 7.
6. British Library. Add. MSS. General Convention of the Industrial Classes. 1839. Papers 34245A.

Meanwhile, Chartists in Rochdale decided to arm themselves with a variety of weapons including pikes and guns, pistols, powder and ball. They claimed to have in their possession more than four thousand instruments of warfare.[7] It was reported that pikes were being manufactured cheaply in Lancashire and Yorkshire and were being openly sold in the marketplace for prices ranging from sixpence to one shilling and sixpence each.[8] Similar reports were received from London, Wigan, Trowbridge, Truro and Rochdale. Significantly, as it would transpire, arms were also being sold in Monmouth and a letter from the Home Secretary to the Lord Lieutenant of Monmouthshire pointed out that any person attending a meeting for drilling, training or selling of arms was liable to transportation or imprisonment.[9]

Bull Ring Violence

On 13 May the Convention moved from London to Birmingham. Twelve days later a massive meeting of some 300,000 people that was to become part of Chartist folklore was held at Kersal Moor under the slogans: "Slavery versus Liberty" and "Peace, Law and Order". Twenty bands and 200 banners were present with one banner displaying an image of the Peterloo Massacre with the words, "Murder demands Justice".

The government became alarmed and on 4 July a special body of London police was sent by train to Birmingham where it brutally attacked a demonstration in the city's famous Bull Ring. Bloody clashes resulted which led to rioting and the burning of houses. Several policemen were injured and troops were brought in. Dozens of people were arrested although most were subsequently discharged or acquitted by the courts. Nevertheless, three men, one with a wooden leg, and a boy were tried on charges of arson and sentenced to death. This was later commuted to transportation on the grounds of possible mistaken identity[10] which, on the basis of proof being required "beyond reasonable doubt", should surely have secured their pardon and release.

---
7. *The Times*. (29 March 1839). p. 3.
8. *Ibid*.(2 April), p. 7.
9. *Ibid*. (10 April), p. 4.
10. *Northern Star*. (10 and 31 August 1839).

After the Bull Ring violence and Chartist arrests the Convention returned to London. Here it presented to the House of Commons the first National Petition which called for the implementation of the six demands of the Charter. One hundred and forty three yards in length, the Petition contained 42,884 signatures. However, it was brusquely rejected by the Commons by 235 votes to 46.

The disturbances then spread to Glasgow, Newcastle and a number of other northern towns. The secretary of the Chartist Association at Ashton-under-Lyne, near Manchester, was arrested by police for possessing a large quantity of muskets, bayonets, fowling pieces, rifles, single-barrelled guns and pistols. The Chartists in Cheshire were reported to be keeping up intimidatory agitation and a number were arrested and committed for trial.[11] Three Chartists, Francis Roberts, Joseph Howell and John Jones were sentenced to death at Warwick Assizes. In Bolton, rioting broke out in which two men were killed, a number wounded, shops gutted and the hall of the council chamber almost destroyed by fire.[12]

The prime minister, Lord Melbourne, warned Queen Victoria that troubled times were approaching and that there were fears of a revolutionary outbreak.

The Newport Rising

Despite all the arming and violence, and the fears of Lord Melbourne, the fire of the "physical force" men who seemed to be in the ascendancy failed to stand the test of time. Fergus O'Connor, for instance, advocated violence but was careful never to become involved in it and always walked away when the crunch came. The miners of South Wales erupted in the belief that it was part of a general insurrection but no other part of the country joined in.

John Frost led the Newport Rising of South Wales' miners, but, as if fearing the outcome, he did so with great reluctance. The rising was ostensibly to free the charismatic Chartist leader Henry Vincent from Newport Gaol where it was alleged he was being treated with great cruelty. According to

---

11. *The Times.* (9 July, p. 6).
12. *Ibid.* (15 August, p. 5).

the Chartist leader and historian R. G. Gammage, Vincent was regarded as "the young Demosthenes of English democracy".[13] At the time he was known to be imprisoned in Monmouth which is some 20 miles from Newport and from which one contingent of miners was moving away during the march to Newport.

The whole rising is shrouded in mystery. Frost really favoured a mass demonstration and not force but when he was urged not to take action by the irresolute O'Connor he is said to have been afraid of being seen as a traitor to the miners and responded, "I might as well blow my brains out as try to hold back the Monmouth lodges now".[14] The anger of the miners is undoubted and it was understandable when their lives, as well as their livelihoods, were often at risk when working in dangerous conditions underground. And not surprisingly their feelings towards the coalowners were bitter. Even in October 1913, when serious breaches of the Coal Mines Act by colliery owners and managers were proved to have caused the Senghenydd pit disaster in South Wales which resulted in the death of 439 men, the owners were merely punished by fines amounting in total to £24, or just over a shilling per head of the dead![15]

In the middle of the night of 3-4 November 1839 many thousands of colliers marched down their valleys in the unusually heavy blustering rain and storms of the moonless sky. One of them, George Shell, a 19-year-old miner, wrote to his parents from Pontypool, "I hope this will find you well as I am myself at this present. I shall this night be engaged in a glorious struggle for freedom, and should it please God to spare my life, I shall see you soon; but if not, grieve not for me. I shall fall in a noble cause. Farewell"![16]

Frost's detachment had assembled at Blackwood. Others, under the leadership of Zephaniah Williams, both a collier and an innkeeper, met at Nantyglo and yet more, led by the erratic and militant William Jones, at Pontypool. Whilst some were armed with muskets, pikes and pitchforks, many had no

---

13. R. G. Gammage. (1894) *History of the Chartist Movement 1837-1854*. London, Truslove and H anson. p. 11.
14. G. D. H. Cole and Raymond Postgate. (1938) *The Common People 1746-1938*. London, Methuen & Co. Ltd., p. 280.
15. Mines and Quarries. S. Wales Division Reports. Cmd. 8023-iv. pp. 58-9.
16. John Hostettler. (1998) *At the Mercy of the State: A Study in Judicial Tyranny*. Chichester, Barry Rose Law Publishers Ltd. p.167.

weapons of any kind. All were marching to meet at Risca, above Newport. However, the unprecedented weather not only drenched them to the skin but delayed their progress and prevented them meeting at the rendezvous on time.

Eventually, with dawn breaking, Frost, who had been the first to reach Risca, decided to proceed to Newport at the head of some 5,000 men without waiting any longer for the other two groups. Unknown to him in that fateful night Williams was only a short distance away. Unfortunately for the miners, as a consequence of the delay, the authorities were fully warned of what was happening and the dishevelled men walked into an ambush in the square outside the Westgate Hotel in Newport. Unaware that troops had been stationed in the hotel by the mayor only a few minutes earlier, the men approached the building (some gaining access) and stood exposed to bullets from soldiers of the 45th regiment and police who were sheltered behind the hotel shutters. The groans of the dying and the shrieks of the wounded filled the air with blood spilling everywhere. Estimates of the number of miners killed, including young George Shell, vary between 11 and 33 and many more were injured.

High Treason

The miners were dispersed and the government immediately flooded South Wales with troops. Frost and 13 others were captured and brought before a hastily appointed special commission at Pontypool and charged with high treason in waging war against the queen. To discredit Frost before his trial fantastic rumours about him and his family were circulated by the press including to its shame *The Times*. One such rumour claimed that Frost's wife and daughters had joined the miners disguised as peasants. The newspapers found Frost guilty long before his trial had even commenced. Yet public support for him was widespread throughout the country.

Frost was brought to trial first and the case lasted eight days. But no evidence was offered to sustain the theory that the rising was a green light for a general insurrection throughout the country. The Attorney-General, Sir John Campbell (who was later Lord Chancellor), alleged that the revolt was to begin in Wales and the signal for its extension was to be the non-arrival in Birmingham of the coach carrying the Welsh mails.[17] However, this allegation was discredited by the fact that no coach at that time ran from Newport to Birmingham as was pointed out by defence counsel, Sir Frederick Pollock. Moreover, not even the slightest disturbance occurred in Birmingham or elsewhere. Nevertheless, Frost and the others were found guilty of high treason and were sentenced to death.

The queen and Lord Melbourne concurred in the sentence but popular campaigning for a reprieve soon reach great intensity with mass meetings throughout the country. Indeed, Frost's proposed execution threatened to mar the celebrations to honour the royal wedding of Queen Victoria and Prince Albert four days later, and possibly bring down the government. Defence counsel and the Lord Chief Justice appealed to the Home Secretary, now the bureaucratic Lord Normanby, who, under tremendous pressure and concerned about the queen's marriage and the fate of the government, granted a reprieve. *The Times*, no longer the "thunderer" of the Reform agitation, misreported the rising and called for the resignation of Lord Normanby for being too sanguine about it. It also claimed that the mayor, Thomas Phillips, was shot whilst reading the Riot Act when in fact it never left his pocket.[18]

In the event, Frost, Williams and Jones were transported for 14 years to Van Diemen's Land where they were each to be appointed to official positions. Following nationwide campaigning and an impassioned speech in the House of Commons by Thomas Wakley, Frost was finally pardoned in 1854. He died in England twenty three years later, aged 96.

About this time a great series of strikes erupted across the country in mines, mills and factories across Scotland, Wales, the Midlands and the North of England as a consequence of wage reductions and an economic depression. In Lancashire, in what was known as the "Plug Plot", the cotton spinners went from mill to mill, first raking out the fires from beneath the boilers and then knocking the boiler plugs out to bring the steam-engines and the mills to a standstill.

---

17. David J. V. Jones. (1985) *The Last Rising. The Newport Insurrection of 1839*. Oxford, The Clarendon Press. p. 190. By far the best account of the rising.
18. *The Times*. (6 September 1839) p. 5.

Chartist Leaders Gaoled

Although the Chartist leaders had not started this latest movement, meetings of strikers began to pass resolutions that "all labour should cease until the People's Charter becomes the law of the land". The government had already ordered the arrest of some 500 more Chartist leaders, including O'Brien and O'Connor, who were gaoled. Reports of cruelty against the prisoners began to circulate. O'Connor was said to be suffering from ill-treatment at York Castle and Henry Vincent at Millbank. But the treatment of Joseph Crabtree appeared to be even worse and a form of torture. He was held in Wakefield's House of Correction, said to be the most severe prison in Britain. The punishment inflicted was indeed dreadful. He was locked in a six foot by eight foot cell from 6 pm until 6 am when he was taken to the day room where he had to sit on a form all day and face one direction. At six in the evening he was returned to his cell. He was not allowed in the yard unless sick. If he hung down his head or looked at another prisoner in the face he was placed in a dark cell in solitary confinement for three days with only half a pound of bread and some water a day.[19] Not surprisingly, with so many leaders in prison the impact of the movement temporarily declined.

However, many of the prisoners were subsequently released and Chartism revived with the *Northern Star* achieving a circulation of 50,000. But there arose an acrimonious dispute between O'Brien and O'Connor, both of whom remained confined in prison. Nevertheless, a second petition was taken to the House of Commons which was over six miles long, having been signed by 3,317,702 people, more than half the adult male population. Its bulk was so great that the doors of the House were not wide enough for it to be carried through and it had to be unrolled. When it was divided up on the floor of the Commons it rose above the level of the table and the chamber looked "as if it had been snowing paper".

It was presented to the MPs by Thomas Duncombe with a motion that six petitioners be heard by themselves or by counsel at the bar of the House. Lord John Russell expressed both his respect for the petitioners and his abhorrence of the doctrines of the petition. His respect did not extend to

---

19. *The Times*. (6 July 1840) p. 10.

allowing the petitioners to speak to the House, however, and he denied that anybody had the "right" to vote; thus confirming the correctness of the nickname "Finality Jack" given to the author of the Great Reform Act. Despite a lively debate the petition was rejected on 4 May 1842 by 287 votes to 49. Disraeli had not been present but the leader of the Liberal Party, William Ewart Gladstone, supported Russell and voted against the motion.

Despite these setbacks women were continuing to show a growing interest in the movement. A meeting of female Chartists was held for the purpose of forming an association to co-operate with the all-male association. A Mr. Cohen caused a "sensation among the ladies" when he asserted that women would be more in their proper character and station at home than in the political arena. He did not consider, he said, that nature intended women to partake of political rights. When Miss Susanna Inge, who became secretary to the association, asked Mr Cohen why he considered women unqualified to vote as this required little physical force, he replied that if she were in the House of Commons a man could sway her vote by playing on her affections. Mary Ann Walker responded that she would treat such a man with womanly scorn and then to loud cheers gave a spirited speech and appealed to her countrywomen to come out and enrol their names in favour of the Charter.[20]

Kennington Common

By 1848 another petition was ready and O'Connor was delirious with excitement at the millions of signatures he claimed were appended to it. A monster meeting on Kennington Common, south of the Thames was called for 10 April to precede a procession to Parliament to present the petition and call upon Queen Victoria to dissolve Parliament. The government declared the meeting illegal and the Duke of Wellington, now 78 years of age and commander-in-chief of the army, brought 9,000 troops from outlying barracks and enrolled 70,000 men as special constables. Over four days some 4,000 police guarded the bridges over the river, as well as Palace Yard and Trafalgar

---

20. *The Times.* (20 October 1842). p. 3.

Square. Heavy gun-batteries were ferried over the Thames from Woolwich Arsenal and placed at various strategic points.

Despite all this military activity some hundred thousand or more people gathered on the common ready to march to Westminster with the petition. O'Connor then met with the metropolitan police commissioner, Richard Mayne, at the nearby Horns Tavern where he agreed to abandon the procession to Westminster if the meeting were allowed to continue peacefully, which presumably meant if the police did not disrupt it. The anger of the crowds at this surrender was manifest and it needed all O'Connor's powers of persuasion and demagogy to placate them. However, he did so, rain fell and the meeting broke up peacefully.

According to O'Connor the petition had 5,706,000 signatures but when it was presented to the House of Commons and examined by clerks it was found to have only 1,975,496 names of which many were bogus. These included "Victoria Rex", "the Duke", "Sir Robert Peel", "Mr Punch" and "Pug Nose". Many others were in the same handwriting. Chartism was now largely a spent force although it managed to linger on for a few more years after the price of wheat rose to very high levels. At this point it had found a new leader in Ernest Jones.

Ernest Jones, the Chartists' Advocate

A distinguished radical lawyer, Ernest Jones was born in Berlin on 25 January 1819, the son of a British Army major and his wife, the daughter of an influential Kent landowner. He received an extensive private education and was fluent in a number of languages. Nothing seemed to indicate that he would later become interested in radical politics. However, in 1831, at the age of eleven, he disappeared from home and was found three days later in the Black Forest with a bundle under his arm going, he said, to "assist the Poles" in their insurrection against the Russian occupiers of their country. At 25 years of age he was called to the Bar at the Middle Temple on 20 April 1844. Under the influence of O'Connor, he was an advocate of physical force and in 1843 he had been sentenced to two years solitary confinement in prison for seditious speeches. What he had said was, "Only organize, and you will see the green flag floating over Downing Street; let that be accomplished and John Mitchell[21] shall be brought back to his native country, and Sir G. Grey and Lord John Russell shall be sent out to exchange places with him".[22]

He broke away from his class saying he found them unworthy of the privileges they enjoyed, and of the powers they appropriated. He said that as an honest man he could not support a system by which, "the poor are robbed of their labour for the benefit of the rich, and slaves are still further insulted by being told that they are free".[23]

Jones also wrote songs and poems that were often sung and recited at Chartist meetings. One example, known as "Our Rally" includes the following lines:

> My countrymen! Why languish
> Like outcasts of the earth,
> And drown in tears of anguish
> The glory of your birth?
> Ye were a freeborn people
> And heroes were your race:
> The dead — they are our freemen –
> The living — our disgrace.[24]

He lost both his parents within months of each other in 1846 and his uncle disinherited him, in favour of his gardener, after he refused to give up the politics the uncle said brought discredit to the family. As a consequence he joined the staff of the *Northern Star* at a salary of £250 a year which kept the wolf from the door and he continued to enjoy a happy family life.

In July 1847 he stood as a Chartist candidate in the Parliamentary election in Halifax. He was defeated at the poll after having won a large majority at the hustings. He helped plan the meeting at Kennington Common and supported O'Connor in abandoning the procession to Westminster. In analysing

---

21. John Mitchell founded the United Irishman in Dublin and was an active Chartist agitator who was transported for making seditious speeches.
22. George Jacob Holyoake. (1892) *Sixty Years of an Agitator's Life*. London, T. Fisher Unwin. p. 250.
23. *Northern Star*. (9 May 1846).
24. Ernest Jones. (1846) *Chartist Poems: Our Rally*.

the failure of the 1848 petition Jones blamed the dispute between the physical force group and those advocating moral force. However, times were changing and Chartism was no longer a human convulsion of despairing workmen but a spent force, succumbing to the advance of Victorian prosperity. The "Hungry Forties" were followed by the "Age of Equipoise" as the 1850s were labelled. Britain began to flourish as the workshop of the world.

"The Charter and No Surrender"

In 1848, however, neither the Chartists nor the government saw that the end was in sight. Despite the setbacks, Jones continued his work in the Chartist movement and on 6 June 1848 he was arrested after speaking at a meeting in Manchester and charged with sedition. His trial, with five other Chartists, was heard the following month and he was sentenced to two years solitary confinement in the Millbank Prison for speaking, he said, three words, "Organize, organize, organize". He would go to prison, he wrote in an open letter, with the words, "The Charter and No Surrender" on his lips. In prison he was treated with great brutality and after his release a pamphlet gave some idea of his suffering:

> He was kept in solitary confinement on the silent system, enforced with the utmost vigour; for 19 months he was neither allowed pen, ink, nor paper but confined in a small cell, 13 feet by 6, in utter solitude, varied only by a solitary walk in a high-walled prison yard. He obeyed all the prison regulations in a most exemplary manner, excepting one, that as to picking oakum, observing that for the sake of public order he would conform to all external forms and rules, but he would never lend himself to voluntary degradation. Again and again he was imprisoned in a dark cell, on bread and water, in consequence, even the Bible being taken away from him.[25]

Whilst in prison he contracted dysentery but he also managed, despite the restrictions upon him, to write some poetry. He made pens from feathers

---

25. Ernest Jones. *Who is He? What has he Done?* (no date) Manchester, Manchester Reform League. p. 7.

he picked up from the prison yard and sometimes wrote in his own blood. Here are extracts that exemplify his attachment to the cause of the working people and his optimism:

The Prisoner to The Slaves

What fetters have I that ye have not as well
Though your dungeon be larger than mine?
For England's a prison fresh modelled from hell,
And the jailors are weakness and crime.

They may shut out the sky—they may shut out the light
With the barriers and ramparts they raise:
But the glory of knowledge shall pierce in despite,
With the sun of its shadowless days.
They may stifle the tongue with their silencing rules,
They may crush us with cord and with block:
But oppression and force are the folly of fools,
That breaks upon constancy's rock.

They shall hear us again on the moorland and hill,
Again in street, valley and plain:
They may beat us once more—but we'll rush at them still,
Again—again—and again![26]

He later claimed he went into prison a Chartist and came out a republican.[27]

Red Republican

On his release from prison Jones joined a group connected with the *Red Republican* edited by George Julian Harney. This went beyond the Chartist call for a reform of Parliament to demanding a revolutionary change in British

---
26. Ernest Jones. (ed.) (1852) *Notes to the People*. London, J. Pavey.
27. *Northern Star*. (26 October 1850)

society. Through Harney he met Frederick Engels and Karl Marx, who had a high regard for his talents, and he continued to campaign tirelessly across the country. However, with the decline of Chartism it is perhaps not surprising that Jones and Harney broke their collaboration and became radically hostile to each other. Then, in the end Jones returned to his legal practice at the Bar where he was successful as a popular radical lawyer, often appearing for political prisoners and trade unionists. After developing pleurisy, he died on the day after his 50th birthday on 26 January 1869. His remains were taken to Ardwick Cemetery, Manchester five days later with up to 100,000 people crowding the streets on his last journey to pay their respects.

Towards the end of the century the influence of Chartist radicalism on the reviving trade union movement and the eventual birth of the Labour Party was considerable and, as we have seen, five of the Charter's six point were eventually adopted. In the words of one writer, Chartism,

> represented the first genuinely democratic movement for social reform in modern history and has a real place in the development of modern English politics and society.[28]

---

28. Mark Hovell. (1925) *The Chartist Movement*. Manchester, University of Manchester Press. p. 312.

CHAPTER 21

THOMAS WAKLEY — AN ENEMY OF INJUSTICE

An Improbable Radical

Thomas Wakley was born into a wealthy family and always retained the outward trappings of his class. Notwithstanding his background, however, he became a prominent advocate, not only of medical, social and political reform but also of the deepest aspirations of a working class resolutely excluded from political power. In other words, he was not only a battling surgeon but also an improbable radical. He was a colourful and controversial character and in his day the mere mention of his name was likely to inspire heartfelt praise from some or paroxysms of rage in others. He was a radical figure with an acute reforming zeal and his keen onslaughts on injustice and his unfailing humanity were to win enthusiastic praise from many contemporaries including Sir Robert Peel and Charles Dickens.

The village of Membury in Devon, where Wakley was born on 11 July 1795, gave little promise of the improbable future that lay in store for young Thomas. Indeed, strikingly little of his destiny was to be revealed by his childhood and youth. His father, Henry Wakley, was a wealthy farmer, a leading authority on agriculture in the West Country and a commissioner for the enclosure of waste lands. Thomas was the youngest of the eleven children of Henry and his wife.

On leaving school, Thomas chose medicine as his career and was apprenticed to an apothecary at Taunton. However, at the time, many practising apothecaries received no professional education and possessed no medical qualifications of any kind. And Thomas was ambitious to be a surgeon and persuaded his father to let him become a pupil of his brother-in-law, Mr. Phelps, a surgeon at Beaminster. In 1817, at the age of 22, he obtained his surgeon's diploma at the United Hospitals of St. Thomas's and Guy's in London and on 5 February 1820 he married Elizabeth Goodchild at St. James's Church in Piccadilly.

The Lancet

Wakley soon became appalled by the open nepotism and jobbery he saw practised by many of the leading surgeons and in 1823 he founded *The Lancet* with the primary objects of publicising new medical knowledge and exposing the corruption prevalent in the hospitals. Editorials were written in Wakley's controversial and campaigning style. New discoveries in medicine were reported. Frequent articles appeared on the causes and treatment of many diseases of both the mind and the body. Quacks and myths were exposed and destroyed. At least three important clinical lectures were published in each issue. Campaigns were initiated to improve the standards and qualifications of apothecaries and surgeons as well as conditions in hospitals. And theatrical criticisms and chess problems were not ignored.

With *The Lancet* Wakley raised controversy into an art with his attacks upon the medical oligarchy and their often flawed surgery. As a consequence the leading surgeon of the day, Sir Astley Cooper, called the journal "the Reptile Press" whilst other surgeons referred to it as "that notorious publication". Nevertheless, after a series of libel actions against him, Wakley was successful in the end in achieving a settled policy of medical reform. And 12 years later Queen Victoria granted a new charter to the Royal College of Surgeons with a more democratic system of election of Fellows in place of the previously self-electing Council and widespread nepotism.

The Ballot

Wakley's radicalism took flight, however, with the agitation for the 1831 Reform Bill dealt with earlier in chapter 18. Whilst the political unions were seeking an alliance between the middle and working classes, some radical working class elements were opposed to such an alliance. Accordingly, on

2 April 1831 William Lovett and others formed the National Union of the Working Classes (NUWC) to press for a working class male franchise. In response, and to counter their influence, Francis Place founded the National Political Union (NPU). Following the rejection of the Reform Bill by the House of Lords, Wakley decided to join the NUWC. Its programme called for an end to the "system of exploitation of wage slaves by masters and proclaimed that everything produced belonged to those whose labour produced it and it should be shared amongst them". In an echo of Gerard Wynstanley it further declared that all men were born equally free and demanded universal manhood suffrage. All men, it continued, had certain natural, inherent and inalienable rights on which all governments should be founded. Other demands they pressed for included the secret ballot.[1]

Despite joining the NUWC, Wakley went with some 2,000 people to the inaugural meeting of Place's NPU held at the Crown and Anchor tavern in the Strand on 31 October. Here he called for a "marriage of the middle and working classes". He also moved that 50% of those to be elected to the Council to run the NPU should be drawn from the working class and 50% from the middle class. Place was aghast at the damage he thought this would do and he described Wakley as obnoxious. He was less than pleased when Wakley was elected to the committee formed to devise plans for the election of the Council. In the event, Place eventually secured the exclusion of Wakley from the Council but was unable to prevent the election of 52% of the Council from members of the working class.

During the agitation for the Bill Wakley had produced his own weekly newspaper called *The Ballot*. Remarkably like *The Times* in size and appearance and with front page advertisements, the first number rolled off the presses on Sunday, 2 January 1831 priced at seven pence. Its first leader stated in uncompromising tones that the paper's title declared in one word its political creed and that it would be independent and impartial until corruption was destroyed. To his dismay, however, the secret ballot was not included in the final Reform Act 1832 as it was enacted and was not in fact achieved until forty years later in 1872.

---

1. John Hostettler. (1993) *Thomas Wakley: An Improbable Radical*. Chichester, Barry Rose Law Publishers. p. 62. Much of the material in this chapter is taken from that book.

Tolpuddle Martyrs

The first general election after the enactment of the Reform Act was held in December 1832. Wakley decided to stand in his home constituency of Finsbury as an independent radical. He declared himself in favour of a further extension of the suffrage, the removal of the property qualifications for candidates, the repeal of the Corn Laws, the abolition of slavery and the suspension of stamp duty on newspapers. At the time Finsbury had a population of 330,000 of whom 16,000 had the vote following the Reform Act. He was not elected, however, but stood again in the January 1835 election when he was returned as a joint member with Thomas Duncombe, another radical.

Wakley's upbringing in the Devon countryside on the borders of Dorset made him well qualified to champion the cause of the Tolpuddle Martyrs. Six agricultural labourers in the small Dorset village of Tolpuddle had been arrested in 1834 for swearing men into a trade union lodge. They had not threatened to strike but merely combined to resist a reduction in their wages from nine shillings a week to six shillings. Yet the full power of the state, using the Mutiny Act 1797, was brought to bear upon them. And clearly, if the Dorset labourers were guilty of swearing illegal oaths, then so were the members of other trade unions, Orange Lodges and numerous other societies who were left in peace.

On 19 March 1834 the six labourers were convicted at Dorchester Assizes and all sentenced by Mr. Baron Williams to seven years' transportation. Williams actually declared that it was not for anything they had done, or had intended to do, but as an example to others that he considered it his duty to sentence them to transportation.[2] Had they been tried by magistrates in the normal way for belonging to an unlawful combination under the Unlawful Societies Act 1799, the maximum sentence would have been three months imprisonment.

The nation was stunned and the sentences finally alienated the working class from the Whig government. Whilst the prisoners languished in the decaying hulks at Portsmouth awaiting transportation, more than 30,000 people, led amongst others, by Wakley joined a vast demonstration in

---

2. George Lovelace (One of the accused). (1837) *The Victims of Whiggery*. London.

Copenhagen Fields, King's Cross to protest against the savage sentences. And by 27 May 1835 Wakley was able to present to the House of Commons 16 petitions with over 13,000 signatures for the reprieve of the convicts. He made a short speech in which he disclosed that the wives and families of the men had not only been reduced to poverty but had even been refused parish relief.

He then gave notice that in a month's time he would move a resolution that the sentences should be annulled. The Home Secretary, Lord John Russell, requested Wakley to postpone his motion since the government had already recommended a partial remission and he was supported by the Member for Dorset. Wakley refused since the partial remission was conditional upon some of the men remaining in Australia for some time and the Lovelaces, whom Russell called "the greater criminals", until they died. Wakley also expressed his astonishment that the Member for Dorset, who had been the foreman of the grand jury, should intervene between the sufferers and the "seat of mercy" (i.e. the House of Commons).

Wakley told the House of the biased charge delivered by the judge to the grand jury and referred to the Act of 1824 which made combinations in trade unions legal for all purposes. He then quoted at length from a compassionate letter written from the hulks by George Lovelace to his wife. "Was it fitting", he asked, "was it just, that such a man as this, for a doubtful offence should be torn from his loved family, and expatriated for the lengthened period of seven years? It was enough to drive the working millions into madness and revenge".

And hear it, he continued,

> Ye Gentlemen of England, who are husbands, and fathers, and brothers—who have wives and children of your own—one woman—ah! poor creature, how painfully is she figured in my mind at this moment—having a husband and six children, and taken from her, her two brothers, her husband, and her eldest son, all at "one fell swoop", and this my Lord [addressing Lord John Russell] is your boasted England! This is your country of equal laws and equal justice.

Wakley continued speaking from the heart for two and a half hours and when he sat down he received unrestrained applause from MPs. Nine months later he drew from Russell a statement that the six men had received a free pardon and were returning to England at the government's expense. Proof, Wakley called it, of the sovereignty of the people. On 25 April 1836 a public dinner of thanksgiving for the remission of the sentences was held at White Conduit House, London with nearly 2,000 people attending. Wakley presided and was enthusiastically fêted. A copy of the poster proclaiming the dinner now fittingly hangs in the T. U. C. Memorial Museum in the village of Tolpuddle.

Friend of Chartism

Wakley played a prominent part in the birth of Chartism and when leaders of the movement, including Fergus O'Connor and Henry Vincent, were imprisoned he and Duncombe moved in the Commons for a full inquiry into the harsh conditions in which they were held. He also called for the return of the transported Chartists; Frost, Williams and Jones, the leaders of the Newport Rising.

Nonetheless, although Wakley counted O'Connor as a friend, he always opposed the "physical force" arm of the movement in the belief that its actions were counter-productive. For him action had to be taken constitutionally and the place for achieving reform was Parliament. He told his constituents that whereas lawless rebellion stirred up enmity to good causes among the people, constitutional agitation generally obtained its just demands. Indeed, many Chartist leaders themselves abjured violence and Chartist posters and literature constantly proclaimed the slogan, "Peace, Law and Order". Clearly, without distancing himself from mainstream Chartism, he had drawn important lessons from the agitation for the Reform Bill.

The People's Judge

Wakley became the coroner for West Middlesex in 1839. At the time coroners were lawyers without the medical skills often called for in that office. Moreover, inquests on deaths were frequently held in tap rooms and taverns where alcohol was freely available. The "Sol's Arms" in Dickens's *Bleak House* gives a grim and potent picture. A typical case was reported in *The Times* for 6 June 1839 when, in an inquest on a particularly gruesome body, the "courtroom" in "The Rough" public house in Westminster was adjourned in uproar because of the oppressive atmosphere. Wakley was alarmed that many such inquests degenerated into farce from a surfeit of gin and the incompetence of lawyer coroners. For years he had campaigned for medical coroners in the columns of *The Lancet* and had reported numerous inquests which made clear his reasons.

In one case, for example, a family ate a pie from which two of them died at once, a third some 24 hours later, and a fourth was seriously sick. The remnants of the pie were thrown out into the yard where some chickens ate them and died instantly. All the evidence pointed to arsenic poisoning, yet the lawyer coroner directed the jury to bring in a verdict of "death by the visitation of God". Later, when the bodies were exhumed, poisoning by arsenic was established and the divine intervention exploded. Wakley claimed that this travesty of justice could never have occurred with a medical coroner. In another case where a woman named Elizabeth Chalk had died from cholera, which was prevalent at the time, the coroner told the jury to return a verdict of manslaughter after refusing to admit the testimony of four medical witnesses but allowing three young children to say she was pushed about. These are just two of such cases reported in *The Lancet*.

It is interesting to note that in her novel *Middlemarch* George Eliot reveals some of the contemporary attitudes to Wakley and the coronership of lawyers. She writes:

> I hope, says Mr. Chiceley, you are not one of *The Lancet's* men, Mr. Lydgate—wanting to take the coronership out of the hands of the legal profession: your words appear to point that way. I disapprove of Wakley, interposed Dr. Sprague, no man more: he is an ill-intentioned fellow, who would sacrifice the respectability of the profession, which everybody knows depends upon the London Colleges, for the sake of getting some notoriety for himself…But Wakley is right sometimes, the

Doctor added, judicially. I could mention one or two points on which Wakley is in the right.³

The group continued to discuss the relative merits of legal against medical coroners with Lydgate adding, "A lawyer is no better than an old woman at a post-mortem examination. How is he to know the action of a poison? You might as well say that scanning verse will teach you to scan the potato crops".⁴

Coroner for West Middlesex

In the district of West Middlesex 9,000 freeholders had the vote in a far-flung division stretching from Farringdon Road adjoining the City in the east to Uxbridge in the west and comprising over 300 square miles. There were also political obstacles for Wakley. The Middlesex magistrates, who paid the coroner's fees, were openly hostile to the Radical candidate and decided to intervene. Without warning, on 7 February they petitioned the Lord Chancellor, Lord Cottenham, to withdraw the writ he had issued to commence the election on 18 February. They asked him to declare that two coroners should be elected for the one vacancy, each to act for one half of the division. This would at least have ensured the election of their own candidate. The bias was only too obvious, however, since they had been satisfied with the previous coroner, a Mr. Stirling, who had not only acted alone, even at the age of 94, but was also a practising solicitor and clerk to the very same magistrates. It was not only *The Lancet* that pointed to the prejudice but also *The Globe, The Examiner* and *The Morning Chronicle.*

It cannot have escaped the Lord Chancellor either since he brusquely rejected the request. In consequence, after Wakley had secured 2,015 votes to 582 for his solicitor opponent, the latter retired from the contest and on 25 February Wakley found himself elected coroner for West Middlesex. Even at that stage his enemies had still been trying to persuade his opponent to continue the hopeless contest.

---

3. George Eliot. (1972) *Middlemarch*. London, Folio Society edition. p. 168.
4. *Ibid.*

Soon after the election Wakley issued new regulations providing that the coroner should be informed of deaths occurring within his jurisdiction in the following cases:

1. When persons died suddenly.

2. When persons were found dead.

3. When persons died from any acts of violence or any accident.

4. When women died during labour or a few hours after delivery.

5. When persons were supposed to have died from the effects of poisons or quack medicines.

6. When persons died who appeared to have been neglected during sickness or extreme poverty.

7. When persons died in confinement, as in prisons or police offices.

8. When lunatics or paupers died in confinement, whether in public or in private asylums.

Such a measure was long overdue and would quickly produce excellent results but the magistrates and sections of the press were in uproar at the increase in the number of inquests that they predicted would occur. Wakley responded by telling one of his juries that the coroner was the people's judge, the only judge they had the power to elect or appoint.

And within 24 hours of the regulations coming into force Wakley was vindicated. On 30 September 1839 Thomas Austin, aged 79 and a pauper, died in the Hendon Workhouse. In fact, he had fallen into the copper in the laundry and did not survive the scalding he received. In breach of the new regulations no notice was given to the coroner and with indecent haste the workhouse guardians ordered that the body be buried in the Hendon churchyard without delay. Wakley heard of the death, however, and swiftly attended the workhouse to hold an inquest. The guardians resisted but Wakley demanded that the body be exhumed and an inquest was held. The jury returned a verdict of accidental death but added a rider that the workhouse authorities were guilty of contributory negligence in not placing a railing around the copper.

The master of the workhouse endeavoured to embarrass the coroner and exclaimed in triumph, "The jury have found a verdict but have not identified the body", to which Wakley blandly inquired, "If this is not the body of the man who was killed in your vat, pray, Sir, how many paupers have you boiled"?

The magistrates then returned to the attack. They alleged he was holding too many inquests in order to obtain more fees and they proposed to petition the Lord Chancellor to dismiss him. They appointed a committee to inquire into the increase in inquests and to consider the fees which could only be paid if approved by them. To their astonishment when the committee published its report it revealed that Wakley was holding fewer inquests than his predecessor, that less money had been paid for the attendance of medical witnesses and that Wakley's expenses were considerably lower than those of Mr. Baker, the coroner for East Middlesex.

Death by Flogging

Floggings in the army and navy, as well as in prisons, were a regular occurrence. They could involve up to 200 lashes with a cat-o'-nine tails. It was on 25 February 1836 that Wakley first moved in the House of Commons that flogging in the army should be abolished. He had seen, he told the House, the body of William Saundry who had died from a flogging at Woolwich Barracks. He had been sentenced to 200 lashes with the cat which had nine thongs treated until they resembled wire. In the course of the "punishment" his screams were so loud that the files and drums were ordered to drown them. Yet they could still be heard 1½ miles away. After 100 lashes, or 900 thongs, had been passed over his lacerated back Saundry had to be taken down. The Member for Dumfries, continued Wakley, had said flogging was not degrading to a soldier. If it was not degrading to the men, asked Wakley wryly, why was it not applied to the officers?

The motion was defeated but ten years later Wakley was in a position to take action. On 15 June 1846, Frederick John White, a private of the Seventh Hussars, received a severe and cruel flogging of 150 lashes with the cat-o'-nine tails at the Cavalry Barracks on Hounslow Heath. Unfortunately for the government the death was within Wakley's jurisdiction as coroner. White died on 11 July. The local vicar, to whom the death had been reported to be the result of a liver complaint, discovered that the flogging had occurred, refused permission for the funeral and informed the coroner. Wakley promptly attended the scene and summoned a jury to hold an inquest. Without properly examining White's back, three army doctors declared that the flogging had nothing to do with the death and in answer to a question this was reported to the House of Commons on 20 July. A local surgeon, who examined the body at Wakley's request, also suspiciously failed to examine the back and spine and Wakley rejected his report.

He then called in a specialist, Erasmus Wilson of the Middlesex Hospital, who, after examining the lacerated body, had no difficulty in convincing the jury that the flogging had caused the death. In giving their verdict the jury, who had also seen White's body, took their cue from Wakley and publicly expressed their "horror and disgust" at the law which permitted the "revolting punishment of flogging to be inflicted upon British soldiers". They implored every man in the kingdom to join "hand and heart" in forwarding petitions to Parliament praying for the abolition of such a disgraceful practice, which was a "slur upon the humanity and fair name of the people of this country". Wakley now received public acclaim with even the Middlesex magistrates finally supporting him and flogging in the army largely fell into disuse until it was abolished by the Army Act 1881.

Wakley continued to attack injustice and malpractice as an MP; as coroner; and through the columns of *The Lancet* until his death in Madeira, where he had gone for his health, on 16 May 1862. He was buried on 14 June, alongside his wife and daughter, in the catacombs of John Nash's Kensal Green Cemetery in London. His neighbours in death include Feargus O'Connor, Joseph Hume, Sydney Smith, Thackeray, Trollope, Thomas Hood, James Leigh Hunt, Wilkie Collins, Thomas Barners, Emil Blondin,

Isambard Brunel and George Cruikshank. If only their shades could enjoy each others company!

The Lancet continues as a prestigious medical journal and we all benefit today from the many inspiring actions, of which only a few are recorded here, of the radical Dr. Thomas Wakley, MP.

CHAPTER 22

KEIR HARDIE

Self-help

James Keir Hardie was born in a one-room cottage at Legbrannock near Holytown in Lanarkshire on 15 August 1856, the illegitimate son of a farm servant, Mary Keir. His mother later married David Hardie, a ship's carpenter who became the boy's father. Without any schooling, at the age of eight Keir was working as a baker's delivery boy and by the age of eleven he was employed in the mines as a "trapper". This involved him in opening and closing a door during a ten hour shift to maintain the air supply for the miners in his section of the pit. In spite of his lack of formal education, with extraordinary persistence he had taught himself to read and write by the time he was 17 years of age. In time he was to become the heroic face of late nineteenth century radicalism.

Hardie was a radical to whom other miners in Scotland looked as a spokesman for their grievances. However, sensing his potential as a leader the Scottish mine owners soon blacklisted him with the result that he could get no work in the pits. Their philosophy was expressed in saying, "We'll hae nae damned Hardies in the pit".[1] However, because of this blacklisting, in August 1879 he was appointed Miners' Agent and began his career as a trade union organiser. In the same year he married Lillie Wilson, a dark-haired Lancashire girl but she was not happy with public life and played little part in his career. In 1881 he led the first ever strike of Ayrshire miners which lasted for ten weeks. The miners' demand was for a 10% raise in wages but they returned to work without achieving it. Nevertheless, soon after their

---

1. William Stewart. (1925) *J. Keir Hardie*. London, Independent Labour Party. p. 8.

return, wages were raised so that the strike was to that extent considered to have been successful. Five years later, in August 1886, largely as a result of Hardie's efforts the Ayrshire Miners Union was established with Hardie as its organising secretary at a salary of £75 a year.

The Cloth Cap

As was not uncommon for a radical-minded working man at the time, in politics Hardie supported the Liberal Party and urged the miners to do the same. However, he quickly became disillusioned with Gladstone's economic policies and came to believe that the Liberals could not adequately represent the working class and introduce radical reforms. As a consequence in 1888 he stood as an independent labour candidate in Mid-Lanark. Although he came bottom of the poll his faith remained undiminished and when a Scottish Labour Party was formed in that same year he became its first secretary. In 1892 he was unexpectedly invited to stand as an independent labour candidate for West Ham South in the East End of London—a constituency with a large population of gasworkers, dockers and Irishmen. He was chosen probably because of his recent declarations in favour of the eight-hour day, an important issue at the time. In the event, the Liberals did not run a candidate and Hardie defeated the sitting Conservative, major George Banes, by 5,268 votes to 4,036.

He celebrated his success by taking his seat in the House of Commons on 3 August wearing, not the usual black frock coat and top hat but, yellow tweed trousers, serge jacket, a red tie and a tweed cap (later to become the legend of the "cloth cap"). In an early speech he advocated a graduated income tax on incomes over £1,000 a year, free schooling, women's franchise, old age pensions and abolition of the House of Lords. There are echoes here of Tom Paine's *The Rights of Man*. He told the House of Commons that the people were called upon to decide the question put by Jesus in the Sermon on the Mount as to whether they would worship God or Mammon. The present day, he said with some prescience, was a Mammon-worshipping age which corrupted people. Of great significance, a year later he joined others to form the Independent Labour Party in an endeavour to break the practice of working men voting for Liberal candidates in elections.

The Independent Labour Party

The Independent Labour Party (ILP) was founded by a delegate conference at the Bradford Labour Institute on 13 January 1893. There were 120 delegates including, as well as Hardie, Ben Tillett, Robert Blatchford and George Bernard Shaw. However, Hardie was the dominant personality in bringing it to life. As a consequence, he was elected conference chairman and in his opening address called for a Party made up of men of labour to be independent of the Liberal Party. A socialist demand for the collective ownership of the means of production, distribution and exchange was adopted almost unanimously. To demands that would have had the support of the Chartists such as the payment of MPs, adult suffrage and shorter Parliaments[2] were added social measures including the abolition of child labour, an eight-hour day and a graduated income tax.

Hardie fought off a call for the party to be named "The Socialist Labour Party" and ensured that a wide range of bodies like trade unions, Radical clubs, trades councils and other groups could affiliate to an all-embracing ILP. At its second annual conference at Manchester in 1894 he was re-elected chairman by a huge majority. The new party was regarded as his personal creation — he was its symbol and its prophet.[3]

In 1894 an explosion at the Albion Colliery in Cilfynydd, east Glamorgan killed 251 miners including boys. In the Commons Hardie called for a message of condolence to be sent to the relatives of the victims and added to the address of congratulations on the birth of the future King Edward VIII. The request was refused and Hardie made a speech attacking the monarchy which caused uproar. He said:

---

2. Until the Parliament Act 1911 Members of Parliament were elected for seven year terms.
3. Kenneth O. Morgan. (1984) *Keir Hardie: Radical and Socialist*. London, Weidenfeld & Nicolson, p. 65.

> From his childhood this boy will be surrounded by sycophants and flatterers by the score—[Cries of "Oh, oh!"]—and will be taught to believe himself as a superior creation. [Cries of "Oh, oh!"] A line will be drawn between him and the people whom he is to be called upon some day to reign over. In due course, following the precedent which has already been set, he will be sent on a tour round the world, and probably rumours of a morganatic alliance will follow—[Loud cries of "Oh, oh!" and "Order!"]—and the end of it all will be that the country will be called upon to pay the bill. [Cries of "Divide!"].[4]

This led to the press depiction of him as an irresponsible fanatic and in the temper of the times may well have ensured his defeat in the 1895 General Election.

The Birth of the Labour Party

After his defeat at West Ham in 1895, many of Hardie's critics predicted that his career was over. He was, however, indefatigable in his efforts for the unemployed and before long took to a new level the recognition the vital importance of adequate labour representation in Parliament in place of the existing Liberal-Labour (Lib-Lab) alliance.[5] In consequence of this recognition on his part, Hardie played a major part in the formation of the Labour Representation Committee, subsequently known as the Labour Party, by organizing a meeting of various trade unions and socialist groups to meet on 27-28 February 1900. One hundred and twenty nine delegates gathered at the Memorial Hall in Farringdon Street, London. They were made up of 41 trade unions with a total affiliated membership of 353,070, together with seven trades councils and socialist societies with a total membership of 22,861. Strongly represented were railway workers, dockers, printers and gasworkers. The common factor for them all was a desire to see working men better represented in the House of Commons but the miners and tex-

---

4. Jeremy Paxman. (2006) *On Royalty*. London, Penguin Books. p. 58.
5. Manual workers who secured election to Parliament with the support of the Liberal Party, in the absence of recognition by the trade unions, were known as Lib-Labs.

tile workers remained outside as favouring the Liberal Party in which they had some influence.

During the meeting Hardy proposed the establishment of a distinct Labour group in Parliament who should have their own whips. This was narrowly adopted by 53 votes to 39 with 37 abstentions. But it was an historic step forward towards working class political activity in Parliament and the birth of the modern Labour Party. The Labour Representation Committee (LRC) was then elected comprising seven trade unionists, two members of the ILP, two members of the Social Democratic Federation and one of the Fabian Society. Ramsay MacDonald became its secretary.

Almost immediately the LRC was involved in what was known as the "Khaki Election" in the Autumn of 1900 for which it was hardly prepared. With the welter of jingoism that was sweeping the country the new Party was running against the tide. But two of its 15 candidates were successful, Keir Hardie at Merthyr Tydfil and Richard Bell at Derby. Bell soon defected to the Liberals which left Hardie as the only Labour MP, but as a Radical rather than as a Socialist. There were also two Lib-Labs and five miners' MPs but they stood aloof from Hardie. It is interesting that the mining, cotton and engineering trade unions also kept their distance and did not join the LRC at that time. However, there were firm links with other trade unions and with the ILP. Nevertheless, there was no commitment to socialism and Hardie's proposal ensured that the LRC would co-operate with any party engaged in promoting legislation which was in the interests of labour. Hardie had prophesied for years that a living party of labour acting together in Parliament would focus labour aspirations in a way that no amount of theoretical propaganda could do.[6] This set the tone for the Labour Party which the LRC soon became.

In this same year of 1900 Hardie was elected to the House of Commons as ILP and LRC candidate for the formerly Liberal constituency of Merthyr Tydfil in South Wales, which he would represent for the remainder of his life. This was a marked success for the LRC as only one other Labour MP was elected that year and Hardie was fêted as a working class hero. Sixty-five

---

6.   Sir Robert Ensor. (1936) *England 1870-1914*. Oxford, The Clarendon Press. p. 266.

trade unions and 21 trades council were now affiliated to the LRC. Yet for the first time Hardie became a lonely figure remote from day-to-day decisions.[7]

Nevertheless, from 1900 to 1906 membership of the LRC increased from 376,000 to 921,000 and increased fees enabled the National Executive Council to offer a £200 salary to its MPs, thereby strengthening its control over candidates, a key step in transforming Labour into a conventional political party.[8]

Then came the decision of the Liberal Party not to stand against Labour candidates in 30 constituencies in the next General Election to avoid splitting the anti-Tory vote. In the General Election in January 1906 the Liberals obtained 377 seats a majority of 84 over all other parties combined. The Conservatives were completely overwhelmed and 20 years of Tory rule came to an end, but the sensation of the time was the return of 53 labour members. Of these 29 were members of the LRC sitting as an independent party whilst the other 24 were largely officials of the miners' unions which were still not affiliated to the LRC.

The Labour Party and the *Taff Vale Case*

The successes in this election transformed the LRC into the modern Labour Party. The trade unions had a large affiliated membership and contributed substantial funds to the new party. Naturally they wanted the chairman to come from their ranks. But Hardie disagreed considering that in effect he had created the new party. The ILP shared this belief and nominated Hardie to be the first annually elected chairman. The other candidate was David Shackleton of the Weavers' Union. The election represented a conflict between socialist and trade union activists and it took three votes before Hardie won by a majority of one.

In Parliament the Labour Party, under Hardie's guidance, generally supported the Liberal government's legislation. However, on one issue the party helped score a considerable victory which still reverberates today. In 1901 the Taff Vale Railway Company sued the Amalgamated Society of Railway

---

7. Kenneth O. Morgan. *Keir Hardie: Radical and Socialist. Op. cit.* p. 122.
8. Martin Pugh. *Speak for Britain: A New History of the Labour Party. Op. cit.* p. 62.

Servants for damages following a strike, despite it being the general view among lawyers that a trade union could not be sued in its registered name. This view was upheld when the case reached the Court of Appeal which had already ruled in *Temperton v. Russell* [9] that equally no representative action against a union's members could succeed. However, the Company appealed to the House of Lords where the accepted law was overturned so that trade unions could be sued. This caused fury and uproar in the labour movement and contributed substantially to the overriding success of the Liberal Party in the January 1906 General Election.

Accordingly one of the first tasks the Liberal government set itself was to reverse the Taff Vale judgment and Hardie referred to the urgent need to do so in his maiden speech. The Attorney-General thereupon introduced a Bill which gave the unions most of what they were demanding. It fell short of expectations, however, by providing that they would continue to be liable for tortious acts committed with the authority of their officials. Despite this setback Lord Halsbury over-enthusiastically claimed that, "immunity is sought for what is practically civil war in another form", adding that, "This is a Bill for the purpose of legalising tyranny".[10]

On behalf of a highly critical Labour Party this omission was instantly countered by Walter Hudson when he introduced a Private Members' Bill, signed by Hardie and others, to give the unions complete immunity from any form of civil liability whatever, despite a royal commission having reported strongly against any such general exemption. Pressure from the Labour Party forced the prime minister, Henry Campbell-Bannerman, to oblige the Attorney-General to commit a U-turn in favour of what he had earlier called a "privileged proletariat". The Bill then duly passed and became law as the Trades Disputes Act 1906.

Aftermath

In 1908, Hardie resigned as leader of the Labour Party and was replaced by Arthur Henderson. He spent the remainder of his life campaigning for votes

---

9. 1 QB (1893) 435.
10. Hansard. [166] (3 August 1906) col. 704.

for women and had a close passionate relationship with Sylvia Pankhurst despite his being 50 years old and she a 24-year-old student. At this time he was constantly at odds with his colleagues and, when in 1907 the party conference rejected a proposal to enfranchise single women he had astonished them by stating that he was considering whether he could remain a member of the parliamentary party. This undoubtedly diminished his influence in the party. But, in any event, the former party chairman, Bruce Glazier, had described Mrs Pankhurst as "the Delilah who cut our Samson's locks". And party secretary, Ramsay MacDonald, commented that "I have the very strongest objection to childishness masquerading as revolution" and dismissed the suffragettes as "pettifogging middle-class damsels".[11]

International Impact

Whilst the new Labour Party was concerned almost entirely with domestic issues, Hardie was an early Labour internationalist. From July 1907 to April 1908 he travelled throughout the greater part of the world, always making contact with socialist and trade union movements. As part of this tour he visited the United States, Canada, Japan, Malaysia and Singapore (as they now are), Australia, New Zealand and South Africa. In each country he made an impact and increased the strength of his own anti-imperialism. As a consequence his reputation grew in international organizations and he made a particular contribution to the colonial freedom movements in India and South Africa.

As a pacifist Hardie joined socialists in other countries in trying to organize an international general strike to stop the First World War. And when Britain entered the war he made a dissenting speech in the House of Commons. This was not popular in the Labour Party or his Welsh constituency but he continued to speak at anti-war demonstrations across the country.

---

11. Martin Pugh. *Speak for Britain: A New History of the Labour Party. Op. cit.* p. 93.

Folk-hero

After a series of strokes, James Keir Hardie died of pneumonia in hospital in Glasgow on 26 September 1915, aged 59. He was cremated at the Maryhill crematorium in Glasgow where he was referred to as the greatest agitator of his time. Since his death he has been a folk-hero in the Labour Party he did so much to bring into existence and remains a legend in modern British politics. Although not entirely at home in the House of Commons he was a true radical in his activities both inside and outside Parliament.

In the words of his biographer, Kenneth O. Morgan, his image has become enshrined in the collective memory of the British working class movement.

> He seemed certain of immortality as the one acknowledged folk-hero of the labour movement and of the under-privileged throughout the world.[12]

His pioneering role reached its apogee when, on 22 January 1924, Ramsay MacDonald formed the first Labour government. Although this did not prove to be a success Labour had come of age. It was now ready to be a party of power when women's final franchise reform in 1928 at last ensured a huge catchment area for Labour with the working class of the time making up the enormous majority of British people at 78.29 per cent of the population.

---

12. Kenneth O. Morgan. *Keir Hardie: Radical and Socialist. Op. cit.* p. 276.

CHAPTER 23

THE PANKHURSTS AND THE SUFFRAGETTES

Votes for Women

One of the most dissenting and radical groups of modern times was the suffragettes. But, as we shall see there was a negative side to them. According to Martin Pugh, "the explosive mixture of idealism, self-sacrifice and strategic insight", of the Pankhursts that enabled them, "to contribute so notably to national life also made them ruthless, high-handed and self-righteous".[1] Nevertheless, their dissent was justified and for it they are celebrated in the political world of today. At the same time they were largely conventional middle class women with the single cause of votes for women, but in many ways that was their strength. However, except for Sylvia Pankhurst, they played little part in securing women's wider rights, the serious struggle for which came later in the twentieth century with the feminist movement. How the fight for the women's franchise would have played out without the suffragettes and the coming of the First World War can only be a matter for conjecture. That they made their mark at the time cannot be denied.

It can be argued that the women's vote was an ancient constitutional right and, as we have seen, it was the Reform Act of 1832 that first legally confined the suffrage to males. In any event it was in February 1884 that a conference of women held in a committee room of the House of Commons resolved to work to secure for women the parliamentary franchise on the same terms as for men.[2] This was the start of the movement for women to be able to exercise the right to vote. It became a movement that was to shatter the complacency of the establishment for the next 30 or more years. Four months after

---
1. Martin Pugh. (2001) *The Pankhursts*. London, Allen Lane, The Penguin Press. p. xiii.
2. *The Times*. (8 February 1884, p. 11.

that conference, on 11 June, William Woodall proposed in the Commons a motion to extend the suffrage to women[3] but it was defeated by 271 votes to 135. And that was to be the parliamentary pattern for the next 35 years.

However, the movement for women to have the vote took a more significant turn in 1897 when Millicent Garrett Fawcett, sister of Elizabeth Garrett Anderson the pioneer woman doctor, drew together all the existing women's suffrage bodies to form the National Union of Women's Suffrage Societies (NUWSS) which attracted the affiliation of some 500 groups. Fawcett believed in peaceful protest and campaigning for democratic reform by lawful means and its members became known as suffragists or constitutionalists. Public meetings and petitions were their weapons.

That year another women's franchise Bill, proposed by a Conservative MP, passed a second reading in the House of Commons for the first time but Lord Salisbury's Conservative government refused to allow it to proceed.

Birth of the Suffragette Movement

The next stage occurred in October 1903 when a more militant Women's Social and Political Union (WSPU) was formed in Manchester by Emmeline Pankhurst, a politically-minded member of the Independent Labour Party and the mother of Christabel and Sylvia. However, the real birth of the suffragette movement and their militant tactics came with the imprisonment of Christabel Pankhurst and Annie Kenney, a cotton mill operative, on Friday 13 October 1905.[4] With a banner emblazoned with the legend "Votes for Women" they "yelled and shrieked" at Sir Edward Grey who was speaking at a Liberal Party meeting in the Free Trade Hall built on the site of the Peterloo Massacre in Manchester. The purpose of the meeting was to endorse the candidature of Winston Churchill in the forthcoming General Election. Ironically, both Grey and Churchill were at the time keen advocates of women's suffrage.

---

3. Hansard. [289] col. 92.
4. The term "suffragette" was first used by Charles E. Hands, a *Daily Mail* journalist. The WSPU adopted it to distinguish themselves from the suffragists.

Both women were removed by stewards and police officers to an ante room where they were asked to behave like ladies and told they could leave. However, that was not what Christabel wanted and she spat at two police officers and struck one in the mouth. Taken out of the hall they were again told they were free to go but Christabel again struck Superintendent Watson. Only then were they arrested and charged. Christabel with the assault on Watson, Annie with creating a disturbance. Annie said, "Never mind, we have got what we wanted" and Christabel replied, "Yes, I wanted to assault a policeman".[5]

Taken to court, both were convicted and fined. However, they refused to pay the fines and were sent to Strangeways Prison in default, Christabel for seven days and Annie for three. Their incarceration in such circumstances, even though for short periods, aroused intense sympathy and publicity throughout the country. When Christabel was released she returned to the Free Trade Hall which was filled in her honour and Keir Hardie made a speech in support. All this breathed fresh and defiant life into Mrs Pankhurst's Union.

Emmeline Pethwick-Lawrence, a wealthy socialite and suffragette, chose the colours of the WSPU, namely, green (for hope), white (for purity) and purple (for dignity). Dresses were run up in these colours and were worn with matching sashes and ties.

So extensive did the activities of the organization become that no Liberal meeting or Cabinet minister could escape the attention of its members, usually unexpectedly in indoor meetings from underneath the platform or high up in the rafters. Liberals were chosen for their attentions, they said, since only the Liberal government could enact a suffrage Bill. Consequently, even meetings of ministers favourable to their cause such as Grey, Churchill and Lloyd George were subjected to disruption.

In time, the tactics of the suffragettes became more violent. Windows were broken and the proceedings of Parliament disrupted from the galleries of both Houses. Such actions produced a backlash but that only stimulated them more. Eventually they would alienate Churchill and Lloyd George,

---

5. *Manchester Guardian.* (16 October 1905).

who initially were their partisans in the Cabinet as well as George Lansbury and even Keir Hardie.

The Mud March

On Saturday 9 February 1907, the constitutional societies held a march from Hyde Park to Exeter Hall in the Strand two days before the State Opening of Parliament. Despite heavy rain, between 3,000 and 4,000 women, dressed mainly in black, joined the procession which was a great success although dubbed by the press "The Mud March". As a counterblast to the march, a few days later Mrs. Pankhurst called "A Women's Parliament" to be held in the Caxton Hall. After a number of speeches she and Mrs. Charlotte Despard led the women present in a march to the precincts of Parliament. Here the police rode into them on horseback and scattered them. Some 54 women were arrested and, after refusing to pay fines, they were sent to Holloway Prison. This heavy-handedness inflamed the suffragettes and their supporters who refused to bow to violence and began more and more to turn to violent action themselves.

Schism and Successes

By the summer of 1907 there were complaints within the WSPU that the executive committee never met and that the Pankhursts dominated the emergency committee which ran the union as dictators. As if to prove the critics' point, at the next meeting Mrs Pankhurst simply abolished both the constitution and the annual conference of members and announced that in future she would not have anyone on the emergency committee who did not agree with her. This caused a split in the movement and a number of members, including the prominent and formidable Charlotte Despard, broke away in the September to form the more democratic Women's Freedom League of which Mrs Despard became president. As Mrs. Pethick-Lawrence said, "a society that was founded upon a desire for the extension of democracy [turned] into an enthusiastically supported dictatorship".[6]

In the following year Londoners saw two impressive demonstrations in favour of women's right to vote. On 13 June the NUWSS organized a march of 13,000 women from The Embankment to the Albert Hall. Eight days later, on a Sunday, the suffragettes held a rally in Hyde Park which was attended by more than a quarter of a million people, including some prominent men such as Thomas Hardy, George Bernard Shaw and H. G. Wells. Mrs Flora Drummond, known as "The General", had advertised the meeting to MPs by mooring a motor-boat opposite the terraces of the House of Commons and using a megaphone to invite members having an *al fresco* tea to attend.

In Court

Against a background of growing unemployment and hunger marches, the struggle now grew more intense. The suffragettes called a meeting for 13 October in order, as they put it, to "rush the House of Commons". In response, the government had all the approaches to Parliament sealed off and obtained from the Bow Street magistrate, Mr Curtis Bennett, a warrant for the arrest of Emmeline and Christabel Pankhurst and Flora Drummond. They were charged with conduct likely to cause a breach of the peace. The case against them opened on 21 October at Bow Street magistrates' court when Christabel, who had read law, subpoenaed the Chancellor of the Exchequer, Lloyd George, and the Home Secretary, Herbert Gladstone, to give evidence. As Lloyd George had taken his six-year-old daughter, Megan, to see the demonstration he seemed well placed to say that no breach of the peace was likely but as it happens he miscalculated. However, both witnesses agreed that they had not seen anyone attack either people or property.

During the case Christabel revealed that another magistrate had admitted that in sentencing a suffragette he had, "done as I was told" by the government. She also complained that they were being tried by a "Star Chamber of the twentieth century" and were being denied trial by a jury who would

---

6. E. Sylvia Pankhurst. (1931) *The Suffragette Movement: An Intimate Account of Persons and Ideals.* London, Longmans & Co., p. 214.

acquit them. For her part, Emmeline Pankhurst told the court, "I come here not as an ordinary law-breaker. We are here in our effort to become law-makers".

In giving his decision, Mr Curtis Bennett said that in the fracas at the meeting ten people had to be taken to hospital, seven policemen were injured, 37 people were arrested and 40 had property stolen. A serious breach of the peace had occurred, he said, and he ordered Mrs Pankhurst and Mrs Drummond to be bound over in their own recognisance of £100 each and to find two sureties of £50 each to ensure they kept the peace for 12 months with the alternative of three months imprisonment. Christabel was asked to find sureties in half these sums with the alternative of ten weeks in prison. As they all refused to accept the binding over they were sent to prison for the terms stated.

A week later, in a gesture of solidarity with their former colleagues, three members of the Women's Freedom League, chained themselves to the grille of the ladies' gallery in the House of Commons and commenced shouting "Votes for Women". This continued until officials found they were unable to break the chains and release the women and instead removed the entire grille with the women attached to it.

Forced Feeding of Hunger Strikers

Despite the huge success of the suffragettes' Hyde Park rally in June 1908 the Women's Freedom League and the constitutional societies outnumbered the WSPU both in the number of branches and members. However, a turning point in militancy occurred in June 1909. Marion Wallace-Dunlop, a suffragette in prison, on her own initiative went on hunger strike against the harsh second-division treatment reserved for serious criminals which she was receiving in place of the more lenient first-division treatment. Among other things, she had to wear a prison dress with broad arrows and was not permitted to receive visitors. After she had fasted for 91 hours, ministers, fearing that she would die whilst in their charge, released her. Not surprisingly, other suffragette prisoners were quick to follow her example.

Now faced with a new dilemma, the government decided that hunger strikes should not result in freedom. Instead they introduced forcible feeding with meat extract and lime cordial passed through tubes; a practice that could prove dangerous.

Suffragette Mary Leigh described the procedure she suffered:

> There were about ten of them. The doctor then forced my mouth so as to form a pouch, and held me while one of the wardresses poured some liquid from a spoon...the wardresses forced me on to the bed and two doctors came in with them, and while I was held down a nasal tube was inserted. It is two yards long with a funnel at the end...the end is put up a nostril, one one day, and then other nostril, the other. Great pain is experienced during the process...the drums of the ear seem to be bursting, a horrible pain in the throat and the breast. The tube is pushed down about 20 inches.[7]

As a response to forced feeding the WSPU decided to attract greater publicity by destroying property. Initially this was confined to breaking glass windows of shops but was soon to go much wider.

In the year 1910 Winston Churchill replaced Herbert Gladstone as Home Secretary. One of his first actions was to introduce improved prison conditions including a change whereby non-serious offenders would no longer have to wear prison clothing, would not be searched, would be permitted to receive food from outside and allowed to take regular exercise during which they could talk. Women suffragettes, he explained, were included among those who would benefit.

In March 1912 the suffragettes revoked the truce they had declared during the passage of two Conciliation Bills in the House of Commons and extended militant activity to include arson. At the same time the Pankhursts forced out of the WSPU Mr and Mrs Pethwick-Lawrence, their hitherto valued comrades, who then formed the "Votes for Women Fellowship". *The Times* now weighed in with a leading article entitled "Insurgent Hysteria". In a large number of cases, it said, "even though insanity was not present" among militant suffragettes there was a tendency to hysteria and morbid

---

7. Rosen, Andrew. (1974) *Rise Up Women! The Militant Campaign of the Women's Social and Political Union 1903-1914*. London, Routledge & Kegan Paul. p. 123.

moods. "Physicians", the writer claimed, "came across many cases in which there was so much mental instability that any public excitement disturbed the balance and produced fits of hysteria that showed itself in violent conduct or loquacity".[8]

Whilst questions were being raised in the House of Commons on 25 June 1912 about the forcible feeding of suffragette prisoners, the Labour MP, George Lansbury, left his seat below the gangway and walked to the ministerial bench above the gangway. Face to face with Prime Minister Asquith he cried,]

> You call yourselves gentlemen, and you forcibly feed and murder women in this fashion! You ought to be driven out of office...It is the most disgraceful thing that ever happened in the history of England! You will, go down in history as the man who tortured innocent women.[9]

Two days later Keir Hardie produced in the Commons a copy of a document sent to the Home Secretary by 117 medical practitioners. In part it read:

> We, as members of the medical profession, strongly protest against the forcible feeding to which certain prisoners are at present being subjected. We consider that tube feeding in cases where the operation is resisted by the patient, is accompanied by immediate risk to life, in addition to the danger of permanent damage to the health, both of body and of mind. We urge that this practice be discontinued.[10]

Nothing was done and by the following year, two hundred and forty suffragettes were in prison of whom 57 were being forcibly fed.[11]

King George V was also disgusted by the practice of forced feeding. Although normally avoiding politics he caused his private secretary, Lord Stamfordham, to write to Reginald McKenna, the Home Secretary, to say:

---

8. *The Times.* (28 March 1912) p. 7.
9. Hansard. [40] cols. 217-19.
10. *Ibid.* cols. 650-51.
11. *Ibid.* [50] col. 1663.

The King desires me to write to you upon the question of "forcible feeding". His Majesty cannot help feeling that there is something shocking, if not almost cruel, in the operation to which these insensate women are subjected through their refusal to take necessary nourishment. His Majesty concludes that Miss Pankhurst's description of what she endured when forcibly fed is more or less true. If so, her story will horrify people otherwise not in sympathy with the Militant Suffragettes. The King asks whether in your "Temporary Discharge of Prisoners Bill" it would not be possible to abolish forcible feeding.[12]

McKenna replied that he hoped that under the Act it would be possible to restrict forcible feeding to a few exceptional cases, but that was not achieved, as he may have anticipated.

More Violence

As a consequence of the forcible feeding the suffragettes decided to increase the violence. This involved more extensive and secret arson with paraffin-soaked rags being placed in pillar boxes, houses, pavilions, a grandstand, a railway station and schools. It was secret because the suffragettes were no longer actively seeking arrest although they were prepared for it if caught. Before long bombs were being used, pictures in public galleries, including the "Rokesby Venus" by Valesquez, were slashed, the Tower of London and the British Museum were attacked, and golf greens were damaged. Four postmen were badly injured in Dundee when the letters they were sorting burst into flame. According to *The Times* tubes containing phosphorus inside envelopes addressed to Asquith were found among the letters.[13]

The refreshment rooms at Regents Park were burned down. The Orchid House at Kew was destroyed. Telephone wires were cut in Dumbarton, Birmingham and other areas and hundreds of windows of government buildings and of shops in London's West End were smashed. After Lloyd George's new house at Walton Heath was bombed causing extensive damage, and a

---

12. Harold Nicolson. (1952) *King George the Fifth: His Life and Reign.* London, Pan Books Ltd. pp. 285-6.
13. *The Times.* (6 February 1919) p.6.

second bomb failed to explode, Mrs Pankhurst, who disliked the secrecy, publicly declared, "We have tried blowing him up to wake his conscience. I have advised, I have incited, I have conspired. The authorities need not look for the women who have done what they did last night. I accept full responsibility for it". Arrested for incitement, she was tried at the Old Bailey and on 3 April 1913 was sentenced to three years penal servitude whilst her supporters in court sang *The Marseillaise*. She was taken to Holloway Prison where she immediately went on hunger strike.[14]

"Cat and Mouse"

On 26 April 1913 the ingenious Prisoners (Temporary Discharge for Ill-health) Act was enacted and was quickly dubbed the "Cat and Mouse" Act. With this the Home Secretary could abandon forced feeding in order to avoid hunger-strikers (whose plight was securing them great public sympathy) dying whilst in prison and instead keep them in jail until they appeared to be weakening from starvation. They were then released on licence but could be re-arrested and again submitted to forcible feeding if they made speeches in public. Sylvia Pankhurst now formed a "People's Army" to protect women from such re-arrest. "Athletic Amazons with broomsticks" ridiculed the *Daily Citizen*[15] but they registered some successes.

The Derby

The Derby in 1913, which was attended by the king and queen, was run on 4 June and the race was noteworthy for an unusual incident. Just prior to the end of the race as the horses rounded Tattenham Corner a remarkable young woman rushed towards the king's horse, Anmer, with the apparent objective of seizing the reins. The horse fell and rolled on to its jockey who was lightly concussed when it sprang up and dragged him by a foot caught in a stirrup. The woman, who had also fallen under the horse, was taken unconscious

---

14. Antonia Raeburn. (1973) *The Militant Suffragettes*. London, Michael Joseph, pp. 190-91.
15. *Daily Citizen*. 24 November 1913.

to Epsom Cottage Hospital. She remained unconscious all night and was identified as Miss Emily Davison, a prominent suffragette who had been in prison a number of times for suffragette activity, the last time in November 1912 for ten days for assaulting a Baptist minister whom she mistook for Lloyd George. A graduate of London University with a first class degree from Oxford, she was well known for her militancy.[16] In Holloway Prison she had been force-fed 49 times and on one occasion in 1911 in protest had thrown herself 30 feet down an iron staircase in what was presumably a suicide attempt. She landed on the wire netting that was designed to prevent suicides and that saved her life but the attempt caused severe injuries to her spine. Notwithstanding her record, after the Derby incident the queen sent a messenger to the hospital that evening to inquire after her.

Miss Davison continued to deteriorate and underwent surgery the next day but she died the day after. A number of her friends visited her before she died and draped her screen with the colours of the WSPU which she had joined in 1906. Her funeral took place at Morpeth, Northumberland on 15 June. The body was brought from Epsom by train and escorted across London from Victoria to King's Cross by thousands of sympathisers. The interment at Morpeth was private but after the ceremony suffragettes walked in single file to the graveside each bearing a floral tribute.[17] Her grave bears the inscription, "Deeds, not words".

Less well known is her having hidden in the crypt of Westminster Hall overnight to get herself into the 1911 census as staying in the House of Commons. And that is how she was indeed recorded in the census papers. Although she was still unable to vote, today there is a plaque in the Commons to mark her uncomfortable stay during the night, placed there by Tony Benn, MP, Helena Kennedy, QC, and Jeremy Corbyn, MP.

Appraisal

Apart from Sylvia Pankhurst the leading suffragettes fought, with a great deal of fanaticism, a single-issue campaign. But there were other issues such

---

16. *Ibid.* 9 June, p. 8.
17. *Ibid.* 16 June, p. 5.

as married women's property rights, education for girls and lack of employment opportunities that exercised the minds of many women who did not think the vote was in itself a panacea. Of the Pankhursts only Sylvia linked the franchise campaign with wider social questions of female equality which were left to be tackled later, by the feminists of the 1960s and after. And when Sylvia proclaimed that, "Every day the industrial and suffrage rebels march closer together", Christobel responded with, "Independence of all men's parties is the basis of the WSPU".[18] In fact, unlike the NUWSS, the WSPU confined its membership to women and by the year 1910 had fewer than 1,000 members. There were no male allies within Christabel's vision. Also in contrast to the suffragettes, in 1912 Mrs Fawcett's NUWSS sought a working alliance with the Labour Party in by-elections following the endorsement of women's suffrage at the Labour Party conference in January. They now established an election fighting fund to promote Labour candidates in constituencies where there were anti-suffrage Liberals standing. They sent volunteers to assist their campaigns, provided the Party with much needed finance and experienced working class helpers as well as new candidates in elections for seats held by anti-suffrage MPs. By-election successes followed and by 1914 the NUWSS had 480 branches and 53,000 members.

Emmeline and Christabel have widely been seen as personifying the women's campaign. According to Martin Pugh, however, "what we now know of the rest of the women's movement suggests that the Women's Social and Political Union played a far less significant part than the Pankhursts admitted. Moreover, investigation of the WSPU itself destroys their exaggerated claims.[19] He adds, "Their switch to attacks on property was the Pankhursts' way of obscuring the fact that they had failed to convert, and had abandoned further attempts to persuade, the country.[20] Moreover, their rigid opposition to the Liberal Party in government that caused them to intervene in by-elections in support of Tory candidates who opposed women's suffrage was politically damaging for them. In fact, Emmeline later joined

---

18. Antonia Raeburn. *The Militant Suffragettes. Op. cit.* p. 221.
19. Martin Pugh. (1980) *Women's Suffrage in Britain 1867-1928.* London, Historical Association. p. 22.
20. *Ibid.* p. 24.

the Conservative Party in 1926 and was adopted as a prospective candidate for Whitechapel.[21]

Nevertheless, it must also be acknowledged that they were dedicated to the cause of women's franchise. And although their violent methods alienated many of the public they stirred the suffragists into greater activity. But whilst Sylvia worked among the poor women and working class of London's East End and shared their wider problems her mother and sister obsessively saw poor women only as political fodder.

In the event, public reaction to the suffragettes became so hostile that they ceased to hold meetings. And considerable antagonism from women arose when Christabel launched her "Chastity Campaign" in 1913 urging women to avoid marriage on the ground that three-quarters of men were infected with venereal disease. In doing so she reduced "to absurdity what was in fact a serious issue".[22]

Sylvia Pankhurst

Following the activities of her father, Richard, Sylvia was always more interested in socialist and feminist politics than her sisters. However, in 1906 she gave up her position at the Royal College of Art in order to work full-time for the WSPU. Five years later she became concerned about the increase in violence and, believing the WSPU was losing ground, she left the organization to help build up support for the Labour Party in London. In 1913, with the help of Keir Hardie and others, she launched the East London Federation of Suffragettes (ELFS) and published *The Women's Dreadnought*, a weekly paper for working class women. She wanted a socialist organization tackling wider issues than women's suffrage and she gained considerable support from women and dockers in the East End of London and was arrested eight times. In January 1914 Sylvia finally took her East London Federation out of the orbit of the WSPU.

She disagreed with the WSPU's strong support for the war and in March 1916 she re-named the ELF the Workers' Suffrage Federation with the weekly

---

21. A. N. Wilson. (2005) *After the Victorians*. London, Hutchinson, p. 285.
22. *Ibid.*

now called *The Workers' Dreadnought*. In 1920, after some disputes with Lenin in Moscow, she joined the newly-formed Communist Party of Great Britain but she considered the organization to be too right-wing and was soon expelled after refusing to hand over editorial control of the *Dreadnought* to the party executive. As she put it, "The disciplinarians had set forth their terms".[23]

She continued to be active politically and was involved in movements connected with anti-fascism and anti-colonialism. She gave her support to Ethiopia when it was invaded by Mussolini's Italy in 1935. After the Second World War she moved to Ethiopia at the request of Emperor Haile Selassie and she died in Addis Ababa on 27 September 1960. She received a full state funeral there, being described by Haile Selassie as "an honorary Ethiopian", and a memorial service was held in the Caxton Hall in London on 19 January 1961.

Stream of Dissent

With the outbreak of war in August 1914 the Home Secretary released all suffragette prisoners and Emmeline and Christabel threw themselves into the cause of recruiting men and women into the armed forces. In a significant move the title of their journal, *The Suffragette*, was changed to *Britannia*. At the end of the war the Representation of the People Act 1918 provided for votes for women aged 30 and over. As a consequence, with 13 million men aged 21 and over being given the vote the franchise was now extended to 8.4 million women. Ten years later, when the gender discrimination was removed women were to become the majority of the electorate. Asquith claimed that the changes were brought about by women's service in the war and in a sense they were. But other pressures for democracy were also at work and, indeed, seven countries gave women the vote before Britain, including Australia in 1902.

In Britain, statutory social reforms for women followed the 1918 Act in quick succession. In 1919 the Sex Disqualification (Removal) Act abolished

---

23. *Workers Dreadnought*. 17 September 1921.

all existing restrictions upon the admission of women into professions, occupations and civic positions including appointment as magistrates and selection as jurors. Three years later the Infanticide Act 1922 abolished the charge of murder for infanticide and the Law of Property Act 1925 enabled husbands and wives to inherit each other's property.

One thousand three hundred women now qualified as doctors whilst others began to join the higher ranks of the civil service. Soon, there were 4,000 women magistrates, mayors, councillors and guardians. And also in 1925 the Widows Pension Act gave widows a pension of ten shillings a week with children's allowances of five shillings for the first child and three shillings for each of any subsequent children. It took the feminist movement of the 1960s, however, to bring to the fore the issue of the right of women to enjoy full equality with men although women are still grossly underrepresented in the House of Commons as well as various types of employment.

Nothing, however, can detract from the significant impact the tempestuous tactics of the suffragettes had, and in a sense still has. On the death of Emmeline Pankhurst on 15 June 1928 *The Times* wrote:

> Whatever views may be held as to the righteousness of the cause to which Emmeline Pankhurst gave her life and the methods by which she tried to bring about its achievement, there can be no doubt about the singleness of her aim and the remarkable strength and nobility of her character. The end that she had in view was the emancipation of women from what she believed to be a condition of harmful subjection. She was convinced that she was working for the salvation of the world, as well as of her sex...With all her autocracy, and her grievous mistakes, she was a humble-minded, large-hearted, unselfish woman, of the stuff of which martyrs are made.

That is why the suffragettes are remembered so vividly today and why they form an integral part of the stream of dissent in English history.

CHAPTER 24

MARIE STOPES

Campaigner for Birth Control

Marie Stopes was born in Edinburgh on 15 October 1880 the daughter of Henry and Charlotte Stopes. Her mother had become a women's rights campaigner after she was prevented from attending lectures at university because she was a woman. Instead of a degree she was awarded a certificate after passing exactly the same examinations as the male students despite being denied the benefit of lectures. Her interest in women's rights was subsequently passed on to her daughter.

Marie's own qualifications are even more impressive. As a scholarship student at University College London she studied botany and geology and graduated with a first class BSc. in 1902. Two years later she received a PhD. in palaeobotany at the University of Munich and, in 1903, a DSc. degree from University College. At the time she was the youngest person to have done so. Later, after spending some time at the Imperial University in Tokyo she lectured in palaeobotany at University College and then at the University of Manchester from 1904 to 1907. She was also the first female academic in Manchester University.

She was determined to help better the human race and, in particular, women who suffered from both establishment antagonism to birth control and also the cover up of the horrors of back street abortions. In the 1920s some 39,000 women had died in childbirth in England and Wales.[1] Her own two unhappy marriages impelled in her a desire to spread happiness. And she did so. People from all over the world wrote to her about their most intimate

---

1. Sheila Rowbotham. (1977) *A New World for Women*. Stella Browne: Socialist Feminist, Pluto Press. p. 43.

sexual problems, their fears and their worries. As a global family planning pioneer she played a vital role in breaking down taboos about sex and thus improving knowledge, pleasure in sex and improved reproductive health.

As soon as she was an adult she followed her mother to become a campaigner for women's rights, and also a pioneer in the field of birth control. She edited a newsletter *Birth Control News* which, with its explicit advice, brought her into conflict with both the Church of England and the Roman Catholic Church. Her sex manual, *Married Love*, in which she argued that marriage should be an equal relationship between husband and wife instead of putting an end to a woman's intellectual life, only exacerbated the conflict. The book was an immediate success and had to be reprinted six times in the first year. However, the courts declared it obscene and it was quickly banned. It also caused a storm in the United States and was prohibited there too.

The Mothers' Clinic

Undeterred, and despite the fact that Richard Carlile, Charles Bradlaugh and Annie Besant had been imprisoned for advocating birth control, she opened the first family planning clinic in the United Kingdom in Marlborough Road, Holloway on 17 March 1921. She called it the Mothers' Clinic and to start it going she received financial help from her second husband the aircraft manufacturer, Humphrey Verdon Roe. Here, mothers with marital problems could obtain free advice. Its patrons included Arnold Bennett, Dame Clara Butt, Admiral Sir Percy Scott and Sir James Barr. In 1925 it moved to central London where it still flourishes.

During the ten years following the opening of this first clinic, others were started in various parts of London and in Glasgow, Manchester, Birmingham, Oxford, Newcastle, Exeter, Nottingham, Bristol and Salford. At the time women were finally breaking out of the stranglehold of large families until couples with two children became fairly normal. The use of contraceptives also became more general in spite of dire warnings of the harm of these "filthy things". Apart from so describing them, the Bishop of London told the House of Lords, that "When I hear of 400,000 being manufactured every week, I would like to make a bonfire of them and dance round it".[2]

In 1925 Stopes was involved in a birth control case that became known as the trial of the decade.[3] Because of her birth control clinic she came under attack from Dr. Halliday Sutherland, a well-known and ardent Catholic medical practitioner who was a doctor at the University of Edinburgh and a deputy commissioner for the Ministry of Pensions. He claimed that Dr. Stopes' methods subjected poor women to experiments and that they were "monstrous" and "of a most harmful and dangerous nature". The book, *Married Love*, he said, was an obscene and criminal publication. He became one of many people who used a great deal of energy in trying to get Dr Stopes put behind bars.

In his own book, *Birth Control: A Statement of Christian Doctrine against the Neo-Malthusians*,[4] Sutherland had written that the "decent instincts of the poor are against these practices" i.e. birth control. But he was ignoring the wide appeal of Marie Stopes to numerous women whose husbands forced them to bear often up to as many as 15 children. He also admitted in court that he had no knowledge as a gynaecologist. He simply relied, he frankly admitted, upon the opinion of others.

Despite the likelihood of prejudice against her, Marie Stopes took action and became the first woman in England to sue for libel. She chose as her counsel the renowned Sir Patrick Hastings KC whilst Serjeant Sullivan KC of the Irish and English Bars appeared for Sutherland.

At first instance the jury found the words complained of by the plaintiff, namely, "that Dr. Stopes subjected poor women to experiments that were monstrous, harmful and dangerous", were true in substance and in fact, but were not fair comment made in good faith. They awarded Dr. Stopes £100 damages and half the costs of the action. On this the Lord Chief Justice, Lord Hewart, gave judgment for the defendant and his publisher. This decision was subsequently reversed by the Court of Appeal in Dr. Stopes' favour.

---

2. Hansard. 5th series. vol. xv. col. 818.
3. (1925) Appeal Cases. 47.
4. Halliday Sutherland. (1922) *Birth Control: A Statement of Christian Doctrine against the Neo-Malthusians*. London, Harding & More.

In the House of Lords, where the case finally came to rest, the prejudice of the time re-asserted itself and the original judgment of Lord Hewart was restored. Their Lordships held that a plea that the words complained of were true in fact, and as far as they expressed opinions were fair comment in the public interest, was not a plea partly of justification and partly fair comment but was a plea of fair comment only. Why then, asked Lord Wrenbury perceptively were justification and fair comment separate issues which were put to the jury separately?

The majority of the Lords also held that there was no evidence to support the jury's finding that the comments were unfair. Curiously it was further argued that the jury finding of justification (i.e. that the words complained of were true) itself afforded a complete answer to the action. In the event, Dr. Stopes was ordered to repay the damages and costs first awarded to her. However, Lord Wrenbury dissented and re-asserted that the jury's verdict that the words complained of were true should not be considered in isolation from their correct finding that they were not fair comment. This caused an angry Lord Carson to interject that Lord Wrensbury should not have said anything on the subject of birth control and what Dr. Stopes did about it. Yet, that was, of course, what the case was about. Carson continued by saying he felt bound,

> After listening to the speech of my noble friend, to say that the recital of alleged facts and views he has expressed, which seem to me and will be read by others as being in sympathy with the actions of the plaintiff or her writings or of certain evidence produced on her behalf, must not be taken in any way as presenting my own views if I had thought it necessary or relevant to discuss them.

The vast publicity the case engendered brought Marie Stopes a tremendous volume of support and as it happens history has dealt more kindly with her as a public benefactor than Carson and the majority of his brethren were prepared to.

Stopes also campaigned to prevent education authorities from sacking teachers who married. And she was active in the efforts to persuade the Inland Revenue to tax husbands and wives separately.

Eugenics

Unfortunately, despite all her brilliance and exemplary work for women Stopes, like many others it must be said, was bewitched by Hitler to whom she sent some of her poems. She also became attracted to eugenics and the idea that overpopulation and poverty could be overcome by breeding and limitation of birth. She was drawn to the Eugenics Society which had been founded in 1908 with the aim of eliminating the unfit from future generations. In her book *Radiant Motherhood,* published in 1920, she argued for a sort of Utopia to be achieved through sterilisation of the unfit. She wrote:

> Those who are grown up in the present active generations, the matured and hardened, with all their weaknesses and flaws, cannot do very much, though they may do something with themselves. They can, however, study the conditions under which they came into being, discover where lie the chief sources of defect, and eliminate those sources of defect from the coming generation so as to remove from those who are still to be born the needless burdens the race has carried.[5]

She did say, however, that the main cause of what she described as racial degeneration was overcrowding and sexually transmitted disease.[6]

When her son Harry married a myopic woman Stopes cut him out of her will. His wife, Mary Eyre Wallis, later Mary Stopes-Roe, was the daughter of the famous engineer Barnes Wallis who devised the "bouncing bomb" that destroyed some of the German dams of the Ruhr in 1943. Stopes believed that any grandchildren the couple might have could inherit the condition. It was, she said, cruel to burden children with defective sight and the handicap of goggles, i.e. glasses. And, when she died from breast cancer at her home in Dorking in 1958 a large part of her fortune passed to the Eugenics Society.

Of course, it should be understood that eugenics was a fashionable theory in her day and was supported by such figures as George Bernard Shaw and Dean Inge. In fact, it did not become really discredited until its notorious use by the Nazis, particularly by doctors in the German concentration

---

5. Marie. C. Stopes. (1920) *The Control of Parenthood.* James Marchant (ed.) London, G. P. Putnam's Sons. pp. 208-9.
6. *Ibid.* p. 211.

camps. We cannot know, of course, how Stopes would have reacted to this outrageous misuse of medical knowledge.

International Success

In any event, Marie Stopes' achievements for women and their health the world over justify her inclusion in this book in spite of the serious flaws in her character. The extent of her influence for the common good of women world-wide can be seen in the modern organization that bears her name. "Marie Stopes International" is active in 42 countries and in 2008 there were 560 centres including five in Bolivia, nine in the United Kingdom, ten in Australia, 25 in Kenya, 24 in South Africa, 48 in Pakistan and more than 100 in Bangladesh. Its aim is to protect some 20 million couples from unplanned pregnancies and unsafe abortions each year. Marie Stopes' struggles against entrenched forces and prejudice to improve the quality of life for countless women have borne fruit and entitled her to a place in the roll of honour of dissent.

CHAPTER 25

BATTLE OF CABLE STREET

British Union of Fascists

In the 1920s Sir Oswald Mosley was a formidable and popular Labour MP who became a junior minister in the 1929 Labour government. But when his proposals for dealing with the severe crisis and rising unemployment in the great economic slump of 1931 were rejected in Cabinet, he resigned from Labour and formed his own "New Party". This failed to win any seats at the general election of that year, however, and he then turned to the path of Hitler and Mussolini with both of whom he was in contact. Indeed, he received funds at least from the latter. In October 1932 he founded the British Union of Fascists (BUF) to the applause of Lord Rothermere and the *Daily Mail*. Its members, numbered at some 20,000, wore *blackshirts* on the Italian model and acted as an army with frequent marches and meetings noted for their violence.

An early recruit to the fascists was William Joyce who worked on the blackshirt newspaper, *Action*. Emigrating to Germany in 1939, he became infamous for his subversive and largely false propaganda broadcasts to Britain on Nazi radio and was known as "Lord Haw Haw" from his way of speaking. After he was captured at the end of the war he was tried for treason at the Old Bailey in 1945, found guilty and executed. Whilst in Brixton Prison awaiting the hangman he wrote to his wife, "I salute you Freja, as your lover for ever, Sieg Heil! Sieg Heil! Sieg Heil!".

In the meantime Mosley had become a rabble-rousing speaker with a streak of fanaticism. A series of meetings were to culminate in a monster rally at the Olympia Stadium in West London on 8 June 1934. The *Daily Mail*, which described Mosley as a "new leader of genius" had provided free tickets for the meeting. When he entered the meeting he was greeted with cries of "Hail Mosley". But when he was heckled gratuitous violence was used against the hecklers who were beaten up by Mosley's uniformed stewards. Each heckler was ejected into the street with great violence whilst the police stood by and did nothing. Fifty people were injured and taken to hospital, five of them with serious wounds. Testimony of their disgust at the brutality was given by well-known people who were present at the stadium. These included Canon Dick Sheppard, the Chancellor of the Duchy of Lancaster, Professor Julian Huxley, Vyvyan Adams, MP, Geoffrey Lloyd, private secretary to Stanley Baldwin and a host of others. This had the effect of destroying Mosley's credibility although, curiously, Joyce expressed the view that Mosley was not sufficiently violent.

Nothing daunted, Mosley now decided to concentrate his anti-semitism on the Jewish population of the East End of London where many people were living in miserable, squalid conditions. Against this background, he arranged for a march on Sunday 4 October 1936 to go along Cable Street, in Tower Hamlets, to Bethnal Green. Provocatively Jew-baiting, Mosley planned for three thousand uniformed blackshirts in four columns to march through the area which had a large number of Jewish shops and homes chanting, "The Yids, the Yids, we've got to get rid of the Yids". As soon as the details of the march were announced there were immediate protests. A petition with some thousands of signatures was presented to the Home Secretary, Sir John Simon, and mayors and councillors from the East End went on a deputation to Simon to urge him to use his powers to stop the march. He led them to believe he had no power to do so. Yet, for almost 100 years the police in London had had the power to regulate the routes of processions under the Metropolitan Police Act 1839. And this power was widely used in the 1930s as it is today.

"They Shall Not Pass"

The Labour Party, whilst deploring the BUF, told its members to keep away from the march and take no part in any opposition demonstration. The Jewish Board of Deputies denounced the march but also urged Jewish people to stay away. Nonetheless, anti-fascist Jews along with Irish Catholic dockers (whom Mosley had hoped to use against the Jews) and Communist groups organized to oppose the fascists. Their adopted slogan, borrowed from the anti-Franco forces in Madrid in the Spanish Civil War was: "The fascists shall not pass". Barricades were erected by local residents at three key spots in Cable Street in an endeavour to prevent the march taking place at all. Asked to ban the march the government declined to do so but instead sent in a large force of police to prevent the anti-fascist demonstrators, estimated at 300,000, from disrupting the march. In the event, over 10,000 police, 4,000 of them on horseback, unsuccessfully tried again and again to clear the road with baton charges and it became a battle between the protesters and the police. According to Phil Piratin, who was present and who later became Communist MP for Mile End, women in houses along the street found what weapons they could and bombarded the police, often from balconies, with milk bottles, rubbish, stones, marbles, vegetables and the contents of chamber pots.[1]

BUF Defeat

After a series of ferocious running battles the police used their power, previously denied, to get Mosley to take the marchers on an alternative route to the west. As a result, after saluting their leader the fascists marched off silently through the deserted City of London to the Embankment, where they dispersed. The people of the East End had won the day. But 150 protesters were arrested and a similar number were injured, including police, women and children. Most of those arrested were charged with obstructing the police and fined £5 each whilst several were found guilty of affray and sentenced to three months' hard labour in prison. But the people had won the battle and the BUF was virtually finished after what was widely regarded as a victory for the protesters. That night dozens of victory meetings were held all over the East End, many of them continuing until midnight.

A red plaque which commemorates the battle is in Dock Street and reads:

---

1. Phil Piratin. (1948) *Our Flag Stays Red*. London, Thames Publications. p. 23.

THE BATTLE OF CABLE STREET: The people of East London rallied to Cable Street on the 4th October 1936 and forced back the march of the fascist Oswald Mosley and his Blackshirts through the streets of the East End. "THEY SHALL NOT PASS".

Significantly, the Battle of Cable Street led to the passing of the Public Order Act 1936. Under the Act, from 1 January 1937 it was made illegal to wear a uniform in any public place or at any public meeting in connection with political objects and the offender was subject to imprisonment for up to three months or a fine of £50, or both. The Act also imposed penalties for carrying offensive weapons at public meetings or processions and on offensive conduct at public meetings. Nevertheless, it has to be recognised that the 1936 Act also gave the police wider powers than before to control all processions. But the Statute undoubtedly played a large part in the decline of the BUF. However, it was the people of the East End who caused Parliament to act. In doing so they made the most striking contribution to thwarting the growth of home-made fascism in this country by the strength of their radical action against the threat of Mosley's Blackshirts.

CHAPTER 26

CAMPAIGN FOR NUCLEAR DISARMAMENT

The Atomic Age

The first atomic bomb to be used was dropped by the United States on the Japanese city of Hiroshima on 6 August 1945. Three days later a second devastated Nagasaki. They may have contributed to the end of World War II (which is disputed) but they heralded what became known as the "Atomic Age". In the following decades Russia, Britain, France and other countries all developed and tested atomic weapons. Then came the hydrogen bomb and the disasters in nuclear reactors at Five-mile Island, Chernobyl and recently Japan. During these years fear had been growing not only of nuclear war but of the terrifying effects of widespread radiation. In Britain this fear gave rise to a mounting reaction in favour of unilateral nuclear disarmament, not least in the Labour Party.

At the Labour Party conference in Brighton on 3 October 1957 Aneurin Bevan, Labour's Shadow Foreign Secretary, shocked many delegates when he urged them not to send him, "naked into the conference chamber" by repudiating the nuclear bomb. With soaring oratory, he cried:

> Do it now, you say. Do it now. This is the answer I give you from the platform. Do it now at a Labour Party Conference? You cannot do it now. It is not in your hands to do it. All you can do is pass a resolution. What you are saying is that a British Foreign Secretary gets up in the United Nations without consultation — mark this; this is a responsible attitude! — without telling any members of the Commonwealth, without concerting with them, that the British Labour Movement decides unilaterally that this country contracts out of all its commitments and obligations

entered into with other countries and members of the Commonwealth—without consultation at all. And you call that statesmanship. I call it an emotional spasm.[1]

J. B. Priestley's Call

Bevan succeeded with a conference vote against nuclear disarmament of 5,836,000 to 781,000. But this provoked J. B. Priestley to write an article entitled "Russia, the Atom and the West" for the *New Statesman* of 2 November 1957. In it he attacked Bevan's speech, and said that Britain, having told the world that we had the H-bomb, should announce as early as possible that we proposed to reject nuclear warfare in all circumstances. So instead of giving moral leadership, as we should have done, abroad we cut a shabby figure in power politics. He continued that though it was true as Mr. Bevan argued,

> that independent action by this country, to ban nuclear bombs, would involve our foreign minister in many difficulties, most of us would rather have a bewildered and overworked Foreign Office than a country about to be turned into a radioactive cemetery.

There may, he concluded, "be other chain-reactions besides those leading to destruction: and we might start one".

A large number of readers wrote to the journal in support of Priestley, and according to John Collins, Canon of St. Paul's, in exposing the utter folly and wickedness of the nuclear strategy, the article was the real catalyst for the emergence of a campaign for nuclear disarmament in the tradition of English Dissent.

It was Kingsley Martin, the editor of the *New Statesman,* however, who followed up the article by calling a meeting in the rooms of Canon Collins of interested people who included, J. B. Priestley, Bertrand Russell, Donald Soper, Vera Britain, Michael Foot, Victor Gollancz, E. P. Thompson, Ralph Milliband, Sydney Silverman, James Cameron, Jennie Lee, Canon Collins, Anthony Greenwood, Dora Russell and Fenner Brockway. As a result

---

1. Michael Foot. (1973) *Aneurin Bevan: A Biography, 1945-1960*. London, Davis-Poynter. p. 575.

they, with others, decided to form the Campaign for Nuclear Disarmament (CND). Collins was its first chairman, with Bertrand Russell appointed as its president. The other members of its executive committee were Ritchie Calder, J. B. Priestley, Michael Foot, Kingsley Martin, James Cameron, Joseph Rotblat, Arthur Goss and Howard Davies.

Aldermaston Marches

The CND's first public meeting was held at the Methodist Central Hall in Westminster on 17 February 1958 and was attended by some 5,000 people. There were numerous sponsors of the Campaign including Peggy Ashcroft, Henry Moore, Sir Julian Huxley, Dr. Alex Comfort, the Bishop of Birmingham Dr. J. L. Wilson, Gerald Gardiner QC, E. M. Forster, Doris Lessing, Miles Malleson, Flora Robson, Barbara Hepworth, Dame Edith Evans, John Arlott and Benjamin Britten. Dr. Comfort urged the meeting that within the coming weeks they should raise nationwide an opposition to the strategy of "moral bankruptcy and ceremonial suicide" which the hydrogen bomb epitomised. At the end of the meeting a few hundred left to demonstrate in Downing Street.

The organization quickly inspired wide support from a range of interests including scientists, journalists, academics, writers, actors, musicians, students and religious leaders. Support was also widespread within the Labour Party and the CND symbol, designed in 1958 by Gerald Holton, a professional artist, became an international peace badge. It is based upon the semaphore symbols for "N" and "D" (Nuclear Disarmament) within a circle. According to Holton it also represents an individual in despair with hands outstretched in the manner of Goya's peasant before the firing squad.

At Easter 1958, the first Aldermaston march took place when some 4,000 people left Trafalgar Square on a freezing cold Good Friday to march on a four day journey to the atomic weapons research establishment at Aldermaston in Berkshire. In subsequently years the route of the march was reversed and started at Aldermaston to end in Trafalgar Square. These demonstrations drew very considerable support in the late 1950s and early 1960s and often involved whole families with children either in pushchairs or valiantly marching along with their parents.

Committee of 100

Not all CND supporters, however, were satisfied with the peaceful activities of the organisation. Led by the respected Bertrand Russell, they wanted a campaign to include mass civil disobedience actions including sit-ins and blockades. It was to be called Non-Violent Direct Action. Russell resigned from the presidency of CND in order to form, on 22 October 1960, this more militant group which had one hundred initial signatories when formed on 22 October 1960. Hence, it became known as the Committee of 100. Large sit-down demonstrations were to be organised provided at least 2,000 volunteers pledged themselves to take part. Marches and sit-downs followed in 1961 outside the Ministry of Defence, in Parliament Square and outside the United States and Soviet embassies in London. They reached their zenith on 17 September, Battle of Britain Day, when supporters blocked roads at the Holy Loch Poseidon nuclear missile submarine base in Scotland and at Trafalgar Square. A week earlier, 36 supporters were taken to court for being likely to incite people to commit breaches of the peace. Refusing to be bound over to keep the peace for 12 months, 32 of them, including Russell then aged 89, chose the alternative of going to prison for one month. Russell was released after one week, however, ostensibly on account of his advanced age. At the demonstrations 1,314 people were arrested.

It was then decided to walk on to the airfield base at Wethersfield and sit on the runways to prevent planes from taking off. Three thousand military and civilian police were deployed at the site where they arrested 850 of the 5,000 demonstrators. This proved to be the last act of civil disobedience of the Committee which had tended to disunite CND. After the Committee then widened its objectives Russell resigned in 1963.

A considerable proportion of CND supporters were members of the Labour Party and at its annual conference in 1960 the Party voted in favour of unilateral nuclear disarmament which was the Campaign's greatest influence on national politics. However, the Party leader, Hugh Gaitskell, declared that he would "fight, fight and fight again to save the party we love" against the decision which was overturned at the conference of the following year.

Cuban Missile Crisis

In 1962 the Soviet Union commenced installing nuclear missiles in Cuba, 90 miles from the coast of the United States. A tense confrontation followed and nuclear war was only just avoided by John F. Kennedy and Nikita Khrushchev when the Soviet Union conceded at the last moment and withdrew the missiles whilst shortly afterwards American missiles in Turkey were also withdrawn. Both sides had suffered severe fright and the next year a ban on nuclear testing in the atmosphere was agreed between the United States, the Soviet Union and Great Britain. As a consequence international tension began to relax.

CND support dwindled after the 1963 Test Ban Treaty and it practically ceased to function in 1965. However, in the 1980s American Pershing missiles were deployed in Britain in response to the Soviet SS20s stationed in Eastern Europe and CND support revived and the membership rose from 4,000 to approaching 100,000.

Greenham Common

In 1981, a number of feminist anti-nuclear women marched from Cardiff to the United States air base at Greenham Common in Berkshire to protest at the establishment of a cruise missiles base there. It was to hold 101 missiles each with the power of sixteen original atom bombs used at Hiroshima. At first the women, who were not all members of CND, chained themselves to the gates but then they set up a long-term peace camp at the site. Thousands of women settled at the camp which lasted for 14 years until 1995, outstaying the American base. In 1982 the women staged an "Embrace the Base" event which drew some 30,000 women protesters into a demonstration against nuclear weapons. Fences at the base were regularly cut open as women endeavoured to force their way inside the base and their all-women protest was seen on television around the world. Although the movement was non-violent, and many of the women had their children staying with them, they were often prosecuted and sent to prison after refusing to pay fines or after agreeing to be of "good behaviour" and keep the peace.

So great was the public support for CND that a number of opposition organizations were started up. These included the "Women and Families for Defence" set up by the right-wing journalist Lady Olga Maitland. There was also the government sponsored "Defence Secretariat 19", a special unit set up within the Ministry of Defence in March 1983 by Michael Heseltine mainly to combat CND but also to publicise the government's policy on deterrence and multilateral disarmament. Personal attacks were made on CND leaders and an unsuccessful effort was made to suggest CND was funded by the Soviet Union. Despite lack of evidence of Soviet support, MI5 designated CND as "subversive" and kept a close check on its leaders including telephone tapping which was exposed in 1985 by Cathy Massiter. She was an MI5 officer who had been responsible for the surveillance of CND from 1981 to 1983 when she resigned and made the disclosures on television.

Current Policy

Today, CND not only advocates unilateral nuclear disarmament by Britain but, among other things, campaigns against Trident, calls also for international nuclear disarmament and opposes any military action that might result in the use of nuclear, chemical and biological weapons. It is also opposed to peaceful uses of nuclear power. It remains a national dissenting organization that projects itself as a non-violent body which aims to create genuine security for future generations.

CHAPTER 27

MODERN REVOLT

Rebels

The late twentieth and the early twenty-first centuries have witnessed new attacks on dissent and radicalism. The threat from terrorism has been used as an excuse to introduce legislation to dilute the rule of law and strike at all dissent whether physical, oral or written. Furthermore, although in a sense we have moved away from cruel and unusual punishments, some police officers and private security firms seem to lose control when faced by people exercising their democratic rights and attack with savage violence all forms of dissent and radicalism. We are all also subject to a high degree of surveillance and mass legislation that appears to have got out of hand. In the last decade there have been an astonishing 50 new crime and punishment Statutes and 3,000 new criminal offences created that cover a very considerable range of actions and behaviour. This has led to uncertainty as to what is criminal and sanctionable as have the large number of anti-social behaviour orders (ASBOs) that have been issued.

However, this period has seen fewer dissenters of the type defined in the *Introduction* to this book and more of rebels who resent and resist authority and refuse to conform to generally accepted modes of behaviour. Although they are not primarily the people I am dealing with they are often seen to be a threat to the established order and are attacked accordingly. That they often present no serious threat only emphasises the disproportionate violent treatment they receive from the police whose instructions are frequently politically motivated. A few examples from recent times will be given here.

The Angry Brigade

The background to the Angry Brigade was the anti-Vietnam War demonstrations in London in 1967 and the summer of 1968 outside the American Embassy in Grosvenor Square. Large numbers of those present were students and young left-wing radicals and some violence occurred between them and the police. That was par for the course with this type of demonstration. But the Angry Brigade, a small loose group influenced by anarchism, were something different. The well-known student demonstrator, Tariq Ali, years later recalled being approached at the time by someone claiming to represent a group called the Angry Brigade who he said were proposing to plant a bomb at the American Embassy. Ali claims that he told them it was a terrible idea and that he considered them a distraction from the anti-war movement.[1]

In the event, the American Embassy was not bombed but the Angry Brigade did launch a bombing campaign with small bombs in August 1970 which continued until their arrest a year later. Their targets included banks, embassies, the property of government ministers and the Miss World contest.

The damage caused in a total of 25 bombings was in the main confined to property. After a year the police arrested in Stoke Newington, London four men and four women who were suspected of being members of the group. Although they claimed to represent what they called the autonomous working class they were themselves middle class students. A ninth member, Jake Prescott, was in fact a member of the working class.

Guns, ammunition and explosives were found at the flat of the eight and their trial was to be one of the longest criminal trials in English history. At its conclusion, five of them were found guilty of conspiracy to cause explosions and each was sentenced to ten years in prison. The other three were found not guilty. Despite the bombs, the prison sentences and their links with French "situationists", the Brigade was a very English phenomenon with its targeting of property and not people and one member, Angela Mason, was later awarded the OBE for her campaigning for gay rights.

---

1. David Horspool. (2010) *The English Rebel*. London, Penguin Books. p. 385.

Battle of The Beanfield

This was an example of a pre-emptive action by the authorities that went predictably wrong. Each June travellers in a peace convoy visit Stonehenge in Wiltshire for the Summer Solstice and Druid ceremonials. Prior to the event planned for 1 June 1985 English Heritage, who were custodians of the site, applied to the High Court for an exclusion zone of some four miles around the site and this was granted. Then, on 1 June, when several hundred travellers in convoy in some hundred vehicles, many of them converted mobile homes, reached the outskirts of the zone they were herded into a field by a strong contingent of police. After several hours of inaction it was alleged that the police entered the field in riot gear and proceeded to attack the vehicles using truncheons and sledgehammers to smash windows and damage the interiors of the cars and vans.

Some of the convoy attempted to escape by going through an adjoining field, known as the Beanfield, but they were pursued and arrested by the police. The police claimed that they were responding to attacks on themselves by travellers using wood, stones and petrol bombs. They did not repeat this, however, in any subsequent court cases. Nick Davies, for *The Observer* newspaper reported from the site that, "There was glass breaking, people screaming, black smoke towering out of burning caravans and everywhere there seemed to be people being bashed and flattened and pulled by the hair. Men, women and children were led away, shivering, swearing, crying, bleeding, leaving their homes in pieces".

The response of the police had been politically charged and was disproportionate. As a consequence, 24 of the travellers sued Wiltshire Police for wrongful arrest, assault and criminal damage and almost six years later, after four months of hearings, 21 of the travellers were successful and were awarded £24,000 in damages. Despite heavy media coverage of the event itself, little was reported of this outcome.

Poll Tax Riots

In 1989 the Conservative government of which Margaret Thatcher was prime minister introduced a community charge to replace local authority rates. It was argued that it would be fairer in that everyone on the electoral register would pay the charge instead of say a family of two paying the same domestic rates as neighbours with several wage earners in one family. The stress on the individuals due to pay the charge led to comparisons with the tax that sparked the Peasants Revolt in 1381 and the community charge was quickly dubbed a poll tax.

The tax was first introduced in Scotland in 1989 and the Conservatives were decimated in subsequent general elections there as a consequence. After an All Britain Anti-Poll Tax Federation had been formed the poll tax was then introduced in England and Wales. In response, a series of mass demonstrations and riots then occurred across Britain before the Federation called a demonstration in London for Saturday, 31 March 1990, just before the community charge was due to come into force. From noon onwards on that day an estimated 200,000 demonstrators turned up at Kennington Park in south London and at 1.30 pm began the march to Downing Street where they commenced a sit-in in the street opposite.

The police then moved them on towards Trafalgar Square. It was here that a violent confrontation between police and demonstrators raged until the early hours of the Sunday morning. The police said that the clashes started when they were attacked by militant elements in the crowd and the demonstrators alleged that some unprovoked police officers on horses charged them. One woman protestor claimed that, "the police were going mad. When they charged towards me, everyone ran back. I was grabbed by one and thrown to the floor. I curled in a ball but one hit me with a truncheon across the head and some kicked me".[2]

Police riot vans drove into the crowd who responded by attacking the vans with scaffolding poles. Nearby builders' cabins were set on fire and the violence escalated with anarchists now to the fore. There was considerable looting and vandalism of banks, shops and offices, cafes and wine bars,

---

2. David Horspool. *The English Rebel. Op. cit.* p. 391.

some of which were set on fire. Numerous cars were overturned as battle raged for many hours.

> All sides admit that some marchers were intent on violence, but the police seemed unable to distinguish between trouble-makers and the law abiding majority.[3]

Most demonstrators want to act peacefully but there are often extremists who are looking for trouble with the police. When peace finally settled 400 protestors and 374 police had been injured, and damage to property was estimated at millions of pounds. The greatest single casualty was the person who introduced the poll tax, Margaret Thatcher. The riots played a large part in ensuring her downfall which came when she resigned as prime minister and party leader in 1990 following grave disquiet about the community charge in her own party. In the country at large public opinion polls showed its support standing at two per cent. After her resignation the community charge was quickly brought to an end and replaced with the council tax of today.

Conclusion

Many of the examples given in this book involve people suffering from abuses of the criminal law committed by rulers or governments clamping down on them from fear they might rock the established order, however objectionable it might be. Yet, the struggles of the people whose stories are outlined here have brought us to a more humane system of criminal justice. As a consequence of their actions, persistence and example they have helped establish more certainty in the criminal justice system, due process and the recognition of human rights. In other words, the rule of law and institutional morality.

Nevertheless, in modern times there remain examples of some police officers and private security firms living in a world of their own in terms of who they consider the demons to be. Further, in the United Kingdom many high principles are being eaten away by repressive laws and a diminution of rights. Perhaps the most important are the undermining of the rule of law

---

3. *Ibid.*

and democratic rights in the name of the so-called war on terror. Threats and acts of terrorism have caused the leaders of some democratic countries to weaken fundamental aspects of the rule of law including the absolute requirements of fair trials and the total rejection of torture.

In Britain the former prime minister, Tony Blair, said it was a dangerous misjudgment to put civil liberties before anti-terrorist laws.[4] After the 7 July 2005 bombings in London he said,

> Let no one be in any doubt the rules of the game are changing. Should legal obstacles arise we will legislate further including, if necessary, amending the Human Rights Act in respect of the European Convention of Human Rights.[5]

The rule of law is an expression of the liberal and democratic principles that dissenters have struggled for throughout the centuries. It inhibits arbitrary power and defends citizens from an over-powerful state. It is crucial that it should not be undermined and that principled dissent should always be encouraged as a valuable contribution to liberty.

---

4. John Hostettler. (2011) *Champions of the Rule of Law*. Hook, Hampshire, Waterside Press Ltd. p. 81.
5. Tony Blair. Speech on 5 August 2005.

SELECT BIBLIOGRAPHY

A

A Compleat Collection of State Tryals for High Treason from the reign of Henry IV to the end of the reign of Queen Anne. (1719). 4 vols. London, T. Goodwin and Others.
Annual Register. (1768)

B

Bamford, Samuel. (1844) *Passages in the Life of a Radical,* London, Simpkin, Marshall & Co.
Bernstein, Eduard. (1930) *Cromwell and Communism: Socialism and Democracy in The Great English Revolution.* London, George Allen & Unwin Ltd.
Birmingham Journal. (7 April 1838)
British Library. *Add. MSS. General Convention of the Industrial Classes. 1839.* Papers 34245A.
Bunyan, John. (1827 edn.) *Grace Abounding to the Chief of Sinners.* London, J. F. Dove.
   (1859 edn.) *Works.* vols. i-iii. London, Henry Stebbing.
Burke, Edmund. (1969) *Reflections on the Revolution in France and on the Proceedings in Certain Societies in London Relative to that Event.* London, Penguin Books.
Bush, M. L. (2005) *The Casualties of Peterloo.* Lancaster, Carnegie Publishers.

C

Churchill, Winston. (1957) *A History of the English-Speaking Peoples.* London, Cassell & Co. vol. 3.

Clarkson, Laurence. (1650) *A Single Eye All Light, no Darkness; or Light and Dark One*. London, Gilles Calvert.

Cobbett's *State Trials*. (1792), (1794)

Cockburn, Henry Lord. (1888) *An Examination of the Trials for Sedition which have hitherto occurred in Scotland*. Edinburgh, David Douglas.

Code of Conduct of the Bar of England and Wales. (2004) London, General Council of the Bar.

Cole, G. D. H. and Postgate, Raymond. (1938) *The Common People 1746-1938*. London, Methuen & Co. Ltd.

Coppe, Abiezer. (1649) *A Fiery Flying Roll*. (1973 edn.) Exeter, University of Exeter.

D

Daily Citizen. (1913)

Defoe, Daniel. (1698) *The Poor Man's Plea*. London, A. Baldwin.

(1836 edn.) *The True-born Englishman: a Satire*. Leeds, Alice Mann.

Dick, Oliver Lawson. (ed.) *Aubrey's Brief Lives*. London, Penguin Books.

Dictionary of National Biography. (2004) Oxford, Oxford University Press.

Dyer, Thomas Thiselton. (1891) *Church Lore Gleanings*. London, A. D. Innes and Co.

E

Eagles, John. (1832) *The Bristol Riots, their Causes, Progress and Consequences*. London, Cadell.

Eliot, George. (1972) *Middlemarch*. London, Folio Society edition.

Ensor, Sir Robert. (1936) *England 1870-1914*. Oxford, The Clarendon Press.

F

Firth, Sir Charles. (1900) *Oliver Cromwell and the Rule of the Puritans in England*. London, Oxford University Press.

Foner, Philip Sheldon (ed.). (1969) *The Complete Works of Thomas Paine*. 2 vols. New York, Citadel.

Foot, Michael. (1973) *Aneurin Bevan A Biography, 1945-1960.* vol. ii. London, Davis-Poynter.
Franklin, Caroline. (2004) *Mary Wollstonecraft: A Literary Life.* Basingstoke, Palgrave Macmillan.
Friedenthal, Richard. (1970) *Luther.* (Translated by John Nowell). London, Weidenfeld & Nicolson.

G

Gammage, R. G. (1894) *History of the Chartist Movement 1837-1854.* London, Truslove and Hanson.
Green, J. R. (1874) *A Short History of the English People.* London, Folio Society Edition (1992)

H

Hague, William. (2004) *William Pitt the Younger.* London, Harper Perennial.
   (2007) *William Wilberforce: The Life of the Great Anti-Trade Slave Campaigner.* London, Harper Press.
Hansard. (1817): (1884): (1906); (1913): (1934)
Harding, Alan. (1973) *The Law Courts of Medieval England.* London, George Allen & Unwin Ltd.
Hardy, Thomas. (1832) *Memoir.* London.
Hill, Christopher. (1965) *Intellectual Origins of the English Revolution.* Oxford, The Clarendon Press.
   (1966) *The Century of Revolution, 1603-1714.* London, Thomas Nelson and Sons Ltd.
   (1972) *The World Turned Upside Down: Radical Ideas during the English Revolution.* London, Maurice Temple Smith Ltd.
   (1996) *Liberty Against the Law: Some Seventeenth-Century Controversies.* London, Allen Lane, The Penguin Press.
Hochschild, Adam. (2005) *Bury the Chains, The British Struggle to Abolish Slavery.* London, Macmillan.
Holyoake, George Jacob, (1892) *Sixty Years of an Agitator's Life.* London, T. Fisher Unwin.

Home Office Files, 40/29. Public Record Office, Kew.

(1878) *Wellington Despatches.* 2nd ser. vii. 353.

Horspool, David. (2010) *The English Rebel: One Thousand Years of Troublemaking from the Normans to the Nineties.* London, Penguin Books.

Hostettler, John. (1993) *Thomas Wakley: An Improbable Radical.* Chichester, Barry Rose Law Publishers.

(1998) *At the Mercy of the State: A Study in Judicial Tyranny.* Chichester, Barry Rose Law Publishers Ltd.

(2009) *A History of Criminal Justice in England and Wales.* Hook, Hampshire, Waterside Press Ltd.

(2010) *Thomas Erskine and Trial by Jury.* Hook, Hampshire, Waterside Press Ltd.

(2011) *Champions of the Rule of Law.* Hook, Hampshire, Waterside Press Ltd.

Hovell, Mark. (1925) *The Chartist Movement.* Manchester, University of Manchester Press.

House of Commons Journals. vol. xi. p. 492.

Howell, Thomas. (1809-1826) *Complete Collection of State Trials.*

Hudson, W. S. *Gerard Winstanley and the Early Quakers. Church History.* vol. xii.

J

Johnson, Paul. (1972) *The Offshore Islanders: From Roman Occupation to European Entry.* London, Weidenfeld & Nicolson.

Jones, David J. V. (1985) *The Last Rising, The Newport Insurrection of 1839.* Oxford, The Clarendon Press.

Jones, Ernest. (1846) *Chartist Poems: Our Rally.*

(1852) *Notes to the People.* London, J. Pavey.

Journal of the House of Commons. (1652)

K

Keane, John. (1995) *Tom Paine: A Political Life.* London, Bloomsbury.

Keay, John. (2000) *India: A History.* New York, Grove Press.

Kettle, Arnold. (1951) *An Introduction to the English Novel.* London, Hutchinson's University Library. vol. 1.

L

Latham, Robert and Matthews William. (1973) *The Diary of Samuel Pepys.* London, G. Bell & Sons Ltd.

Lecky, W.E.H. (1882) *A History of England in the Eighteenth Century.* London, Longmans, Green & Co. vols. 1 and 3.

Lindsay, Jack. (1964) *Nine Days' Hero: Wat Tyler.* London, Dennis Dobson.

(1969) *John Bunyan: Maker of Myths.* Port Washington, Kennikat Press.

Lovelace, George. (1837) *The Victims of Whiggery.* London.

M

Manson, Michael. (1997) *Riot! The Bristol Bridge Massacre of 1793.* Bristol, Past and Present.

Manchester Guardian. (16 October 1905)

McFarlane, K. B. (1972) *Wycliffe and English Non-Conformity.* London, Penguin Books.

Mill, James. (1818) "Essay on Government". *Encyclopedia Britannica.* London, Supplement.

Milton, John. (1649) *The Tenure of Kings And Magistrates.* London, M. Simmons.

(1788) *Paradise Lost.* Belfast, James Magee.

(1959) *Complete Prose Works.* (ed.) Don M. Wolfe. New Haven, Yale University Press. Vol. 2.

Mines and Quarries. S. Wales Division Reports. Cmd. 8023-iv.

Morgan, Kenneth O. (1984) *Keir Hardie: Radical and Socialist.* London, Weidenfeld &Nicolson.

Morton, A. L. (1945) *A People's History of England.* London, Lawrence & Wishart Ltd.

(1970) *The World of the Ranters: Religious Radicalism in the English Revolution.* London, Lawrence & Wishart Ltd.

N

Nicolson, Harold. (1952) *King George the Fifth: His Life and Reign.* London, Pan Books Ltd.

Northern Star. (August 1839, October 1850)

P

Paine, Thomas. (1921) *Rights of Man Part 1 — Being an Answer to Mr. Burke's Attack on the French Revolution.* London, Benbow.
   (1792) *Rights of Man Part II — Combining Principle and Practice.* London, J. S. Jordan.
   (1795) *The Age of Reason: Being an investigation of true and of fabulous theology.* London, H.D. Symonds.
Pankhurst, E. Sylvia. (1931) *The Suffragette Movement: An Intimate Account of Persons and Ideals.* London, Longmans & Co.
Parliamentary History. (1653) (1776)
Paxman, Jeremy. *On Royalty.* London, Penguin Books.
Perkin, Harold. (1969) *The Origins of Modern English Society.* London, Routledge & Kegan Paul.
Piratin, Phil. (1948) *Our Flag Stays Red.* London, Thames Publications.
Place, Francis. *Place Papers.* BL. *Add. MSS.* 27,793 fol. 100 and 27,794. fols. 58, 344 and 347.
Postgate, Raymond. (1956) *That Devil Wilkes.* London, Dennis Dobson.
Prentice, Archibald. (1851) *Historical Sketches and Personal Recollections of Manchester.* London and Manchester.
Pugh, Martin. (1980) *Women's Suffrage in Britain 1867-1928.* London, Historical Association.
   (2001) *The Pankhursts.* London, Allen Lane, The Penguin Press.

R

Raeburn, Antonia. (1973) *The Militant Suffragettes.* London, Michael Joseph.
Reeve, John. (1652) *Of the Three Records.* London.
   (1656) *A Divine Looking Glasse.* London.
   with Muggleton, Lolowick. (1711 edn.) *A Transcendent Spiritual Treatise upon several heavenly Doctrines.* London.
Robertson, Geoffrey. (2005) *The Tyrannicide Brief: The Story of the Man who sent Charles I to the Scaffold.* London, Chatto and Windus.

(2007) *The Levellers: The Putney Debates.* London, Verso.
Rogers, E. (1867) *Some Account of the Life and Opinions of a Fifth-Monarchy-Man.* London.
Roots, Ivan. (1966) *The Great Rebellion 1642-1660.* London, B.T. Batsford Ltd.
Rosen, Andrew. (1974) *Rise Up, Women! The Militant Campaign of the Women's Social and Political Union 1903-1914.* London, Routledge & Kegan Paul.
Rotuli Parliamentorum. (1783).
Rover, Constance. (1967) *Women's Suffrage and Party Politics in Britain, 1866-1919.*
Rowbotham, Shelia. (1977) *A New World for Women. Stella Browne: Socialist Feminist.* Pluto Press.
Rudé, George. (1962) *Wilkes & Liberty: A Social Study of 1763 to 1774.* Oxford, The Clarendon Press.
Rutt. J. T. (ed.). (1828) *The Diary of Thomas Burton MP.* London, Colburn.

S

Sabine, G. H. (1941) *The Works of Gerard Wynstanley.* New York, Cornell University Press.
Salway, Peter. (1981) *Roman Britain.* Oxford, The Clarendon Press.
Sharp, Andrew. (1998) *English Levellers.* Cambridge, Cambridge University Press.
Shaw, George Bernard. (1965) *The Complete Prefaces of Bernard Shaw.* London, Paul Hamlyn.
Shaw, Howard. (1973) *The Levellers.* London, Longman Group Ltd.
Shelley, Percy Bysshe. (1968) *Poetical Works.* London, Oxford University Press.
Stebbing, Henry. (1859) *The Works of John Bunyan.* London. vol. 1.
Stewart, William. *J. Keir Hardie.* London, Independent Labour Party.
Stopes, Marie. (1920) *The Control of Parenthood.* James Marchant (ed.) London, G. P. Putnam's Sons.
Sutherland, Halliday. (1922) *Birth Control: A Statement of Christian Doctrine against the Neo-Malthusians.* London, Harding & More.

T

The Catholic Encyclopedia.

The Times. (September 1819); (October 1831); (March, April, July, August, September 1839); (July 1840); (October 1842); (February 1884); (March 1912); (February, May 1913)

Thompson, Dorothy. (1986) *The Chartists: Popular Politics in the Industrial Revolution.* Aldershot, Wildwood House.

Thompson, E. P. (1968) *The Making of the English Working Class.* London, Penguin Books.

Tomalin, Claire. (1974) *The Life and Death of Mary Wollstonecraft.* London, Weidenfeld & Nicolson.

Tomkins, Stephen. (2007) *William Wilberforce: A Biography*, Oxford, Lion.

Trevelyan, G. M. (1946 edn) *England in the Age of Wycliffe.* London, Longmans, Green & Co.

V

Vallance, Edward. (2010) *A Radical History of Britain.* London, Abacus.

Veall, Donald. (1970) *The Popular Movement for Law Reform 1640-1660.* Oxford, Oxford University Press.

Vogler, Richard. (2005) *A World View of Criminal Justice.* Aldershot, Ashgate Publishing Limited.

W

Walker, Clement. (1649) *The Trial of Lt. Col. John Lilburne ... Being as Exactly Penned and Taken in Short-hand, as it was Possible to be Done in such a Crowd and Noise.* London, Theodorus Verax.

Watson, J. Steven. (1960) *The Reign of George III, 1760-1815.* Oxford, The Clarendon Press.

Wharam, Alan. (1992) *The Treason Trials, 1794.* Leicester, Leicester University Press.

Wilson, A. N. (2005) *After the Victorians.* London, Hutchinson.

Wollstonecraft, Mary. (1996) *A Vindication of the Rights of Woman.* London, Constable.

Workers' Dreadnought. (17 September 1921).

Wynstanley, Gerrard. (1649) *A Watch-Word to the City of London and the Armie: Wherein you may see that England's freedome which should be the result of all our victories is sinking deeper under the Norman power.* London.

(1649) "The Levellers' Standard Advanced". In G. H. Sabine (ed.) (1941) *The Works of Gerard Wynstanley.* Cornell University Press.

(1651-2) *The Law of Freedom in a Platform: or, True Magistracy Restored.* London, Giles Calvert.

(1973 edn.) *The Law of Freedom and Other Writings.* London, Penguin Books.

INDEX

A

abortion
    back street abortions *227*
abuse *247*
activists *63*
Adams, John *127*
Addis Ababa *224*
adultery *73*
affray *235*
Age of Reason, The *139*
agitation *54, 127, 128, 157, 178, 209*
    Agitators *57*
Agreement of the People *64*
Albion Colliery *203*
Amalgamated Society of Railway Servants *206*
American independence *127, 152*
anarchy *57, 155, 244, 246*
Anderson, Elizabeth Garrett *212*
Anglo-Saxons *30*
Angry Brigade *244*
Antichrist *33, 41*
anti-semitism *234*
anti-social behaviour orders *243*
Archbishop of Canterbury *48, 49*
aristocracy *152, 164*
arms *177, 178*

Army Act 1881 *199*
arson *167, 217, 219*
Arundel, Thomas *41*
Ashton-under-Lyne *178*
Ashurst, Mr. Justice *134*
Asquith *224*
Atomic Age *237*
attainder *90*
Attwood, Thomas *164, 165, 175*
Austin, Thomas *197*
Australia *224, 232*
Ayrshire Miners Union *202*

B

Badby, John *40*
Ball, John *39, 47, 51, 74*
Ballot, The 165, 190, 191
Bamford, Samuel *159*
Bampton, Thomas *46, 48*
Bangladesh *232*
banishment *75, 108, 132, 149*
banks *244*
Baptism *111*
Barnes *75*
Barnet *69*

barricades *235*
"Bastilles" *173*
Bath *151, 168*
baton charges *235*
Beanfield, Battle of The *245*
Beccaria, Cesare *56*
Bedford *105, 107*
   Bedford Gaol *108*
Bedlam *81*
   Island Bedlam *54*
begging *67, 129*
Belknap, Robert *46*
Bell, Richard *205*
Bennett, Curtis *215, 216*
Bentham, Jeremy *171*
Berkshire *239*
Besant, Annie *228*
Bevan, Aneurin *237*
Bible, The *33, 66, 100*
   Bible Society *136*
   biblical communism *72*
Bill of Rights *89*
binding over *216*
Birmingham *141, 163, 165, 174, 175, 219*
   Bull Ring violence *177*
birth control *227, 228*
   Birth Control News *228*
bishops *40, 228*
   Bishop of Gloucester *146*
Black Death *34, 46*
Blackheath *48*
blacklists *168*
Blair, Tony *248*
Blake, William *105, 130*
blasphemy *20, 72, 82, 88, 90, 111*

blasphemers *22*
blasphemous libel *132*
Blasphemy Act 1650 *72*
Blatchford, Robert *203*
Bleak House *195*
Blood, Fanny *151*
Bloody Assizes *113*
Bloody Mary *44*
Bolivia *232*
Bolton *178*
bombs *219*
   bombing campaigns *244*
Bosworth *69*
Botany Bay *142*
Bournemouth *156*
Bow Street *215*
Bradford *203*
Bradlaugh, Charles *228*
Bradshaw, John *91*
Braxfield, Lord *142*
breach of the peace *215*
Brentwood *46*
Brereton, Colonel *167, 168*
Bridgeman, Orlando *94*
Brighton *237*
Bristol *21, 51, 82, 163, 165*
   Bristol Bridge Riot *165*
   Bristol Political Union *166*
Britain, Vera *238*
Britannia *224*
British constitution *142*
British Museum *219*
British Union of Fascists *233*
Brixton Prison *233*
Brockway, Fenner *238*

brotherhood of man *136*
Brougham, Henry *137*
brutality *132*, *186*, *234*
Buckinghamshire *69*, *119*
Bunhill Fields *111*, *117*, *149*
Bunyan, John *22*, *69*, *76*, *105*, *108*
Burford *72*
Burke, Edmund *128*, *142*, *144*, *152*
burning
   burning at the stake *140*
   burning books *75*, *101*, *116*, *121*
Burrough, Edward *107*
Bushell, Edward *85*
   Bushell's Case *86*

C

Cable Street *233*, *236*
"cab-rank" rule *133*
Calvert, Gilles *74*
Cambridge *73*, *113*, *135*, *137*
Camden, Earl *146*
Cameron, James *238*
Campbell-Bannerman, Henry *207*
Campbell, Sir John *180*
capital punishment *139*, *167*, *177*
  aboliition *56*
Cardiff *241*
Carlile, Richard *228*
Carson, Lord *230*
Carthage
  Council of Carthage *28*
caste system *140*
"Cat and Mouse Act" *220*

catholics *100*, *105*, *235*
   Roman Catholics *20*, *25*, *28*, *44*, *71*
Cavalry Barracks *199*
Caxton Hall *214*, *224*
censorship *73*, *99*, *101*
chaining to public buildings, etc. *216*, *241*
Chancellor of the Exchequer *215*
Charles I *53*, *78*, *89*, *91*, *94*, *99*, *105*
Charles II *94*, *100*, *101*
Chartism *21*, *162*, *173*, *194*, *203*
   Chartist Convention *176*
   Chartist Movement *175*
   women Chartists *183*
Chastity Campaign *223*
Cheshire *178*
Chidley, Katherine *62*
children
   child labour *203*
Christianity *28*, *132*, *133*, *135*
   Second Coming of Christ *76*
   Western Christianity *26*
Chronicle of England, The *47*
church/Church *25*
   Church Missionary Society *136*
   Church of England *71*
Churchill, Winston *147*, *212*, *213*, *217*
civil liberties *248*
Civil War *53*, *54*, *71*, *90*, *97*, *105*
   Spanish Civil War *235*
Clapham Sect *135*, *136*
Clarkson, Laurence *73*
class *161*, *185*, *189*, *205*, *208*, *209*, *211*, *223*, *244*

National Union of the Working
    Classes *165, 191*
clergy *68*
Clerkenwell *50*
clerks *45, 49*
cloth caps *202*
Cobbett, William *134*
Cobham *67*
Cobham, Lord *40*
Cockburn, Lord *142*
Coke, Lord *85*
Collins, John *238*
colonialism
    anti-colonialism *224*
Combination Acts *139, 170*
common birthright *106*
common cause *19*
common good *20*
Common Law *65, 66, 84, 90*
"Common Sense" *127*
Commonwealth *22, 62, 71, 93, 98, 105*
Communism *235*
    Communist Party of Great Britain *224*
community charge *246, 247*
compassing the death of the king *144*
conformity *19*
    nonconformity *31*
conscience *22, 58, 85*
Conservatives *246*
conspiracy to cause explosions *244*
Constantine's Edict of Milan *26*
Constitutional Information Society *146*
Constitutions of Oxford *37*

Conventicle Act 1670 *83, 107, 108*
Cooke, John *89*
    trial and execution *94*
Cooper, Sir Astley *190*
Coppe, Abiezer *74*
Corn Laws *157, 192*
Corresponding Societies *141, 144*
corruption *48, 71, 101, 132, 169, 190, 202*
Cottenham, Lord *196*
Council of Constance *37, 40*
courage *86*
court-martial *168*
Court of Appeal *207, 229*
Court of Common Pleas *86, 121, 167*
courts
    king's courts *42*
Covent Garden *170*
Coventry *168*
Crabtree, Joseph *182*
crime *116*
    crime and punishment
        Statutes *243*
    crimes against humanity *91*
    criminal damage *241, 245*
    criminal law *40*
    new criminal offences *243*
Croker, John *171*
Cromwell, Oliver *53, 56, 57, 63, 77, 82, 90, 100*
cruel and unusual punishments *243*
cruise missiles *241*
Cuban Missile Crisis *241*

D

Dark Ages *25*
Davies, Nick *245*
Davison, Emily *221*
debt
  imprisonment for debt *56*
De Dominio Civili *35*
Defence Secretariat 19 *242*
Defoe, Daniel *22, 110, 113*
degradation *186*
democracy *53, 64, 130, 134, 157, 162, 171, 173, 224*
  democratic rights *248*
demons *247*
demonstrations *157, 177, 215, 234, 241, 244, 246*
  anti-war demonstrations *208*
  peaceful demonstrations *162*
denial as a confession of guilt *92*
Derby *81, 165, 205*
Despard, Charlotte *214*
destitution *105*
destruction
  destruction of property *217*
  Kew Orchid House *219*
Devil worship *119*
Devon *189, 192*
Dickens, Charles *189*
Diggers *53, 65, 72*
disarmament *242*
discontent *160*
disorderly meetings *165*
Disraeli, Benjamin *171*

dissent *19, 69, 77, 88, 105, 113, 135, 148, 156, 162, 211, 224, 243*
dissenters *19, 51, 71, 87*
Dissenters Academy *113*
principled dissent *248*
stream of dissent *224*
tradition of dissent *20*
distress *175*
disturbances *83, 166, 168, 213*
diversity *20*
divine authority/right *26, 90, 105*
Divine Looking-Glass, A *77*
doctrine of the two seeds *76*
Dorset *192*
Drummond, Flora *215*
drunkenness *73*
due process *247*
Duke of Wellington *164, 165, 171*
Dumbarton *219*
Duncombe, Thomas *182*
Dundee *219*
Dunstable *69*
duplicity *49*
dysentery *186*

E

Earl of Sandwich *120*
East Anglia *48*
East End *21, 202, 223, 234*
East London Federation *223*
economy *138*
  economic depression *157*
  economic distress *173*

economic evils *68*
Edinburgh *142, 227, 229*
Edward III *35*
Edwards, Thomas *62*
effigies *168*
egalitarianism *65, 79*
Eikonoklastes 99
Eldon, Lord Chancellor *160*
Ellenborough, Lord *169*
Eltham *43*
Emancipation of Slavery Act 1833 *136*
embassies *244*
"Embrace the Base" *241*
endurance *86*
Enfield *69*
Engels, Frederick *188*
English Heritage *245*
Epsom Derby *220*
equality *193, 225*
   equal electoral districts *174*
   equality before the law *56*
   equality of the sexes *152*
Erskine, Thomas *130, 133, 145*
"Essay on Government" *163*
Essex *47, 51, 83*
established order *71*
esteem *19*
eugenics *231*
   Eugenics Society *231*
evidence
   bar on prisoners giving *85*
exclusion zone *245*
exploitation *191*
expropriation *73*
extremists *247*

Eyre, Lord Justice *145*

F

Fabian Society *205*
facism
   anti-fascism *224*
Fairfax, General *57, 67*
fair trial *248*
family planning *228*
fanaticism *79, 221, 233*
Farren, Elizabeth *158*
fascism *233*
Fawcett, Millicent Garrett *212*
Fawkes, Guy *20*
feminism *156*
   feminist movement *225*
fetters *187*
feudalism *105, 116*
   anti-feudal realism *113*
   feudal aristocracy *53*
Fifth Monarchy Men *76*
Finch, Sir John *94*
Finsbury *192*
fire
   death by *43*
Fisher, William *43*
Fitzwilliam, Lord *161*
Fleet Prison *48, 55*
flogging *82, 116, 198*
Foot, Michael *238*
force *187*
   entrenched forces *232*
   forced feeding *216*

moral force *175*
physical force *21, 175*
forfeiture *131*
Fox, Charles James *137, 146*
Fox, George *75, 81*
France *142*
   French Revolution *21, 128, 130, 141, 152, 156*
   Terror *21*
franchise *55, 56, 123, 125, 141, 152, 157, 162, 163, 171, 174, 208, 209, 212, 222, 224*
Francis of Assisi, St *44*
Franklin, Benjamin *127*
fraternity *156*
freedom *48, 54, 130, 148, 179*
   colonial freedom movements *208*
   freedom of religion *56*
   freedom of speech *100*
   freedom of the press *101*
   freedom of trade *48*
freethinking *132*
Frost, John *176*

G

Game Laws *140*
gaming *152*
Gammage, R. G. *179*
"gaols without guilt" *173*
Garrow, William *145*
Gaunt, John of *32, 34, 39, 45, 49*
   destruction of palace of *48*
gay rights *244*

Geneva *143*
George III *120, 123*
George V *218*
Germany *231*
Gerrald, Joseph *143*
Gladstone, Herbert *171, 215, 217*
Gladstone, William *183*
Glamorgan *203*
Glasgow *175, 209*
Glorious Revolution *63, 71*
Gloucestershire *69*
God as a highwayman *74*
Godwin, William *155*
Gollancz, Victor *238*
good
   good and evil *26*
   public good *95*
Gordon Riots *125*
Grandees *57*
Gray's Inn *89*
Great Fire of London *103*
Great Plague of London *103*
Great Reform Act 1832 *211*
Greenham Common *241*
Greenwood, Anthony *238*
Grenville, George *120*
Greville, Charles *166*
Grey, Lord *164, 213*
Grey, Sir Edward *212*
Grosvenor Square *244*
Guildhall *59*

H

habeas corpus 86, 87, 121, 144
Hague, William 137
Hale, Matthew 108
Hales, Sir Robert 48, 49
Halifax 185
handbills 169
hanging in chains 43
happiness 129, 227
harassment 128
Hardie, James Keir 21, 201, 205, 214, 218
hard labour 134, 167, 235
Hardy, Thomas 133, 141, 144, 148, 215
Harney, George Julian 187
Harrison, Major-General Thomas 77, 96
Hastings, Sir Patrick KC 229
Hellfire Club 119
Henderson, Arthur 207
Hendon Workhouse 197
Henry V 40
Henry VIII 25, 32, 148
hereditary legislators 129
heresy 20, 21, 26, 28, 31, 37, 41, 71, 79
  Statute of Heresy 40
Hereward the Wake 47
heroic aspects 51
Heseltine, Michael 242
Hewart, Lord 229
High Court of Justice 91, 245
High Court of Justiciary 142
high principle 247
Hill, Christopher 54, 73, 100

Hiroshima 237, 241
Hitler, Adolf 233
Holborn 134
Holland 55
Holloway Prison 214, 220, 221
Home Office 168
Home Secretary 160, 181, 193, 215, 217, 218, 220, 224, 234
hooligans 165
Horne Tooke, John 133, 144
horses, use of by police, etc. 122, 158, 166, 214, 235
Horspool, David 23
Hounslow Heath 199
"Householders in Danger, etc." 169
House of Commons 39, 62, 78, 89, 90, 116, 122, 124, 137, 144, 164, 202, 204, 211, 218
  True Commons 48, 49
House of Lords 164, 207, 230
  abolition 202
Howell, Joseph 178
Hudson, Walter 207
Hull 135
humanity 247
human rights 134, 247
  Universal Declaration of Human Rights 57
Hume, David 131
hunger strikes 216, 217, 220
Hunt, Henry 157, 160
Hussein, Saddam 96
Hyde Park 215, 216
hyena in petticoats 154
Hymn to the Pillory, A 116

hysteria *144, 217*

I

idealism *211*
ideas
   tumult of ideas *71*
ignorance *129, 142, 152*
imprisonment *75, 81, 108, 167, 177, 186, 192, 213, 236*
   imprisonment for debt *89*
improving society *64*
incendiarism *123*
incitement *220*
   inciting hatred of the king *148*
Indemnity and Oblivion Act *94*
independence of mind *89*
Independent Labour Party *203, 212*
indolence *154*
indulgences *33, 108*
industrial classes *53*
Industrial Revolution *163*
Infanticide Act 1922 *225*
inflammatory language *176*
Inge, Susanna *183*
inquisition *86*
   ending of the Pope's powers *36*
insurrection *45, 146, 178*
integrity *103*
intellect *20*
intimidation *178*
intolerance *115*
Ireland *89, 128, 152*
Ireton, Henry *58*

Isle of Wight *48*
Islington *117, 149*
Iver *69*

J

Jacobins *144*
James I *67*
Jan Hus of Prague *33*
Jefferson, Thomas *127, 134*
Jeffreys, Judge *113*
Jews *100, 132, 234*
   Jew-baiting *234*
   Jewish Board of Deputies *234*
jingoism *205*
jobbery *190*
Jones, Ernest *184*
Jones, John *178*
Jones, William *179*
Joyce, Jeremiah *146*
Joyce, William *233*
jury *63, 85, 147, 229*
   jury selection *87*
   jury trial *56*
   perverse verdict *61*
   pliant jury *142*
   special jury *121, 130, 133*
   trial by jury *215*
   unfettered jury trial *86*
   women jurors *225*
justice *68, 87*
   common justice *48*

K

Keble, Mr Justice *59*
Kenney, Annie *212*
Kennington *183, 185*
Kennington Park *246*
Kent *40, 47, 48, 127*
Kenya *232*
Kenyon, Lord Chief Justice *130*
Kersal Moor *177*
King's Bench *122, 123, 130*
King's Cross *193*
Kingston-upon-Thames *67*
Kyd, Stewart *133*

L

Labour *204, 208, 233, 237*
   Labour Party *188, 222*
Lafayette *148*
Lambeth Palace
   destruction of *48*
Lanarkshire *201*
Lancashire *177, 181*
Lancaster Assizes *160*
Lancet, The 190
land
   landed interests *142*
   landowners *67*
   land tenure *48*
Lansbury, George *214, 218*
Laud, Archbishop William *97, 100*
law *68, 69, 72, 87, 155*
   law a heathen word for power *116*

Law of Property Act 1925 *225*
   restraining laws *65*
Lecky, W. E. H. *124*
Leeds *141, 163, 175*
Lee, Jennie *238*
Legbrannock *201*
legitimacy *77*
Leicester *89*
Leigh, Mary *217*
Lenin *224*
less eligibility *173*
Levellers *53, 55, 56*
   digging levelling *74*
   sword-levelling *74*
   True Levellers *65*
   women Levellers *62*
Lewes *127*
   Lewes Castle *51*
libel *116, 229*
Liberal Party *202, 206*
liberty *19, 20, 44, 68, 81, 99, 101, 106, 113, 121, 142, 148, 177, 248*
   libertarian sects *55*
   liberty of conscience *22, 58*
   liberty of thought *37*
Lilburne, John *55, 63, 88, 89*
   "Freeborn John" *59*
Lincoln *51*
Lindsay, Jack *109*
Liverpool *141*
Lloyd George *213, 215*
   bombing of home *219*
Locke, John *131*
Lollards *22, 36, 39, 41, 44*
   Lollard martyrs *44*

Lollards Pit *41*
Lollards Tower *41*
London *168*
Londonderry, Marquis of *165*
looting *48, 246*
Lord Chancellor *196*
Lord Haw Haw *233*
Loughborough, Lord *130*
Lovelace, George *193*
Lovett, William *174, 175, 191*
Luther, Martin *30, 33*
Lutterworth *37*

M

Macclesfield *169*
MacDonald, Ramsay *205, 208*
Magna Carta *111*
Maidstone *47*
Maitland, Lady Olga *242*
Manchester *141, 157, 163, 203, 212, 227*
   Free Trade Hall *157*
   Manchester Patriotic Union *157*
Mansfield, Lord *122, 123*
marches *215, 233*
   Aldermaston march *239*
   hunger marches *215*
Margarot, Maurice *143*
Marlborough Road, Holloway *228*
Marlow *119*
Married Love *228, 229*
Marshalsea *48*
Martin, Kingsley *238*
martyrs *123, 225*

Marvell, Andrew *101*
Marx, Karl *73, 188*
Mason, Angela *244*
Masque of Anarchy, etc. *159*
Massiter, Cathy *242*
maximum wage *46*
Mayne, Richard *184*
McKenna, Reginald *218*
Mead, Captain William *83*
meetings *236*
Melbourne, Lord *178, 181*
Membury *189*
Memorial Hall, Farringdon Street *204*
mental health *88, 218*
merchant class *105*
Merthyr Tydfil *205*
Methodism *105*
   Methodist Central Hall *239*
Metropolitan Police Act 1839 *234*
Middle Ages *25*
Middlesex *122, 123, 164, 196, 198*
   Middlesex Hospital *199*
Midlands *48, 181*
Mile End *48, 49, 235*
militancy *216, 217, 221*
military *49, 123, 147, 158, 180*
militia *130*
Millbank Prison *186*
Milliband, Ralph *238*
Mill, James *163*
Mill, John Stuart *163*
Milton, John *97, 131*
Ministry of Defence *242*
Miss World contest *244*
Moll Flanders, etc. *116*

271

monarchy *203*
Monmouth Rebellion *113*
monster meetings *233*
morality *21*, *98*, *132*, *139*
  institutional morality *247*
  moral bankruptcy *239*
  moral force *175*
  moral laxity *26*
  moral leadership *238*
  moral reform *136*
  moral values *72*
  moral victory *161*
More, Hannah *154*
Morgan, Kenneth O. *209*
Morning Chronicle *165*
Morpeth *221*
Morton, A. L. *72*
Morton, Charles *113*
Mosley, Sir Oswald *21*, *233*
Mothers' Clinic *228*
Mud March *214*
Muggletonians *22*, *54*, *76*
Muggleton, Lodowicke *76*
Muir, Thomas *141*
Munich *227*
Mussolini *233*
mutilation *82*
Mutiny Act 1797 *192*
myth *109*

N

Nagasaki *237*
Napoleonic Wars *157*

National Archives *168*
nationalism *27*
Naylor, James *82*
nepotism *190*
Newcastle *175*
  Newcastle, Duke of *165*
Newgate Prison *65*, *83*, *86*, *116*
Newington Green *113*, *151*
New Model Army *67*, *73*, *106*
Newport Rising *178*, *180*, *194*
New Statesman *238*
new thinking *105*
Noakes, Philip *77*
nonconformity *83*, *107*, *108*, *116*
Norfolk *51*
Normanby, Lord *181*
Norman power *66*
Norman Yoke *66*, *114*
Northamptonshire *69*
North Briton, The *120*
Northern Star *182*, *185*
North, Lord *123*
North of England *175*, *181*
Norwich *176*
Nottingham *21*, *81*, *165*, *175*
Nottinghamshire *69*
nuclear disarmament *237*
  Campaign for Nuclear Disarmament *237*
  nuclear, chemical and biological weapons *242*
  nuclear power *242*
Nutley, James *94*

O

oath *55, 85, 88*
O'Brien, James Bronterre *175*
obscenity *228*
O'Connor, Fergus *175, 178, 194*
offensive weapons *236*
Old Bailey *61, 83, 86, 94, 144, 220, 233*
Oldcastle, Sir John *39, 40, 42*
Old Saint Pancras Churchyard *156*
Olympia Stadium *233*
oppression *68, 91, 187*
outlawry *122, 123, 131*
outspokenness *89*
Overton, Richard *55*
Oxford *31, 34, 36, 83, 89, 113*

P

pacifism *208*
Paine, Tom *105, 127, 141, 152, 202*
Pakistan *232*
pamphlets *53, 55, 98, 116, 168, 186*
    "The Case for the Army, etc." *57*
Pankhurst, Christabel *212*
Pankhurst, Emmeline *212, 216, 225*
Pankhurst, Sylvia *208, 211, 220, 221, 223*
Paradise Lost *101*
pardon *113, 181, 194*
    general pardon *101*
Parliament *39, 53, 58, 75*
    Barebone's Parliament *62, 77*
    Long Parliament *55*
    Parliament of Saints *78*
    Rump Parliament *63, 77*
peace convoy *245*
Peasants Revolt *39, 45, 246*
Peel, Sir Robert *189*
Pelagius *25, 31*
penal servitude *220*
Pennsylvania *88*
Penn, William *83, 88*
People's Army *220*
People's Charter *173, 182*
Pepys, Samuel *78*
Perkin, Harold *163*
persecution *75*
Pershing missiles *241*
Peterloo Massacre *21, 139, 157, 177*
Pethwick-Lawrence, Emmeline *213*
petition *178, 182, 234*
    fictitious signatures *184*
    Petition of Women, etc. *62*
Phillips, Thomas *181*
Pilgrim's Progress, The *105, 108*
pillory *55, 82, 116*
    garlanding with flowers *55*
Pinney, Charles *167*
Pinochet, General *91*
Piratin, Phil *235*
Pitt the Younger *135*
Pitt, William *128, 143, 146*
Place, Francis *169, 191*
Plug Plot *181*
police *177, 180, 213, 216, 234, 235, 243, 245, 247*
    assault on police (sugffragettes by) *213*

mounted police *235*
obstructing the police *235*
politics *34, 68, 141, 202, 209, 218, 223*
   National Political Union *170, 191*
   Political Justice *152, 155*
   political opposition *161*
   political prisoners *188*
   Political Unions *163*
   power politics. *238*
poll tax *48*
   All Britain Anti-Poll Tax Federation *246*
   modern-day poll tax *51*
   poll tax riots *246*
   Richard II *45*
Pontypool *176, 179, 180*
Poor Law *173*
poor law commissioners *173*
Poor Man's Guardian *169*
Pope Gregory XI *35*
Portsmouth *192*
poverty *72, 89, 105, 110, 111, 125, 129, 152, 153, 173, 175, 193, 231*
   Poor Man's Plea, The *113*
power *72, 105, 163, 189*
   arbitrary power *248*
   royal power *120*
Pratt, Charles *121*
preaching *83*
pre-emptive action *245*
prejudice *232*
Prentice, Archibald *159*
Presbyterians *62*
Prescott, Jack *244*
Preston *73, 160*

Price, Richard *151*
priesthood *132*
Priestley, J. B. *238*
priests
   enemies of liberty *68*
printers *125*
printing *100*
prison conditions *217*
private property *69, 152*
private security firms *243, 247*
privilege *121*
processions *236*
profanity *133*
propaganda *168*
   false *233*
property qualifications *174, 192*
proportionality *245*
protest *234, 241*
   peaceful protest *212*
Protestantism *44, 100, 108, 113*
   Protestant Dissenting Society *71*
   Protestant ethic *53*
   Protestant Reformation *22*
public meetings *148*
Public Order Act 1936 *236*
publishers *116, 125*
Pugh, Martin *211, 222*
punishment *56, 75, 133*
purgatory *33*
Puritanism *64, 83, 89, 107*
Putney Debates *57, 106*

Q

Quakers *54, 62, 64, 72, 75, 81, 88, 100, 107, 127, 134*

R

rabble-rousing *233*
Radiant Motherhood *231*
radicalism *20, 79, 97, 105, 125, 127, 141, 147, 201, 243*
   Radical clubs *203*
   radical lawyers *89*
   radical tradition *51*
Rainsborough, Thomas *57*
Ranters *22, 53, 62, 71, 72, 110*
reason *156*
   Age of Reason *132*
rebellion *19, 48, 49, 102, 147, 171, 243*
Red Republican *187*
Reeve, John *76*
reform *20, 141, 157, 189*
   Great Reform Act of 1832 *21, 148, 162, 173*
   Reform Bill 1831 *21, 164*
   reforming zeal *189*
   social reform *129*
   torch of reform *161*
Reformation *37*
   Morning Star of the Reformation *31*
   Of Reformation *98*
   Protestant Reformation *31*
Reformation of Manners, A Satyr *115*
refugees *88*

regenerating society *173*
Regents Park *219*
regicides *78, 94, 99*
religion *20, 25, 76, 98, 107, 132*
   freedom of religion *56*
   religious literature *55*
   religious tolerance *100*
Representation of the People Act 1918 *224*
repression *79, 128, 139, 161, 168*
   repressive laws *247*
republicanism *95, 101, 122, 152, 187*
Restoration *53, 71, 75, 78, 81, 94, 101, 107, 116*
reverence *83*
revolution *53, 102, 122, 141, 147, 168*
   Grattan's Revolution *128*
   popular revolt *53*
   social revolution *69*
Richard II *35, 39, 45, 49*
Richmond, Duke of *145*
rights
   ancient rights *61*
   diminution of *247*
   natural rights *66*
   property rights *55*
Rights of Man, The *128, 141, 152, 202*
riot *122, 125, 164, 166, 246*
   Riot Act *122, 165, 166, 181*
   riot gear *245*
Risca *180*
Roberts, Francis *178*
Robertson, Geoffrey *89*
Robespierre *132, 155*
Robin Hood *47*

Robinson Crusoe 116
Rochdale 177
Rochester Castle 47
Rokesby Venus 219
Rome 26
   independence from 27
Rothermere, Lord 233
rotten boroughs 139, 141, 164
Rousseau, John Jacques 153
Royal College of Surgeons 190
Royal power 66
Rudé, George 125
rule of law 87, 148, 243, 247, 248
Russell, Bertrand 238
Russell, Dora 238
Russell, Lord John 164, 169, 176, 182, 193
"Russia, the Atom and the West" 238
Rye 48

S

Salisbury, Lord 49, 212
Salway, Peter 29
Sandwich 127
satire 114, 115
Saundry, William 198
Savage, Mary 175
Savoy (The Savoy) 48
Sawtry, William 41
Saxons 29
schoolmasters 40
Scotland 141, 164, 181, 201, 246
Scottish Labour Party 202

Scott, Sir John 145
secret ballot 174, 191
sedition 120, 141, 142
   seditious libel 116, 128, 130
   Seditious Meetings Act 148
Seekers 71, 72
self-incrimination 56, 75
self-sacrifice 211
serfdom 46, 48, 51
Sexby, Edward 58, 106
Sex Disqualification (Removal) Act 1919 224
Shackleton, David 206
Shakespeare 44
Sharpe, William 146
Shaw, George Bernard 22, 203, 215, 231
Shelley, Mary 155
Shelley, Percy Bysshe 155, 159
Shell, George 179
Sheridan, Richard Brinsley 145
Shortest Way with the Dissenters, etc., The 115
Sidmouth, Lord 160
silence
   right to silence 55, 89
   silent system 186
Silverman, Sydney 238
Simon, Sir John 234
sin 26, 28, 62, 72
   forgiveness of sins 29
Single Eye, A, etc. 73
Six Acts 161
slavery 68, 88, 115, 132, 135, 152, 153, 177, 191, 192

INDEX

abolition *140*
   Emancipation of Slavery Act 1833 *140*
Smithfield *43, 49*
   burning at the stake *41*
socialist groups *204*
social turmoil *141*
Society for the Suppression of Vice, etc. *133, 134, 139*
solidarity *216*
Somers Town *155*
Soper, Donald *238*
South Africa *232*
South Wales *175, 178, 180*
Soviet Union *242*
Sparrow, Joseph *169*
special constables *169*
Special Powers Act *144*
stamp duty *192*
Star Chamber *55, 215*
Starkey, George *94*
starvation *175*
state
   over-powerful state *248*
   State Tryals 44
Statute of Labourers 1351 *46*
St. Augustine *26*
Steele, William *91*
St. George's Fields *122*
St. George's Hill *65, 66*
St. Giles' Field *43*
St. John's Fields *50*
stocks *114*
Stoke Newington *244*
Stonehenge *245*

Stopes, Marie *227*
   Marie Stopes International *232*
St. Peter's Field *157*
Strangeways Prison (Manchester) *213*
strategic insight *211*
Straw, Jack *51*
strikes *181, 201, 207, 208*
Stuart monarchy *63*
subservience *156*
subversion *145, 155, 233, 242*
Sudbury, Simon *48*
Suffolk *51*
suffrage *157, 174, 192, 213*
   universal suffrage *148*
suffragettes *208, 211*
   Suffragette Movement *212*
   Suffragette, The 224
Summa Theologiae 34
Sun 165
Surrey *48, 65, 75*
surveillance *242, 243*
suspicious deaths *197*
Sussex *48, 51, 127*
Sutherland, Dr Halliday *229*
suttee *140*
swearing
   prophane swearing *75*
symbolism *109*

T

Taff Vale Case 206
Tariq Ali *244*
Tattenham Corner *220*

taxation *48*, *73*, *168*, *202*, *203*, *230*
telephone
  telephone tapping *242*
  telephone wires, cutting *219*
Temperton v. Russell *207*
Temple *48*
  Temple Bar *43*
Tenure of King's and Magistrates, The *99*
terror *83*, *141*
  "English Terror" *144*
  Reign of Terror *144*, *155*
  terrorism *243*
  war on terror *248*
Thatcher, Margaret *51*, *246*, *247*
theft *73*
Thelwell, John *144*, *147*
theology *110*, *133*
Thetford *127*, *134*
Thompson, Dorothy *174*
Thompson, E. P. *124*, *161*, *238*
Thorpe Wood *41*
Thoughts on the Education of Daughters, etc. *151*
Tillett, Ben *203*
tithes *68*, *168*
Tokyo *227*
tolerance *100*
Tolpuddle martyrs *192*
Tories *163*, *164*, *170*, *175*, *206*
torture *91*, *182*, *248*
Tower Hamlets *234*
Tower of London *42*, *48*, *49*, *56*, *59*, *83*, *120*, *144*, *219*
trades councils *203*
Trades Disputes Act 1906 *207*

trade unionism *188*, *192*
trade unions *201*, *203*, *204*
  immunity *207*
tradition of dissent *20*
Trafalgar Square *239*, *246*
transportation *142*, *143*, *167*, *177*, *181*, *192*
transubstantiation *41*
treason *92*, *95*, *128*, *130*, *131*, *140*, *160*, *233*
  high treason *79*, *144*, *180*
  Treasonable Practices Act *148*
  Treason Act 1351 *145*
  treason trials *141*
trial
  fair trial *90*
Trident *242*
troublemakers *20*
Trowbridge *177*
True-born Englishman, The *114*
Truro *177*
Tumbledown Dick *101*
tumultuous assembly *85*
turmoil *141*
"Two Acts" *148*
Tyburn *94*
Tyler, Wat *45*, *49*
Tyndal, Sir Nicholas *167*
tyranny *86*, *114*, *123*
  legalising tyranny *207*
  marriage as *155*

U

unemployment *204, 215*
uniforms *236*
universal suffrage *141*
University College London *227*
unlawful assembly *83*
Unlawful Societies Act 1799 *192*
uprising *46*

V

vandalism *246*
Van Diemen's Land *181*
Vaughan, Chief Justice *87*
vengeance *50*
Venner, Thomas *78*
Venn, Rev. Joseph *136*
Victoria, Queen *181, 183, 190*
victory tokens *147*
villeinage *49, 50*
Vincent, Henry *178, 194*
Vindication of the Rights of Woman, A *152*
violence *20, 105, 166, 168, 178, 213, 214, 219, 223, 233, 234, 246*
  non-violence *242*
  violent language *176*

W

Wakefield, Edward Gibbon *169*
Wakefield House of Correction *182*
Wakley, Thomas *165, 181, 189, 196*
Wales *181*
Walker, Mary Ann *183*
Wallace-Dunlop, Marion *216*
Waltham *51*
Walton Heath *219*
Walton-on-Thames *65*
Walworth, William *49*
Walwyn, William *55*
war casualties *88*
war crimes *96*
warrants *147, 215*
  general warrants illegal *121*
Warwick *74, 168, 178*
wealth *73, 74, 97, 105, 115, 121, 135, 168, 189*
weapons *244*
Weavers' Union *206*
Webb, Richard *174*
Wellingborough *69*
Wells, H. G. *215*
Wesley, Charles *113*
Wesley, John *110*
West Ham *202*
Westminster *55, 141, 165*
  Westminster Hall *91, 121*
West of England *48*
West Wycombe *119*
Wetherell, Sir Charles *166*
Whigs *63, 137, 162, 164, 175, 176*
whipping *55, 137, 143*
White, Frederick John *199*
Widows Pension Act 1925 *225*
Wigan *177*
Wilberforce, William *135, 153*

Wildman, John *55*
Wilkes, John *119*
Williams, Mr. Baron *192*
Williams, Thomas *133, 139*
Williams, Zephania *179*
Wilson, Erasmus *199*
Wiltshire *245*
Winchester *41*
  Law of Winchester *50*
windows
  breaking windows *213, 217*
Wollstonecraft, Mary *21, 151, 152, 156*
women
  female equality *222*
  National Union of Women's Suffrage Societies *212*
  votes for women *208, 211, 224*
  Votes for Women Fellowship *217*
  Women and Families for Defence *242*
  Women's Dreadnought, The 223
  Women's Freedom League *214*
  Women's Parliament *214*
  women's rights *227*
  Women's Social and Political Union *212*
Woodall, William *212*
Wood, Robert *121*
Woolwich
  Woolwich Arsenal *184*
  Woolwich Barracks *198*
Worcester *168*
Workers' Dreadnought, The 224
Workers' Suffrage Federation *223*
workhouse *173, 198*

worship *58, 83*
  rejection of *76*
Wrensbury, Lord *230*
writers *55, 147*
wrongful arrest *245*
Wycliffe, John *22, 30, 31, 34, 36*
  death of *37*
  legacy *44*
Wynstanley, Gerard *54, 65, 72, 74, 191*

Y

yeomen *158, 160*
York
  York Assizes *160*
  York Castle *182*
Yorkshire *135, 177*